IMAGES
of America

LUTHERANS IN WESTERN NEW YORK

On the Cover: Following the sudden death of its pastor, Rev. George A. Martin, in 1952, St. Paul's Lutheran Church in Eggertsville called Pastor John L. Kinzel in 1953. He oversaw the rebuilding of the parish hall. The original hall had been the victim of a devastating fire, which ignited when a child placed a coat over a faulty radiator. Pastor Kinzel is pictured preaching during construction, on September 26, 1954. (St. Paul's Lutheran Church, Eggertsville.)

IMAGES
of America

LUTHERANS IN WESTERN NEW YORK

Julianna Fiddler-Woite and
Rev. Jamie Retallack

ARCADIA
PUBLISHING

ISBN 978-1-4671-3388-3

Published by Arcadia Publishing
Charleston, South Carolina

Printed in the United States of America

Library of Congress Control Number: 2015933524

For all general information, please contact Arcadia Publishing:
Telephone 843-853-2070
Fax 843-853-0044
E-mail sales@arcadiapublishing.com
For customer service and orders:
Toll-Free 1-888-313-2665

Visit us on the Internet at www.arcadiapublishing.com

In honor of those who carried the seeds of Lutheranism across the Atlantic and planted them in Western New York . . . look what you have grown.

Contents

ACKNOWLEDGMENTS

As all authors know, it is impossible to tackle a work of this magnitude without the support of those around you. A heartfelt thank you goes out to the churches who donated their images and their time to this project, including St. Paul's Eggertsville, St. Paul's Williamsville, St. John's Akron, St. John's Buffalo/Amherst, Trinity South Newstead, Parkside, Holy Trinity, and Lord of Life. Unless otherwise noted, all images have been donated by the Lutheran Churches of Western New York. We are also very appreciative of the knowledge and memories shared by the Reverend Charles Biegner Jr., Ethel Schleifer, Sue Roesch Mattison, Chuck Roesch, Billy Roesch, Cheryl Roesch, Marty Bauer, and Lois Fiddler. Once again, we thank Jan and Pat Farrell of the Traveling Picture Show for their impressive postcard collection and Kim Retallack for her acute proofreading skills. We would also like to acknowledge the work of our student intern, Alea Tiberi, for her help with layout and pagination. Finally, we must admit that we probably would not have met our deadline without Melinda Harvey and her assistance with captions, her depth of connections, and her enthusiasm for local history.

Most important, we are forever indebted to the last five generations of our Landel, Knoche, Schoelles, and Fiddler ancestors, who meticulously saved and labeled hundreds of precious photographs. Our work has been made richer by their images and propelled by their memories.

INTRODUCTION

The Lutheran Church was born out of the Reformation at the height of the Renaissance. Martin Luther, an aspiring lawyer who became a monk, then a professor, became the unlikely catalyst of change. Luther believed that the Roman Catholic Church had lost its way and had lost sight of the Gospel message. While studying the Bible, and Romans in particular, Luther learned that it was God's grace that was the source of salvation, and not one's actions. This ran counter to the teachings of the day, which focused on earning salvation through supporting the church and its leaders. Specifically, the Roman Catholic Church had begun to implement the system of forgiveness of sins known as indulgences. Martin Luther, deeply troubled by this, set out to help the church refocus on the message of God's grace.

The Reformation began with naive optimism. Luther believed that, when the church in Rome, its leaders, and the bureaucracy that supported it, saw that they had lost their way, they would be eager to change. He was wrong. When Luther posted his Ninety-Five Theses, which describes the errors he saw within the Catholic Church, to the door of the church in Wittenberg, he set off a chain of events that would become known as the Reformation. The ideas contained within the Ninety-Five Theses and Luther's subsequent writings spread rapidly throughout Europe. His ideas were widely translated, allowing many in Europe to read what he had to say. The Roman Catholic Church was surprised by this turn of events, and every attempt to discredit or silence Luther only fanned the flames of change. By the time the dust of the Reformation had settled, the Church was split in two: the Roman Catholic Church in Southern Europe and the Protestant Church in Northern Europe. Those who followed the teachings of Martin Luther became known as Lutherans, the predominant denomination in Germany.

By the end of the Reformation, various denominations of Christianity were flourishing throughout Europe. As Europeans began to settle in America, they brought their faith with them. Initially, settlers arrived seeking religious freedom, people whose faith was not predominant in their native country. Eventually, however, as America grew, people sought opportunities for the American dream. Immigrants made the long trip across the Atlantic in search of the rights guaranteed in the Declaration of Independence: life, liberty, and the pursuit of happiness. Those rights ensured that people arriving in America were free to bring their faith traditions with them. America would be a place where different faith traditions could coexist. So as people from various national and ethnic backgrounds began to settle, they brought to their communities their Christian denomination. The effects of this can still be seen today in communities that contain a variety of churches representing several denominations. The prevalence of any given denomination within a community would depend on the country of origin of the people who settled there. In Germany, Lutheranism was predominant, and so in places where Germans settled, they brought a Lutheran presence with them.

The first Lutheran church in America, Ebenezer Lutheran Church in Albany, was founded in 1649 by Dutch settlers. The church is known today as First Lutheran Church and continues to operate and remains the oldest Lutheran church in America. Lutheranism would not make its way to Western New York for another 170 years. There were two factors involved in bringing Lutheranism to Western New York. The first was an unprecedented wave of immigration from Germany to the United States. The second was the opening of the Erie Canal. Many Germans sought to leave the political and social instability of their homeland and come to the United States for a piece of the American dream. Many of the German immigrants arriving before the 1840s were farmers looking for productive land. The Erie Canal led those immigrants to exactly what they were looking for: large expanses of farmable land. This wave of Germans, following the Erie Canal toward new land, brought Lutheranism to Western New York. With the construction of St. Paul's Eggertsville in 1831, Lutheranism had officially taken root in Western New York. It could, however, be argued that St. John Williamsville was the first congregation in the area. It began church activities, such as baptisms, weddings, and funerals, in 1828; however, it would not officially organize as a congregation until four years later. These two congregations, each holding a particular claim as being first, would not be the only Lutheran churches in the region for long.

Over the next 50 years, Lutheran churches sprang up across Western New York. There were Lutheran congregations in Buffalo, Akron, Tonawanda, and West Seneca and everywhere in between. These congregations shared the trait of practicing their Lutheran faith entirely in the German language. Sermons, scripture, and song could only be heard in German, and Bibles, hymnals, and church records were only written in German. Lutherans in the area may have left their homeland of Germany behind, but they brought the language with them. This may have helped to keep their cultural heritage alive, but it also made it very difficult for those who did not speak German to be a part of a Lutheran church. This meant that Lutheran churches could only grow as a result of families growing and new Germans immigrating to the area. In 1879, a group of Lutherans sought to eliminate this language barrier by offering services in English. They founded English Lutheran Church of the Holy Trinity, most commonly known simply as Holy Trinity. The congregation grew steadily and helped to found other Lutheran churches in the area, such as Parkside Lutheran Church. Lutheranism now had a strong German and English presence in the region. World events, however, would soon result in Lutheran churches leaving behind their distinctly German identity.

In 1917, after nearly three years of remaining neutral, the United States entered World War I and declared war on Germany. Following the declaration, a wave of anti-German sentiment swept across the country, and many Lutheran churches abandoned the use of the German language in their services. In the years following the armistice, even more Lutheran congregations abandoned German, and few if any services or documents could be found in the native language. Events in Germany further hastened this move away from a German identity. Hitler began to appropriate Martin Luther's writings and theology for his own uses as he sought to stir nationalist sentiment. Lutheran churches in America, not wanting to seem sympathetic toward Germany, dropped any remaining vestiges of the German language and distanced themselves from a German identity. The Lutheran Church, brought to America by German immigrants, was no longer tied to a single national identity. Rather, its identity would be rooted in its faith.

The end of World War II brought about a time of population growth. Soldiers returning home from the war got married and started families. As these new families sought homes to live in, the American suburbs were born. Suddenly, Lutheran churches located on the outskirts of the city and in rural communities found themselves in the middle of the suburbs. The church was more than the center of religious life; it was the center of community life as well. The question was not if one attended church, but which church one attended. These new families filling the burgeoning suburbs also began to fill church pews. To meet this growing demand, many Lutheran churches in Western New York began building projects. Sunday school wings, sanctuary expansions, social halls, gyms, and many other additions were made to area churches. As the population boomed and the suburbs grew, church membership soared and church buildings expanded. The Lutheran Church now had a central role within American culture. Christianity was, in many ways, an expectation, but an expectation that was about to change.

The late 1960s in America was a time of great cultural change. Institutions and norms were challenged in ways never seen before. The church was not immune to this seismic shift within American culture. The church quickly shifted from being the American institution to an American institution. Religious practice was an option rather than an expectation and subject to evaluation and critique, just like any other social phenomenon. To Lutherans, this is known as the end of Christendom. Many Lutheran churches in Western New York saw their membership decrease over the ensuing decades. Several Lutheran churches, including some that began during the initial Lutheran expansion following the Erie Canal opening, held their final services and were forced to close their doors. Other Lutheran congregations merged, combining resources in order to survive. Some congregations found novel solutions, such as sharing pastors, hiring part-time pastors, or teaming with a more stable congregation. The Lutheran Church was no longer the center of the community, and it had to figure out how to be "The Church" in a new culture.

The answer to this question was found by looking at the past. In the earliest years of Christianity, immediately after the resurrection of Jesus, those who followed Christ had a similar problem. They had a Gospel message to spread in the midst of a culture that made it challenging to spread that message. The early adherents found a twofold solution. First, they held church services, in which they shared the Gospel message. Second, they served those in need within their community. The Lutheran Church at the end of Christendom responded with the same twofold approach. Lutheran churches in Western New York offered new types of worship services. Essentially, Lutheran worship in Western New York was conducted as often as possible, in as many places as possible, and in as many ways as possible, in order to connect with as many people as possible. The Lutheran Church also responded by serving its communities in new and innovative ways. For instance, Lord of Life Lutheran in Depew opened in the early 1970s as a church and a child development center. In the 1980s, it expanded its service to include an adult health center. It hoped to serve those who helped to care for elderly parents and relatives by providing skilled care during the workday. It was the first facility of its kind in the area. Other churches developed different services supporting those in need. Some churches supported Friends of the Night People, a homeless outreach. Shelters for victims of domestic violence and halfway houses were supported. The national organization Lutheran Disaster Relief (LDR), which responds to disasters on a worldwide scale, was supported. The Lutheran Church engaged in clothing drives, food pantries, Christmas gifts for needy children, and many other special collections and services. Local mission teams were sent to Africa and Haiti to serve the needs of people. In brief, the Lutheran Church sought to serve as many people in Western New York and around the world as possible. The church filled a different societal role than it had until the late 1960s, but it was just as relevant, if not more so, as it had ever been.

The history of the Lutheran Church in Western New York continues. It can be seen in the traditions of the churches in the communities and in the people who are members of those congregations. It can be felt by those who attend the church services and by those who reach out in service to their communities. It is a history that can be experienced in worship within church walls and worship outside of those walls as well. Lutheranism has played and continues to play an important role in the community. The history of the Lutheran Church in Western New York is not a history that happened—it is a history that continues to happen.

One

Pioneers of Lutheranism

As is the case with much of the history of Western New York, the roots of Lutheranism have direct ties to the completion of the Erie Canal in 1825. Almost immediately, colonies of German-speaking immigrants began to thrive in the rural areas outside the city of Buffalo, and two distinct groups of Lutherans were formed. The Getzville region was home to the "Northbushers," who hailed from Alsace-Lorraine. The "Southbushers," predominately of Prussian and central German decent, settled in Cheektowaga and Lancaster. The future of the Lutherans in Western New York was soon bolstered by a very generous gift, when a 50-acre grant was received from the Holland Land Company. Area Lutherans were now proud owners of a spot of land along what was known as the Great Trail, or the Old Buffalo Road. With a place to call home, what began as a backyard fellowship took the first steps toward formal organization. Taking the reins was Rev. Vincent Philip Meyerhoffer. Under his direction, St. Paul's Lutheran Church in Eggertsville was incorporated on December 18, 1827, and took up residence on Main Street. In the following years, Lutheran churches would be established in the city of Buffalo as well as in the communities developing around it. Lutheranism had officially rooted itself in the Buffalo landscape, and the future of the church was bright.

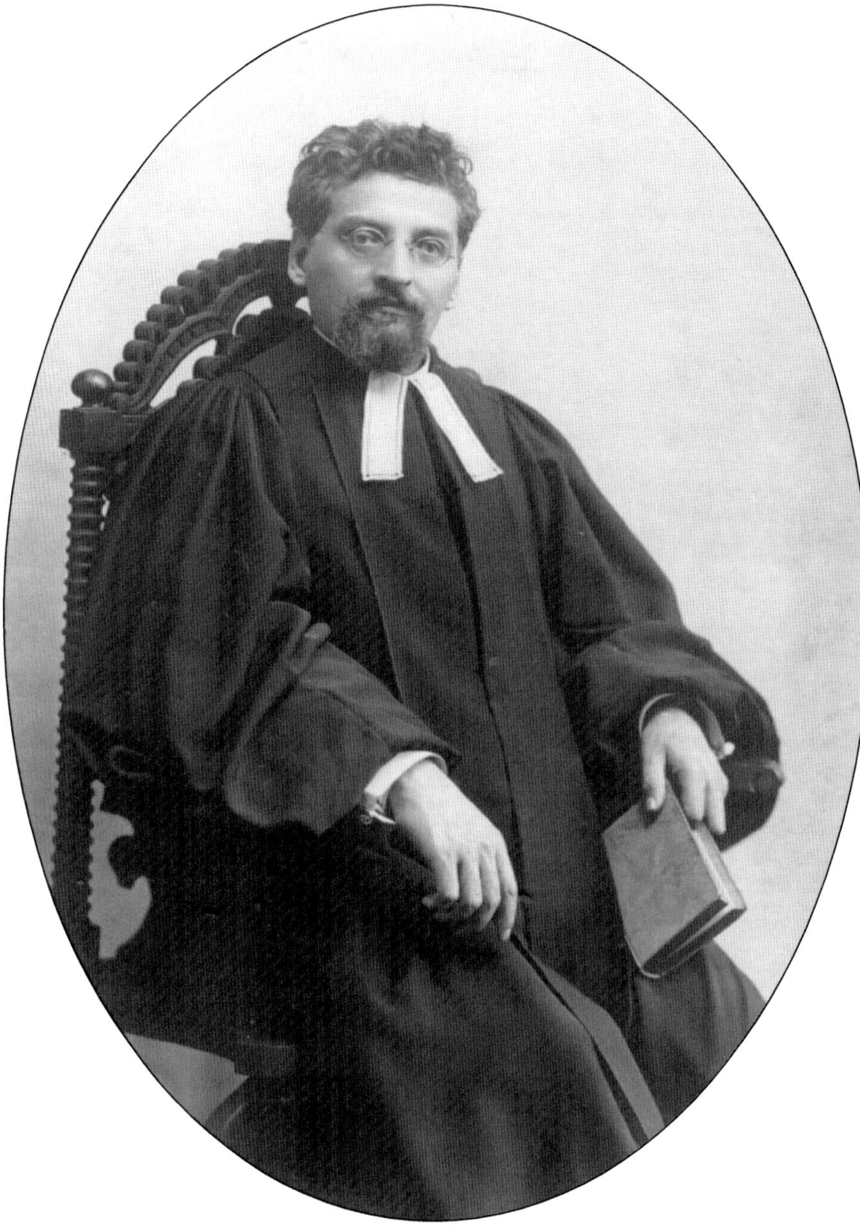

The Lutheran Church has always believed strongly in the education and training of its pastors and leaders. The academic requirement to become a Lutheran pastor is a master's of divinity, a degree requiring significant postgraduate coursework. For many years, this work could only be done at colleges and universities in Germany. This changed in 1826, when Samuel Simon Schmucker founded the Lutheran Theological Seminary at Gettysburg. For the first time, Lutheran ministers could be educated in theology and become pastors without having to leave the country. Disagreements would eventually result in some faculty and students breaking away in 1864 to form a second seminary, Lutheran Theological Seminary, at Philadelphia. Pictured here is the Reverend Heinrich Rudolph Grabau, who served St. Paul's Lutheran Church in Williamsville from 1896 to 1909. Grabau was the grandson of the infamous Lutheran pioneer the Reverend J.A.A. Grabau, who established Trinity Old Lutheran Church and Martin Luther Seminary.

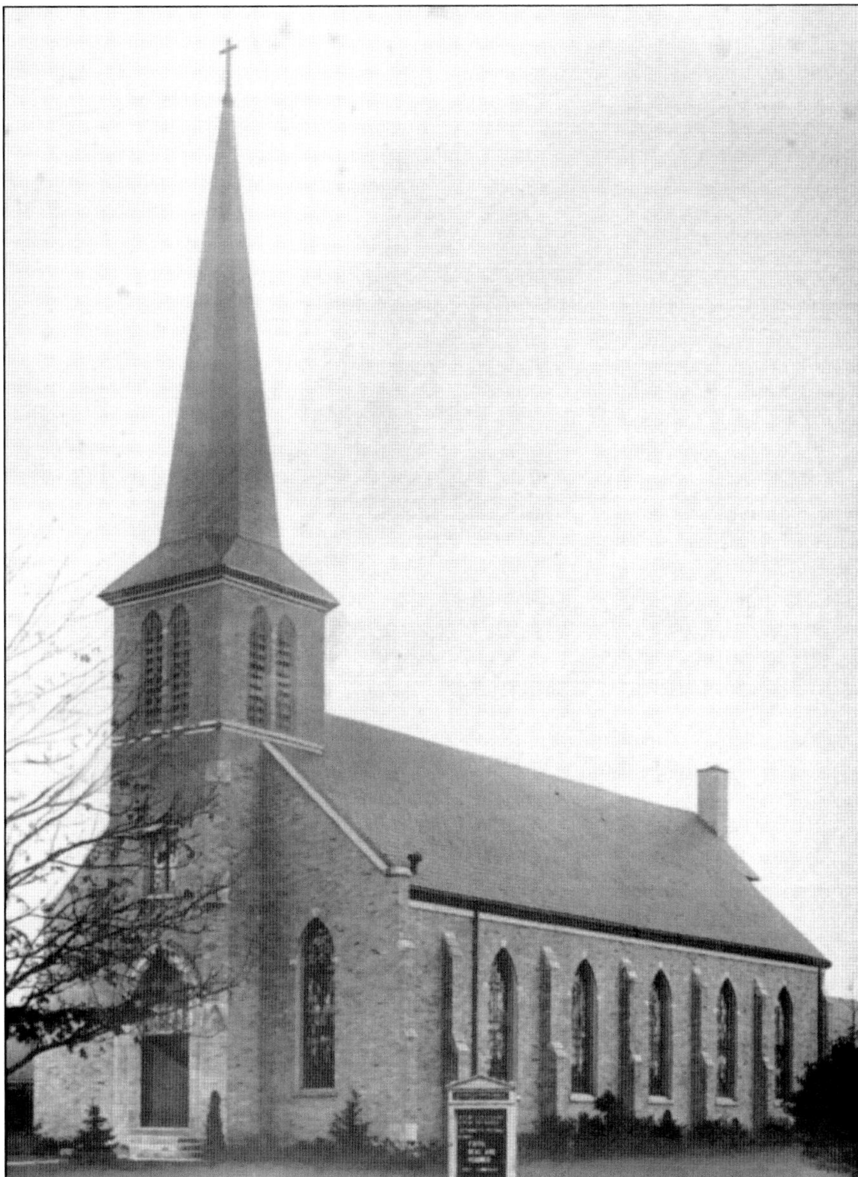

St. Paul's Evangelical Lutheran Church in Eggertsville was incorporated on December 18, 1827, and a church was built in 1833. Under the leadership of the Reverend Vincent Philip Meyerhoffer, the new congregation flourished on Old Buffalo Road, now Main Street. Their earliest recorded baptism was that of Salome Lorenz, performed on April 25, 1829, by the Reverend Keller. Under the direction of Rev. Adolph C. Boettger, a constitution was adopted in 1872. At this time, funds were raided through annual "pew rents," and unconfirmed persons and children were dismissed before the sacrament was administered. As most members of the congregation were farmers, popular social events included husking bees, barn dances, and sleigh rides. A new church building was erected in 1874, but it was destroyed by fire in 1879, after the Reverend Boettger's son Edwin dropped a match in the shed behind the church. Despite a bucket brigade, the church, parsonage, sheds, and a neighboring house all burned to the ground. A new cornerstone was laid later that year, and the present church (pictured) was built.

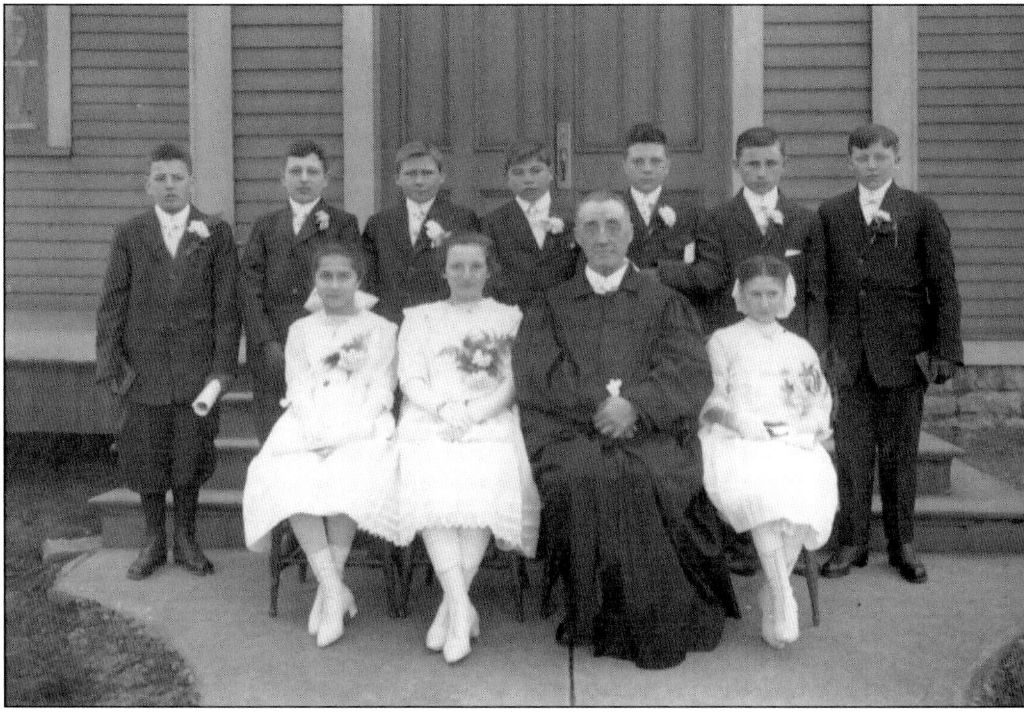

The Reverend Ernst Burke was pastor of St. Paul's in Eggertsville from 1896 to 1919. Under his leadership, a new parsonage was built, and the church and parsonage were electrified in 1911. According to church records, Tiffany-style stained-glass windows were also installed about this time. Pastor Burke is seen here with his 1918 confirmation class.

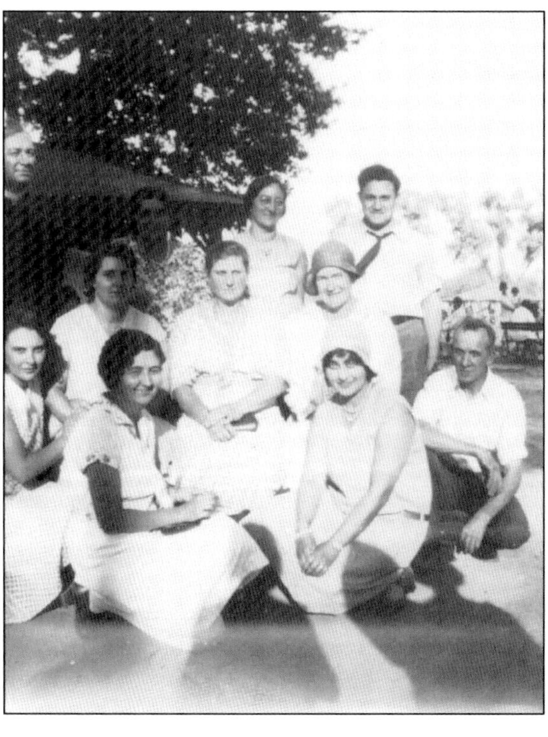

St. Paul's in Eggertsville called the Reverend George E. Schettler in 1919. Under his leadership, Sunday school enrollment flourished and a new parish hall was erected to accommodate the increased enrollment. Prior to this, classes met in a small room located off the back of the church. Shown here are some of St. Paul's faithful Sunday school teachers.

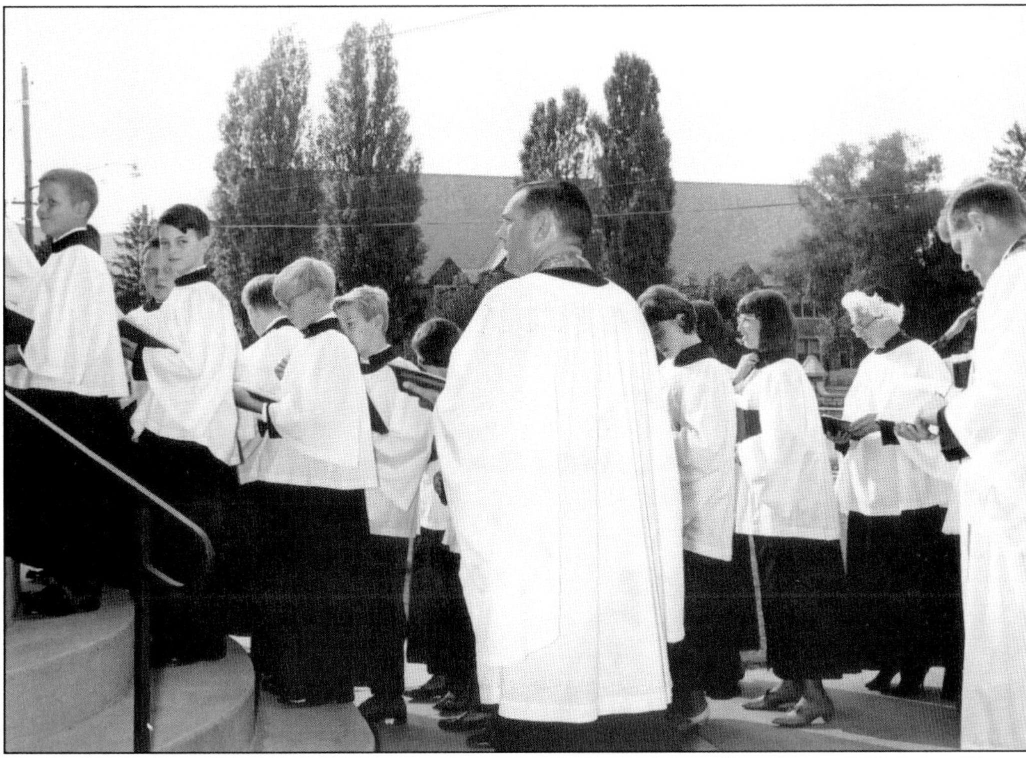

On September 18, 1966, St. Paul's Lutheran Church in Eggertsville celebrated the installation service of the Reverend James Anderson, its new assistant pastor. The above photograph shows the youth choir proceeding into church under the watchful eyes of both Pastor Kinzel and Pastor Anderson. A beautiful balcony view of the installation service is shown below. During his brief time at St. Paul's, Pastor Anderson concentrated on youth work, and a new youth center called "The Place" met in the parish hall on Saturday nights. By 1967, however, Pastor Anderson had resigned from St. Paul's, following the resignation of Pastor Kinzel, who had accepted a call to the campus ministry at the University of Pennsylvania at Philadelphia.

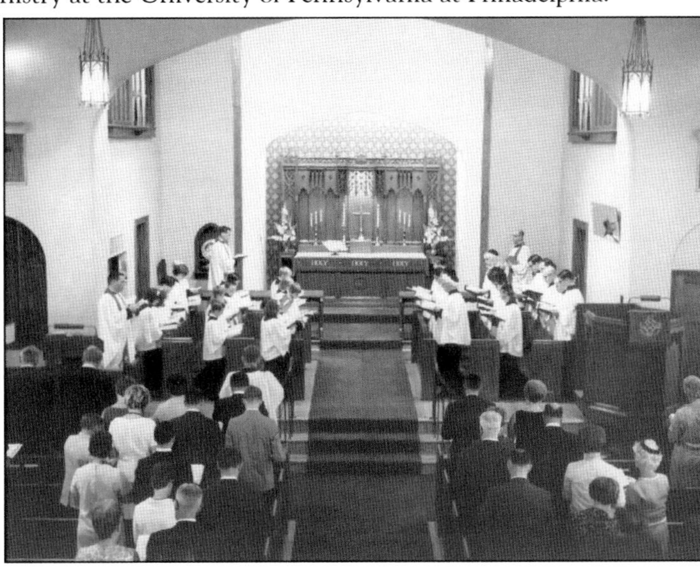

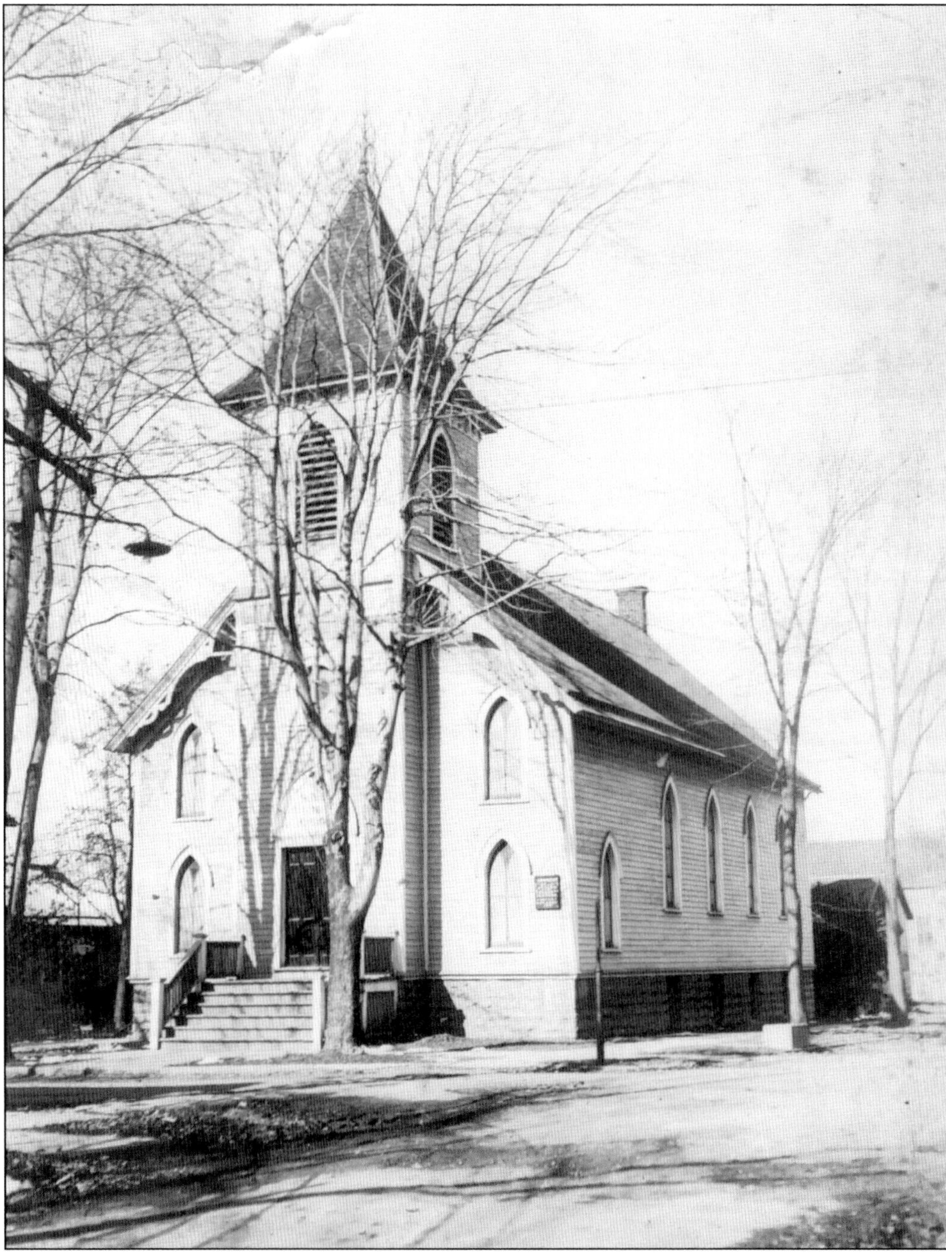

St. Paul's Evangelical Lutheran Church in Williamsville was officially formed as a mission church to St. Paul's Eggertsville on April 4, 1869. While the Reverend Casper Adolph Wolfgang Boettger originally used the Williamsville Baptist Church as a meeting place, the present location at the corner of Eagle and North Ellicott Streets was purchased for $1,000 in 1870, and the new congregation moved into a vacant church on the property. Under the direction of Pastor Grabau, a new plank church was built in 1900, and the first organ was obtained for the Sunday school in 1909. Most important, an entry in the church register verifies that "Today as the 30th of June 1907, the first regular English Service was held and attendance was good." Under Pastor Grabau's direction, English services were henceforth intertwined with the traditional German-based worship. This is an early-1900s image of the current St. Paul's Church building.

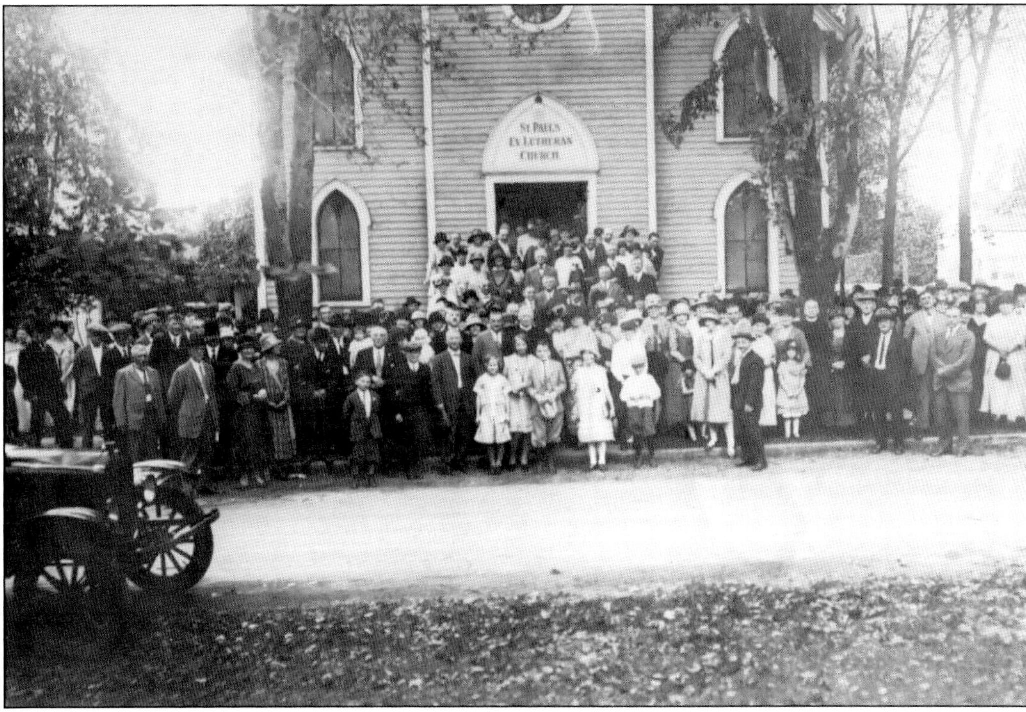

Utilizing a foundation originally laid by the Disciples of Jesus Christ in 1839, construction of the current St. Paul's Lutheran Church in Williamsville began in 1900. The materials and labor cost $2,958. The finished product was dedicated on October 21, 1900. Following his installation as pastor in 1925, Reverend Schleifler proudly posed with his new congregation in front of St. Paul's.

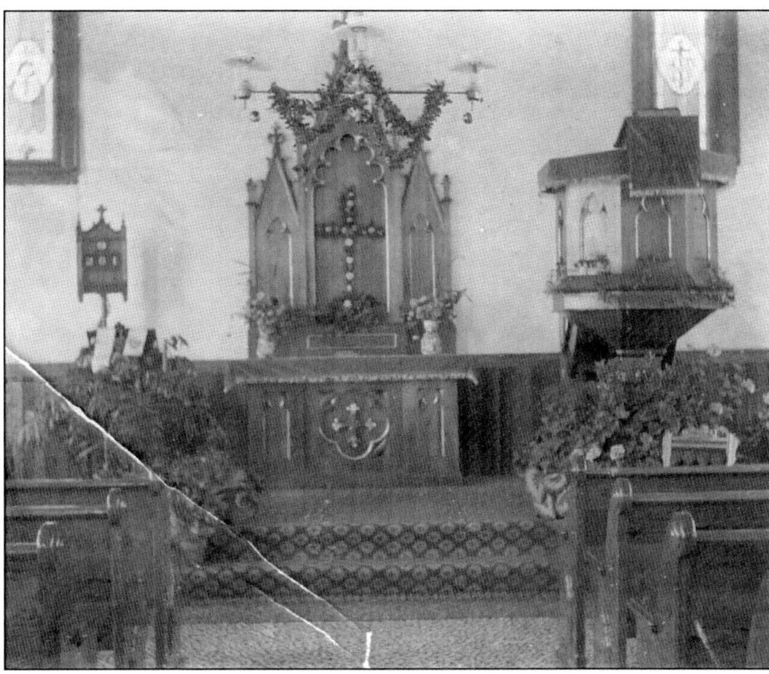

The oldest image of the interior of St. Paul's Lutheran Church in Williamsville dates to 1901, the year after the building was constructed. This is the only photograph known to exist before the installation of the pipe organ. Depicted here is the original positing of the altar and high pulpit, and the original gas chandelier is featured.

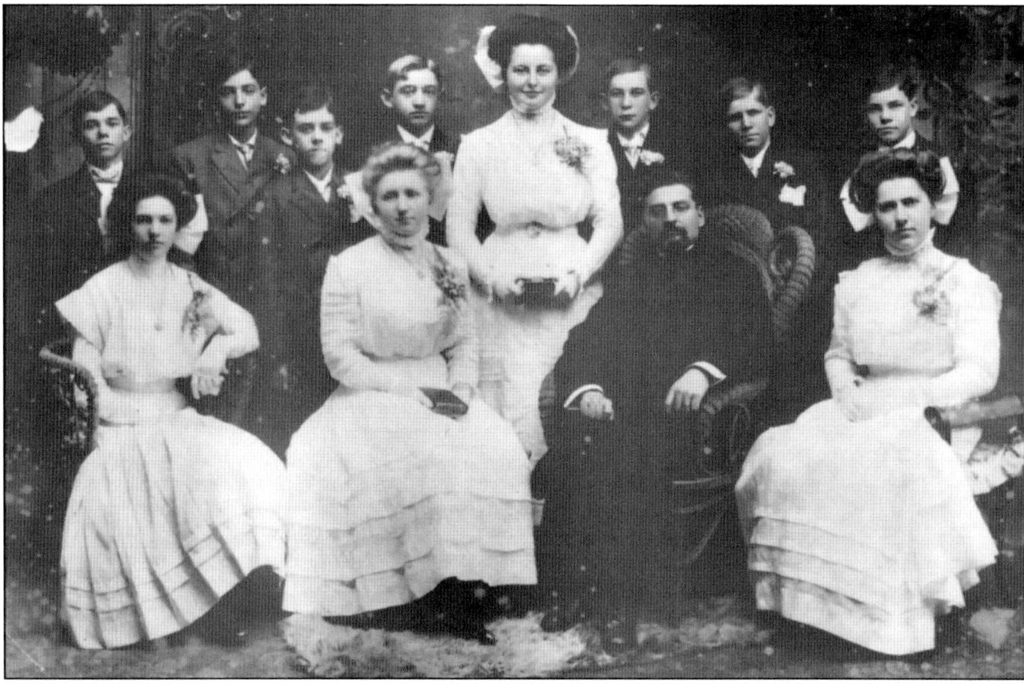

Pastor Grabau's final year of service to St. Paul's was 1909. Before his departure, he oversaw the donation of a simple organ to the Sunday school, marking the beginning of St. Paul's revered music program. His final confirmation class (1909) included Wilhelm Mikolen, James Elheim, Alfred Braber, George Litchkofski, Agnus Schoelles, Ellen Brunner, Henry Brunner, Margaret Wendlum, Mabel Wolf, Florence Kreib, Louise Mikolen, and Monica Oshwald.

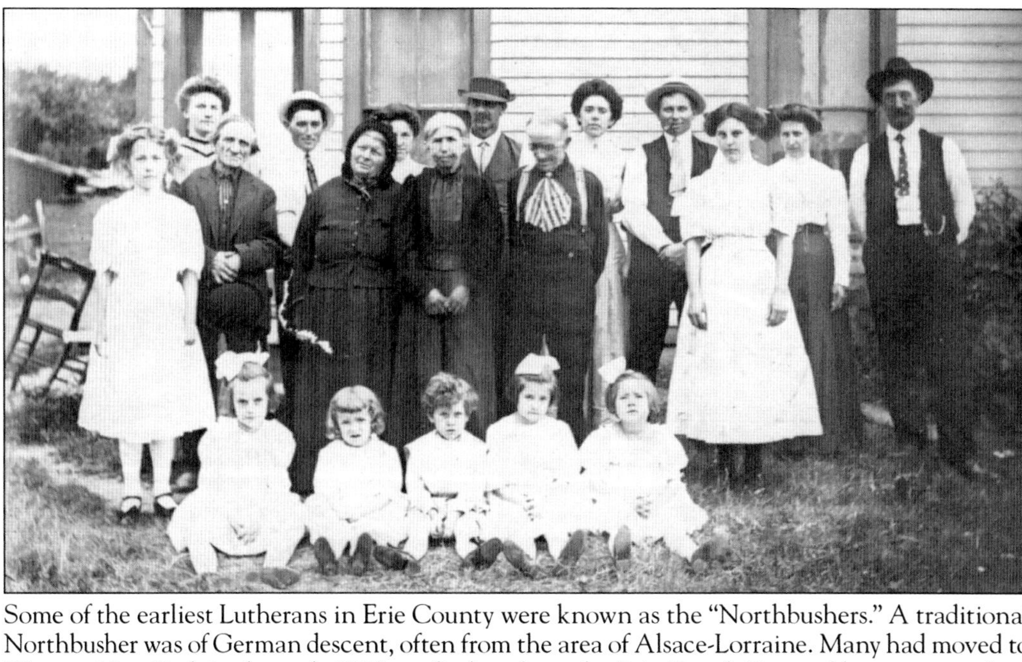

Some of the earliest Lutherans in Erie County were known as the "Northbushers." A traditional Northbusher was of German descent, often from the area of Alsace-Lorraine. Many had moved to Western New York in the early 1800s to find work on the Erie Canal. Pictured here are members of the Loos, Stengel, Hirsch, Hanel, and Spiesz families.

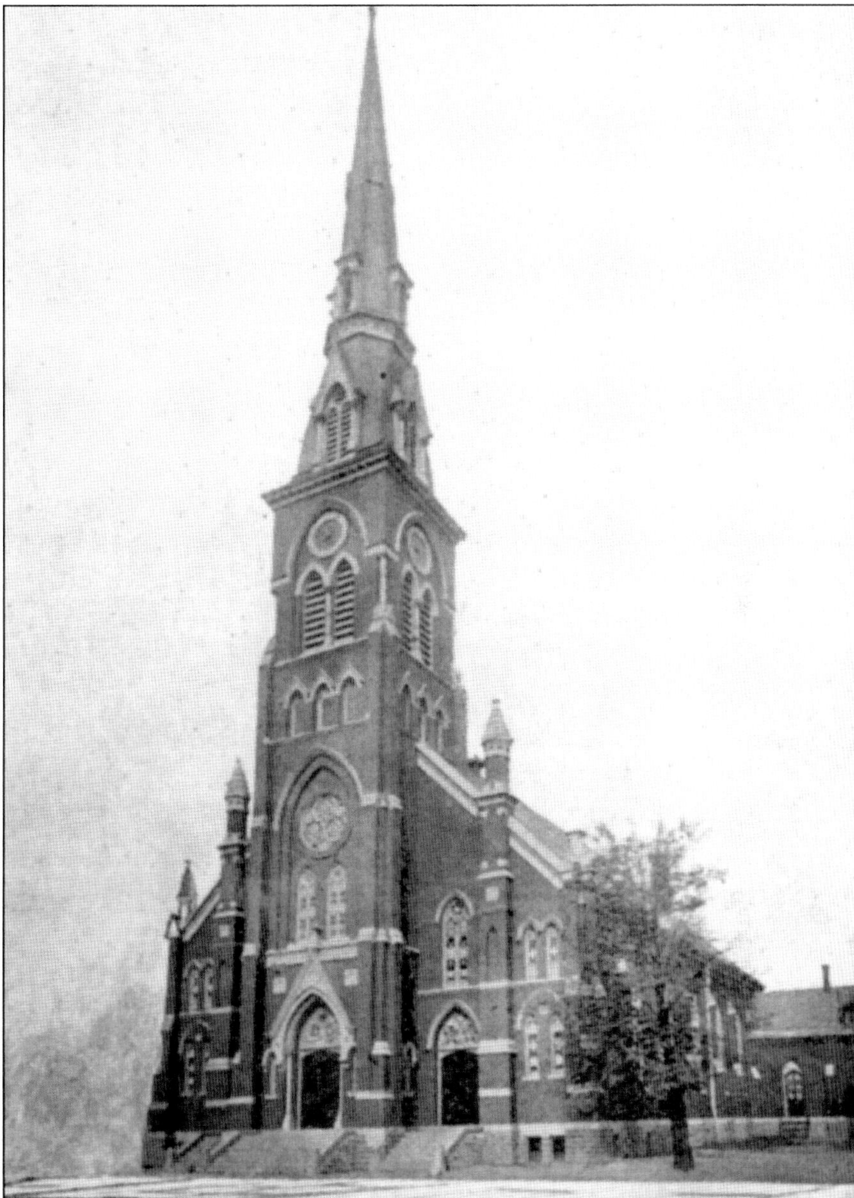

The Evangelical Lutheran St. John's Church of Buffalo was known as "The Mother Church of Buffalo Lutheranism." Its roots trace to 1828, four years before the City of Buffalo was incorporated. The dirt streets were filled with cattle, Native Americans lived in proximity, and wilderness covered most of the land. On September 20, 1828, in a storeroom over Koons & Handel's Grocery on Main Street, near Genesee, the first recorded baptism took place. By 1833, Pastor Francis Guenther was called from Rochester and the constitution for the "German Protestant Congregation of Buffalo" was drafted. Later that year, however, the name was changed to the Evangelical Lutheran Congregation of Buffalo. A half-acre plot was then purchased on Hickory Street for the sum of $500. The cornerstone was laid in 1835, but the building would not be complete or dedicated until May 25, 1843. Situated amid woods and fields, the final project cost $10,000 to construct. Eventually, needing more space, the church shown here was erected in 1873.

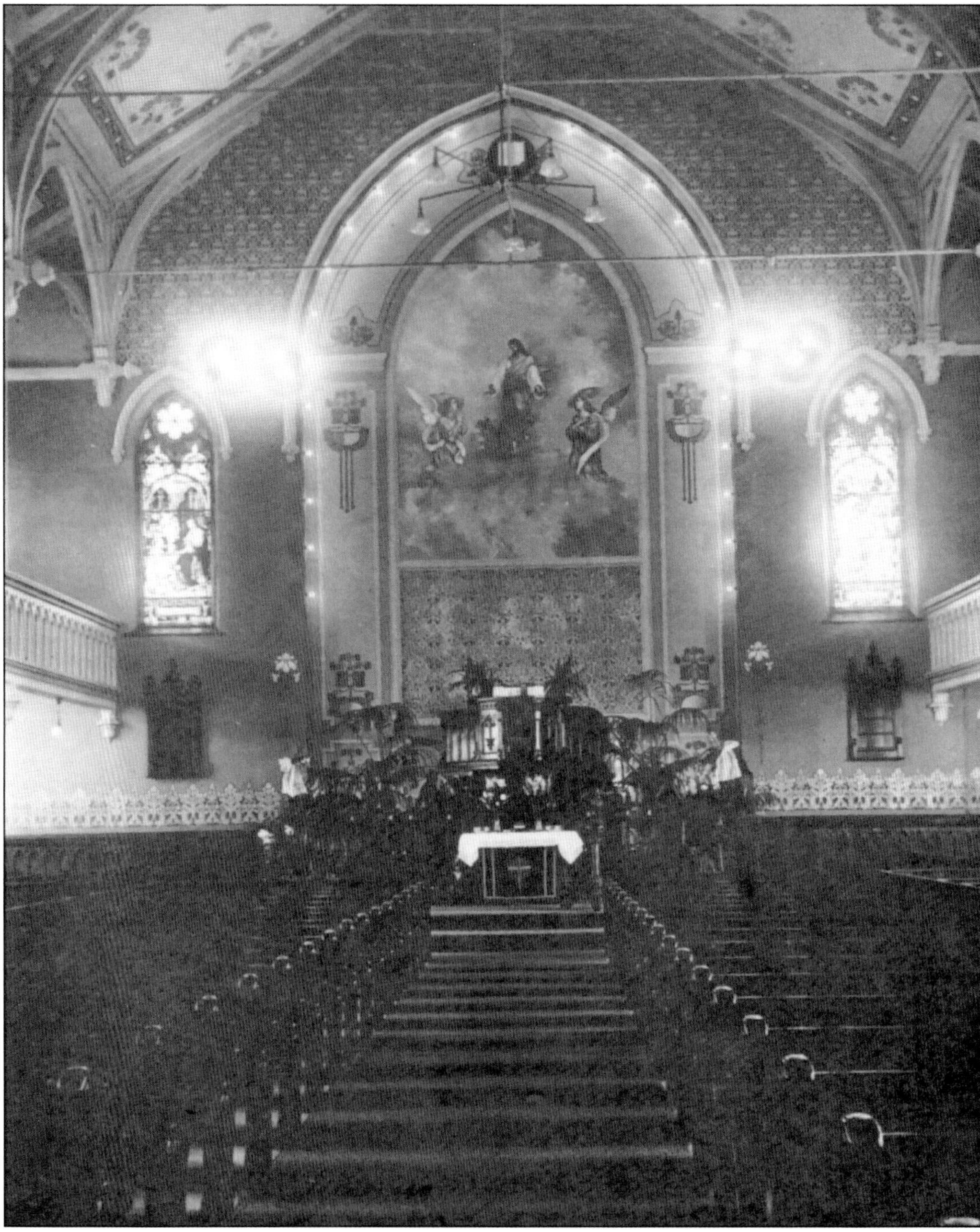

The early years at 285 Hickory Street were very prosperous for St. John's. An extravagant 75th anniversary celebration was held in 1908, and electrical fixtures were installed in July 1910, eliminating the "gloominess" of the gaslit sanctuary. As explained in the church's centennial anniversary booklet, "After all, does not God give us the sunlight by day and the moonlight by night to brighten our existence? Then shall His House also be a place of Light and Happiness, and may St. John's always be a bright and cheerful home for sad and disconsolate hearts." The ambiance of the new lights is beautifully captured here. Unfortunately, disaster struck (literally) a few years later, when lightning hit the church tower and caused $4,000 in damages. According to church records, this continued to be an issue, as the church was struck "repeatedly" in subsequent years.

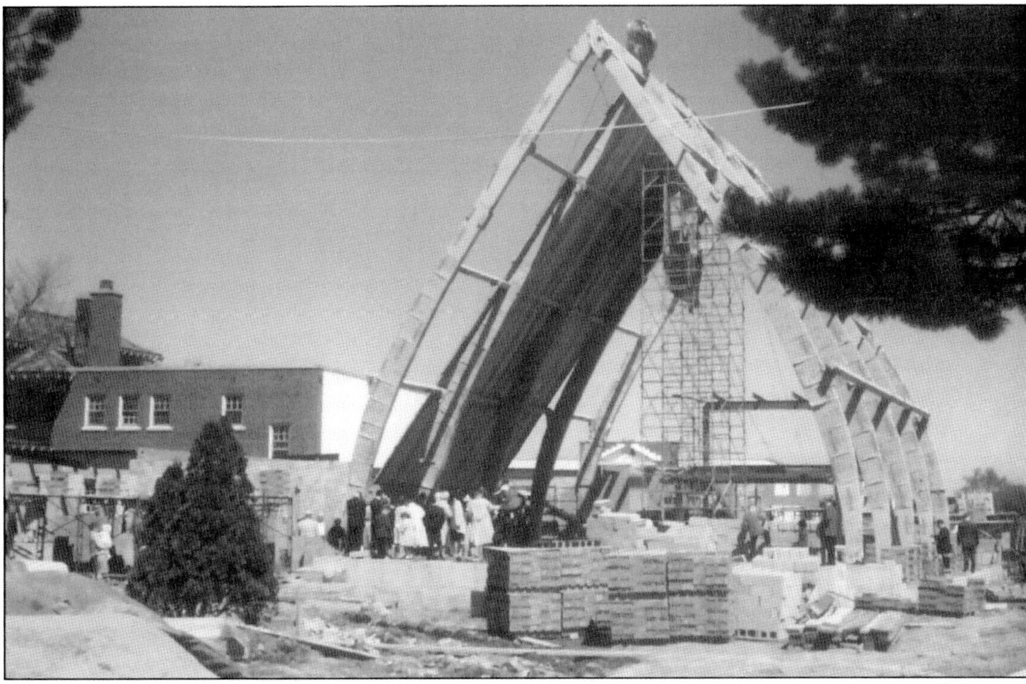

The congregation of St. John's continued to thrive on Hickory Street for the remainder of the 19th century. By the middle of the 20th century, however, a shift was beginning to take place. Many parishioners were moving to other parts of the city or leaving for the suburbs. Feeling that a good church must follow its flock, a plot of land was bought on Main Street in Amherst, and a new chapter began. The congregation utilized an existing house and quickly constructed a fellowship hall where services could be held until the church building was complete. Construction of the new St. John Lutheran Church in Amherst was completed in 1964 and dedicated on January 24, 1965.

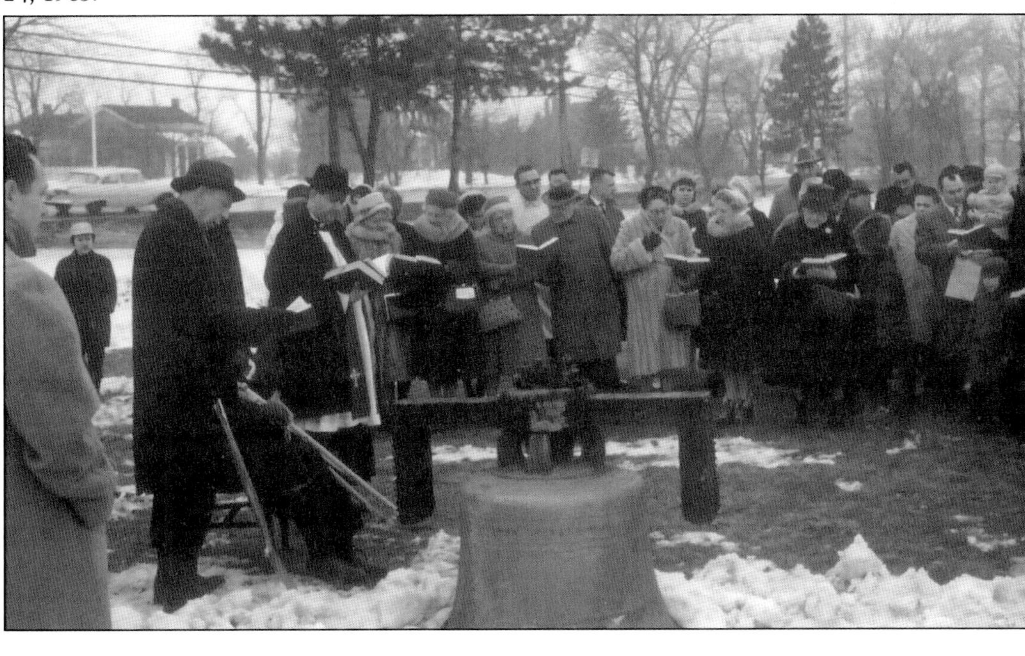

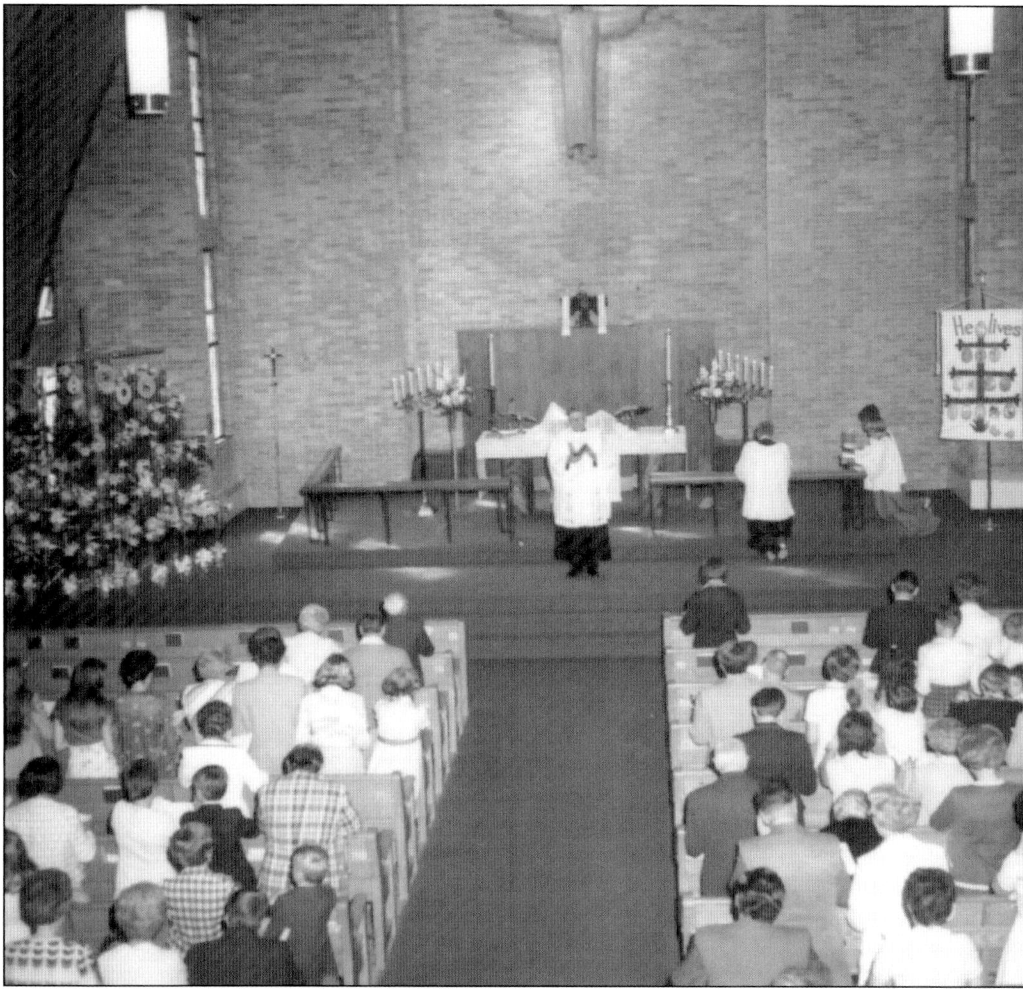

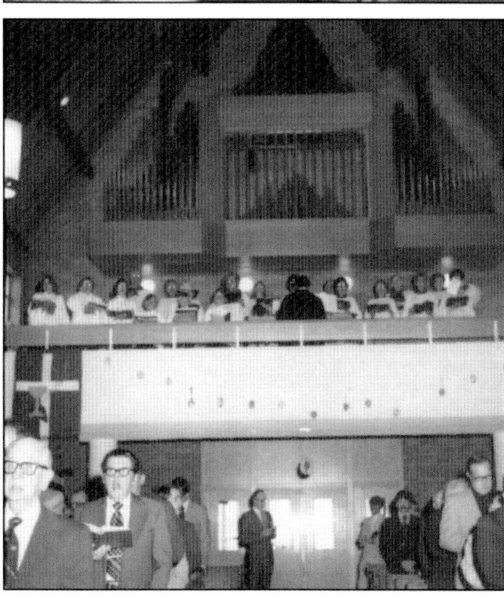

The new St. John church in Amherst was radically different than its predecessor. Utilizing a more contemporary design, this building, designed by Clarence E. Donath, began as the vision of the pastor, Dr. John Schmidt. In alliance with his vision, 10 laminated wooden beams created a "visual allusion" to hands folded in prayer. Church records also declare that "a hand-carved statue of the Risen Lord, arms broadly extended in welcoming forgiveness, evokes an image of the cross where He delivered our salvation." The seven-foot, three-inch sculpture was created by the internationally renowned German artist Otto Flath. At its dedication, Dr. Schmidt observed that, "The figure with outstretched arms emphasizes the living Christ as the companion of His people in every generation." These photographs of the St. John sanctuary were taken on Easter, 1976.

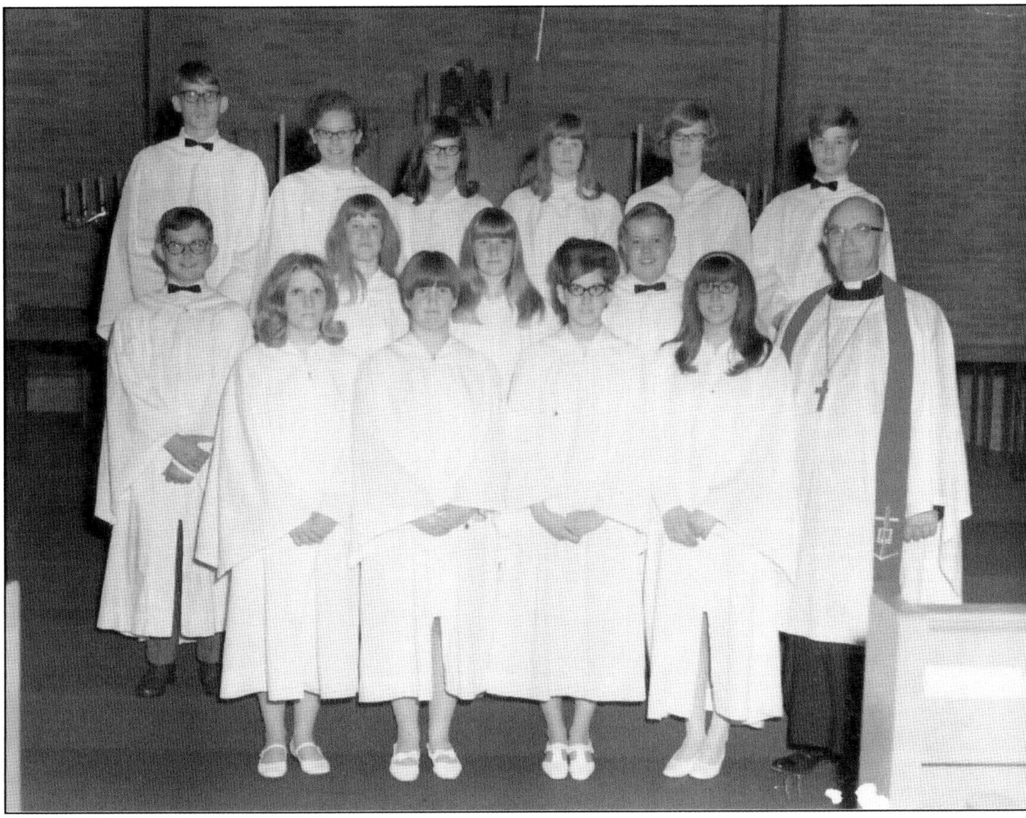

St. John in Amherst celebrated its confirmation class of 1968 (pictured) three years after the church was built. Thriving in its new location, St. John had successfully managed to retain the integrity of its past and embrace the path of its future. Whether in the city or the suburbs, St. John has remained a community institution and continues to thrive in its present location.

St. John's School of Buffalo opened in 1841, and an orphan's home was established in 1864. Here, schoolmaster John Laux and his class pose in the schoolyard on Hickory Street on July 24, 1876. Children were requested to bring 6¢ per week to the schoolmaster to supplement his $100 annual salary.

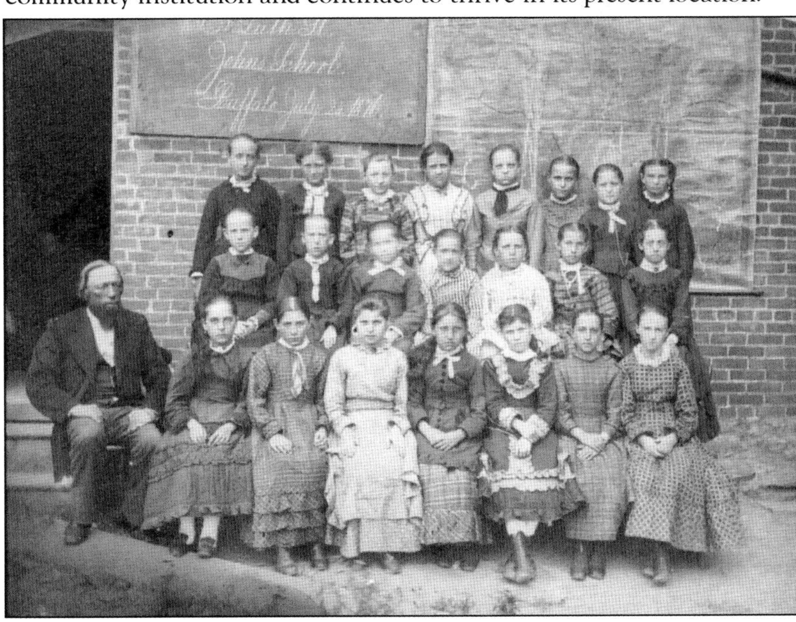

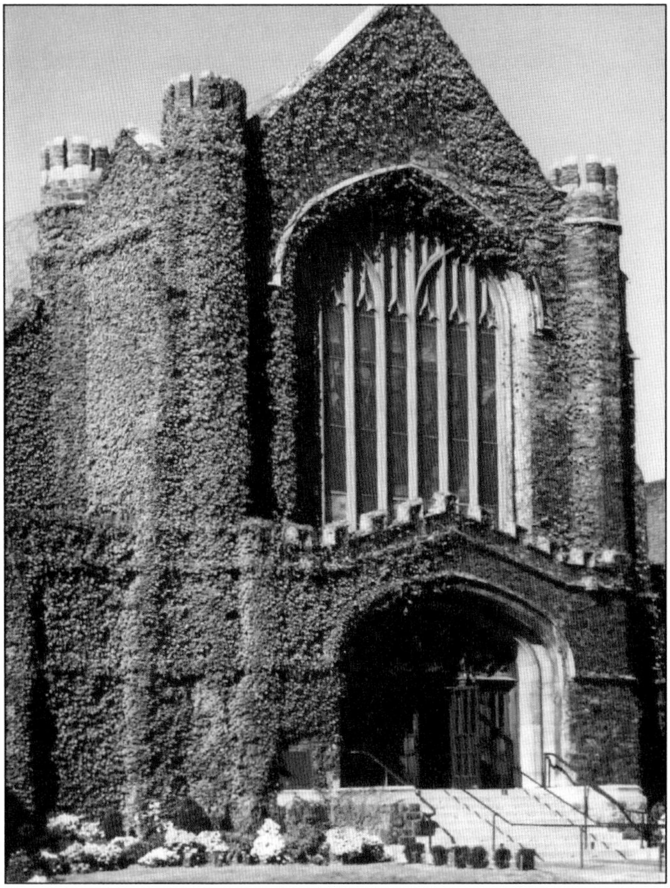

Given the melting pot atmosphere of the city of Buffalo in the late 1800s, some Lutherans began to rethink their strictly German orientation. In 1879, a group of 28 men and women from St. John's on Hickory Street gathered in the choir loft of the old French church and discussed a new beginning. On May 5 of the following year, 67 people attended their first English-spoken service. On May 4, 1881, the group officially became the English Evangelical Lutheran Church of the Holy Trinity. By 1899, the church purchased an old orchard on the west side of Main Street from the Hersee estate at a cost of $26,675. The cornerstone of Holy Trinity was laid on 1903. The first service in the new English Gothic building was held in April 1905, with more than 1,500 people in attendance. (Below, courtesy of The Traveling Picture Show.)

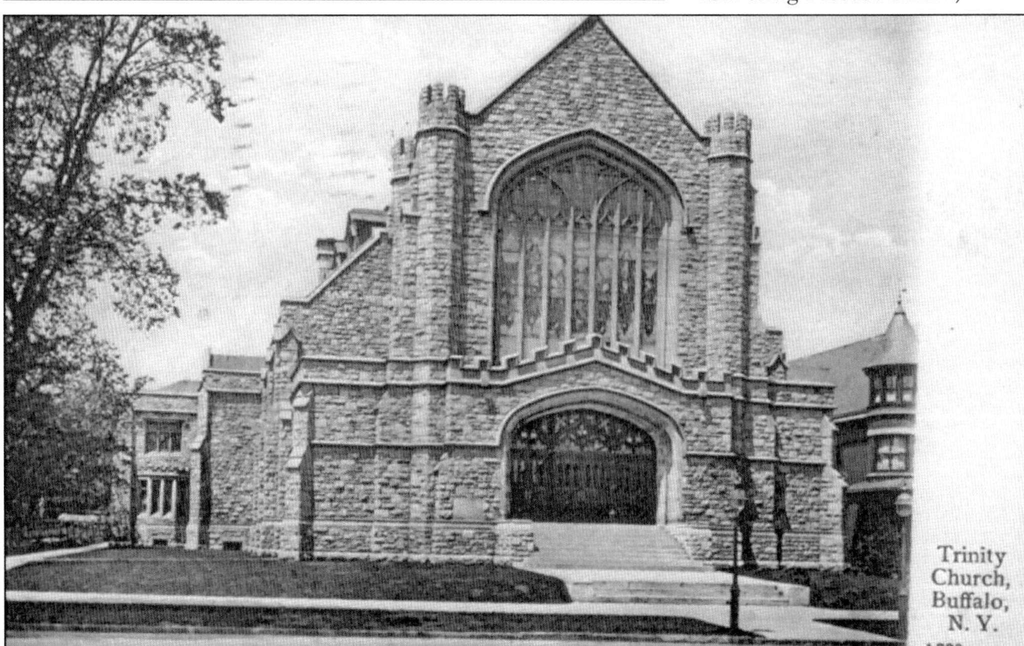

Holy Trinity was the mother church of seven Lutheran congregations: Church of the Atonement, Northland Avenue (1894); Church of the Redeemer, West Ferry (1895); Grace Church, Cazenovia Street (1904); Church of the Reformation, Pine Ridge (1910); Church of the Resurrection, Doat Street (1911); Parkside Lutheran, Wallace Avenue (1912); and Kensington Evangelical Lutheran, Kensington Avenue (1919). These 1936 photographs shows Holy Trinity children's choir (right) and altar (below).

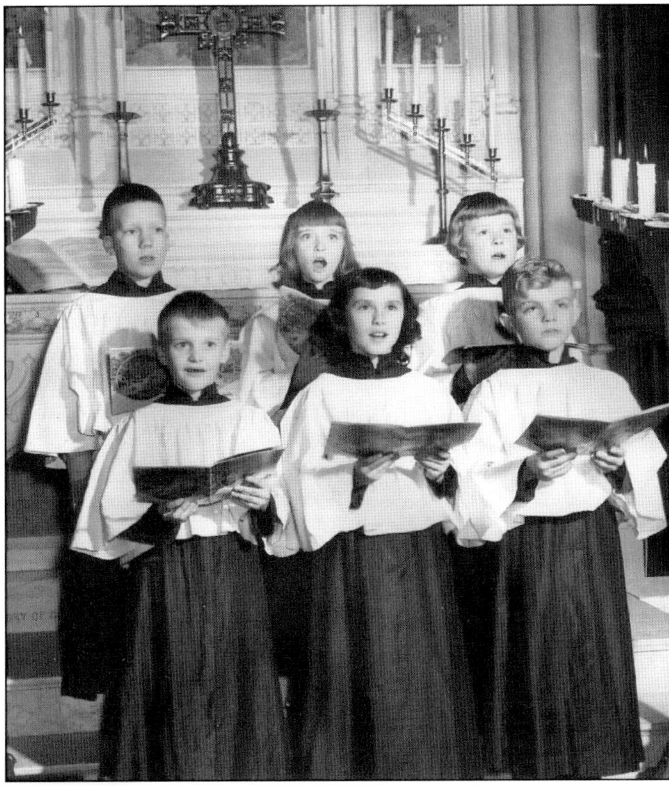

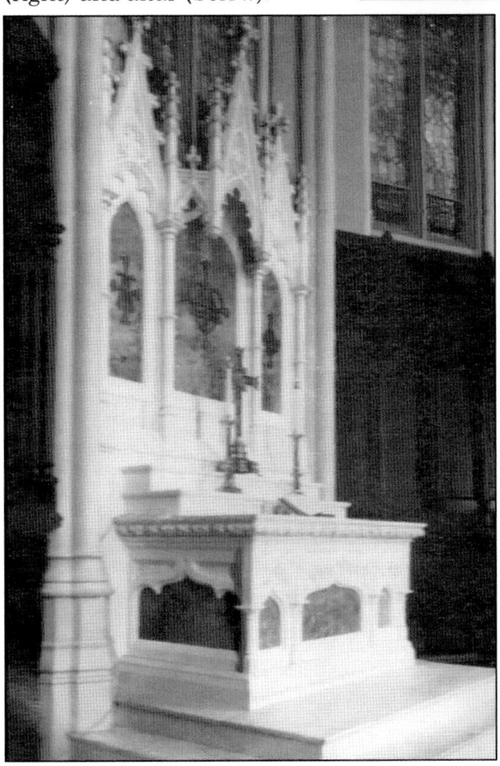

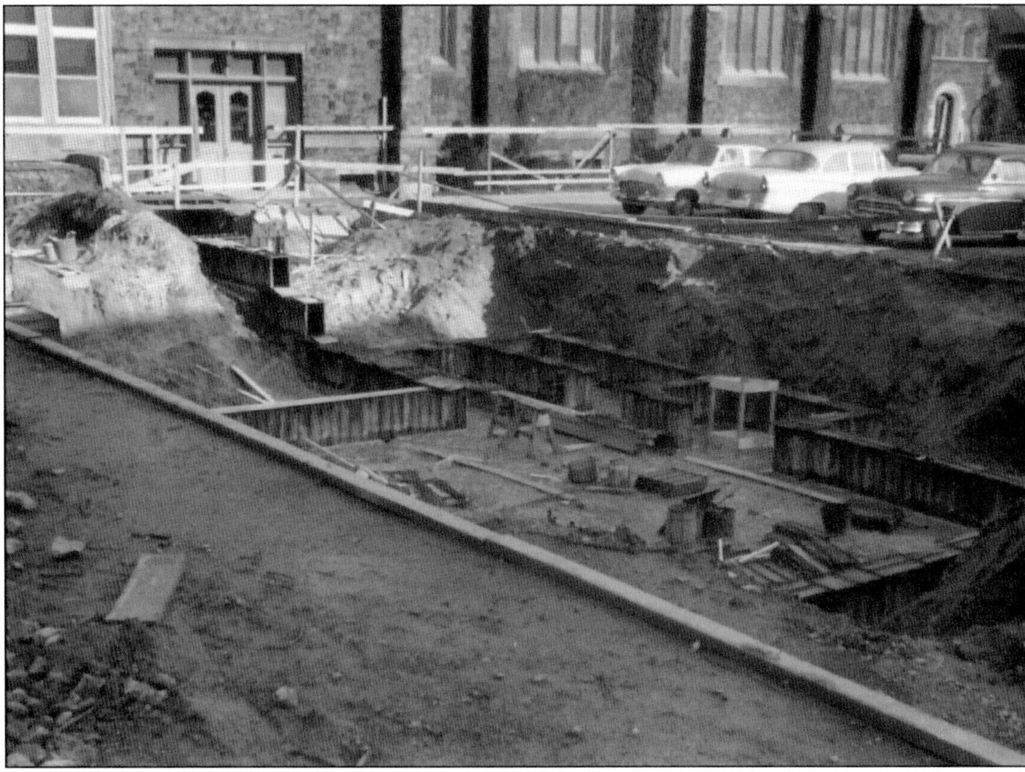

In 1957, construction on the chapel complex began. This project enabled the continuing ministry of word and sacraments in a beautiful, contemporary space. The building was dedicated on January 25, 1959, and named the Mansperger Chapel, after Dr. William Mansperger, who made monumental donations to Holy Trinity and the medical world at large. Dr. Mansperger served as chief of surgery for the Erie Railroad.

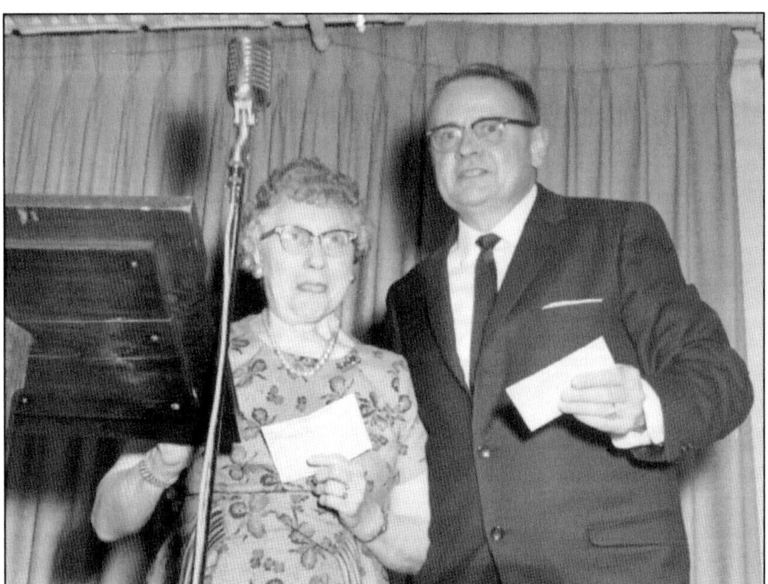

As declared in its mission statement, Holy Trinity remained "determined to meet human needs with a Christian faith translated into the language of a living word for all people through adherence to traditional Lutheran worship, an extensive music program, quality education and Christian fellowship." In 1964, Holy Trinity celebrated its 85th anniversary with many festivities.

The Church of Atonement was organized on May 2, 1895, by 88 members of Holy Trinity Lutheran Church. Department store owner and Holy Trinity founder William Hengerer donated funds for a frame structure at 553 Eagle Street and served with Dr. F.A. Kahler on the building committee. Shown here is the Reverend Hugo Dressler, pastor of the Church of Atonement from 1921 to 1947.

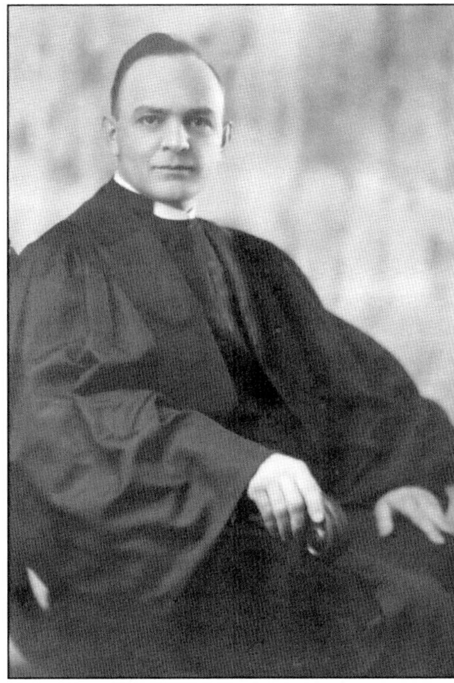

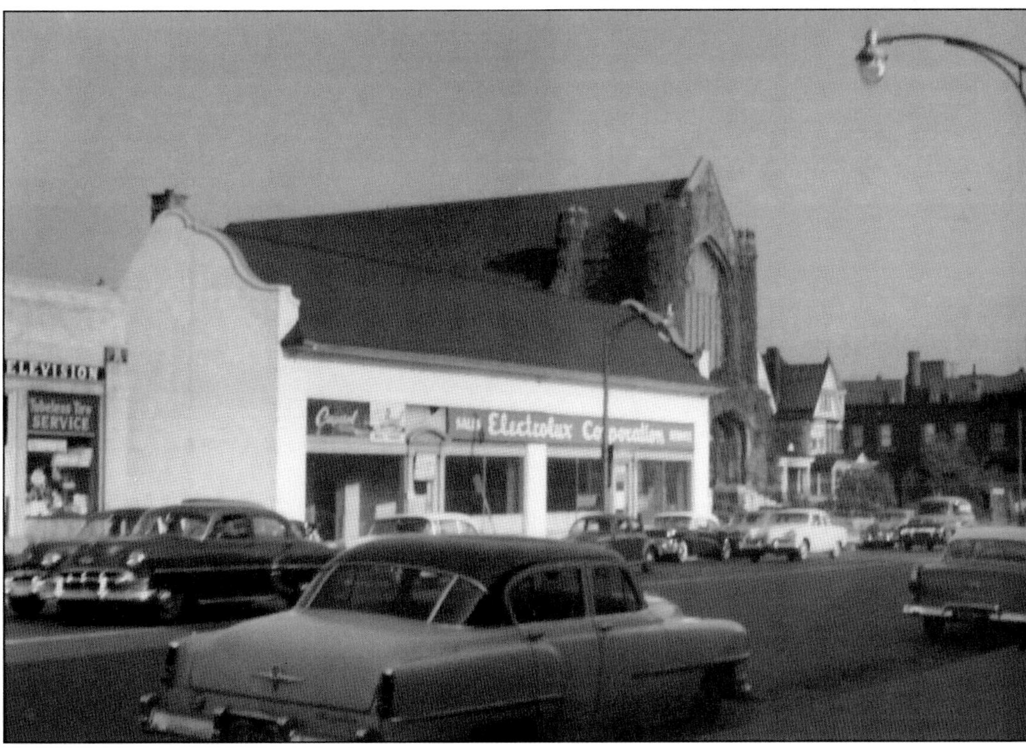

This c. 1956 photograph captures the energy of a busy Main Street. Taken in front of the present-day Anchor Bar, it shows ivy beginning to overtake the facade of Holy Trinity. While life outside the church was bustling, Holy Trinity was experiencing great success inside as well. In April 1957, *Life* magazine published Dr. Ralph Loew's sermon "The Eternity of a Little While."

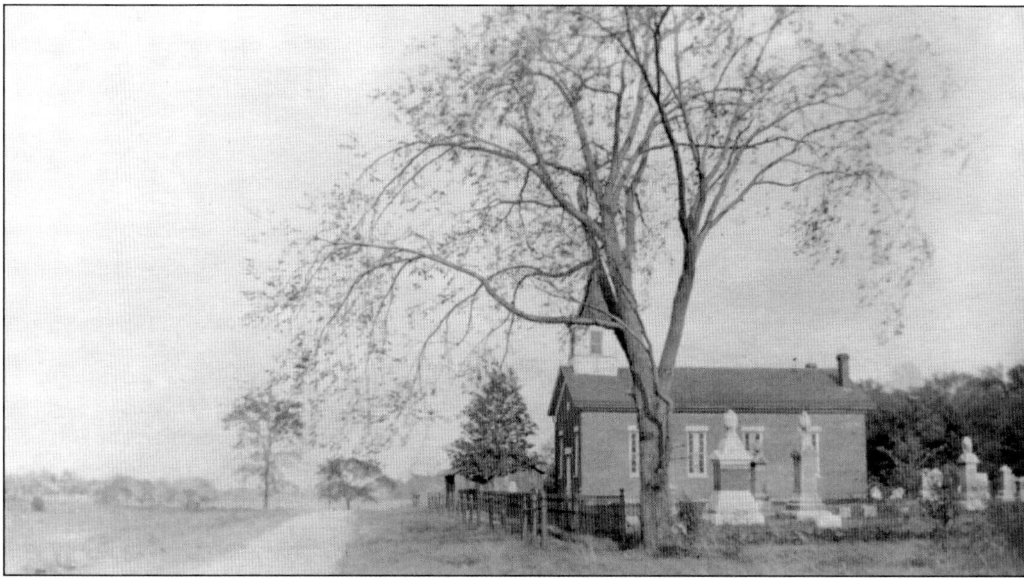

The oldest building in Tonawanda is a church with Lutheran ties. St. Peter's German Evangelical Church was organized in 1830, and this building was erected in 1849 with bricks made of clay from the Ives Pond area. The adjoining cemetery houses graves that predate the church, including that of Martin Zimmerman (1785–1847). The church stands on Knoche Road, just east of Elmwood Avenue, and serves as the Historical Society Museum. (Courtesy of Julianna Woite.)

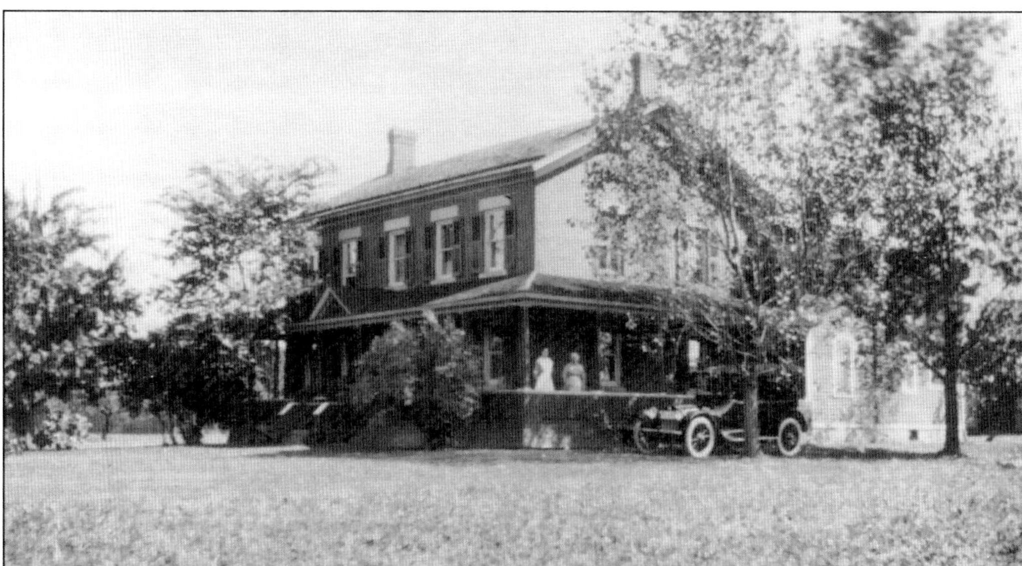

German Evangelical Church served area Lutherans, including the Knoche family, who donated the plot of land on which the church was constructed. Phillip Knoche was born in 1814 in Alsace-Lorraine and immigrated to America as a young man. Originally settling in Buffalo, Knoche built this 50-acre homestead in 1849 as a way to escape the city's cholera epidemic. His daughter Julianna is seen on the porch with an unidentified person around 1918. (Courtesy of Julianna Woite.)

A portion of the financing for German Evangelical Church came from the estate of John Pirson (1782–1849). Born in a German-speaking region of France, Pirson, his wife, and children relocated to America and settled in a log home in Tonawanda. The home was replaced with a brick homestead in 1848, currently standing at 2250 Military Road. Shown here is John's daughter Catherine Pirson (1813–1881). (Courtesy of Julianna Woite.)

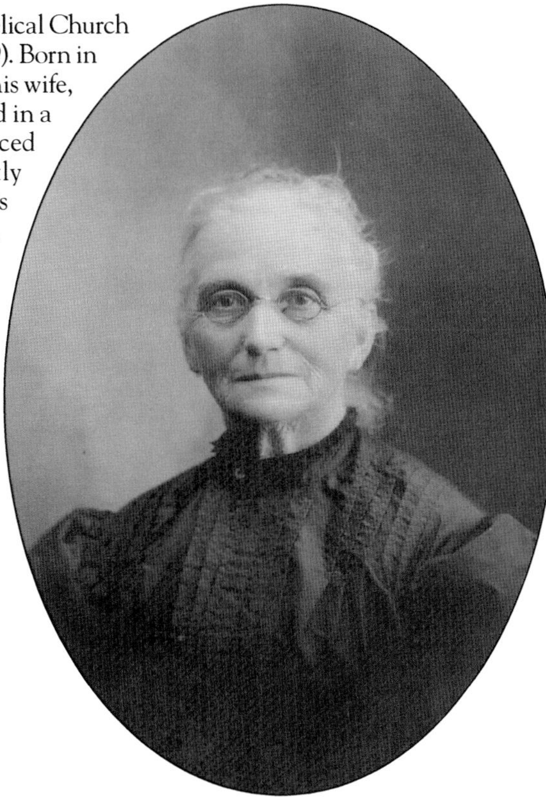

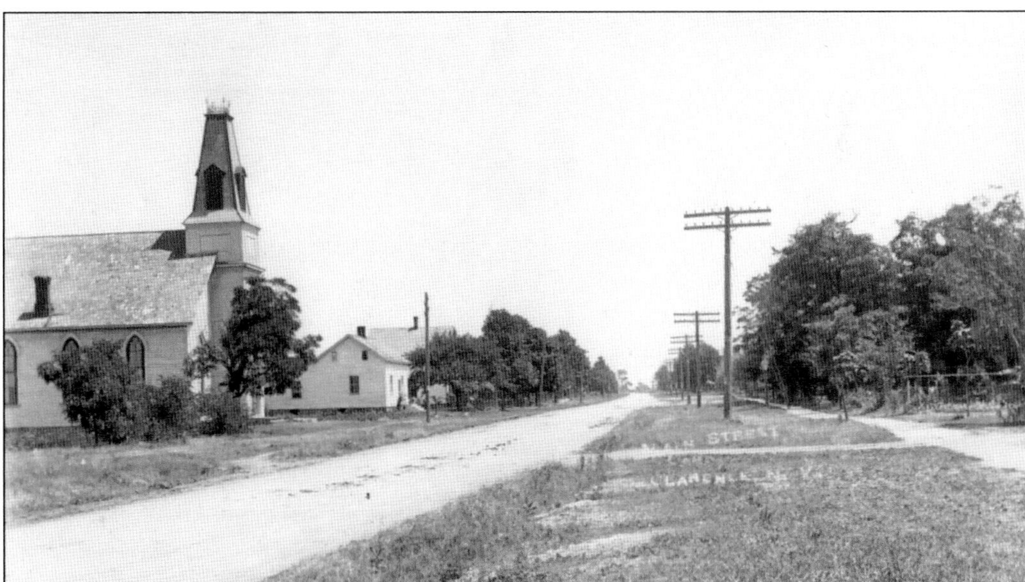

The town of Clarence also had a large German population, and a German Lutheran Church was established in Clarence Center in 1857. A German Reformed congregation was organized around 1859 and, under the leadership of the Reverend Schaad, constructed a church on the East Hill of Main Street in 1886 (pictured). A German Reformed society was founded in Clarence Center in 1865, but it was subsequently disbanded.

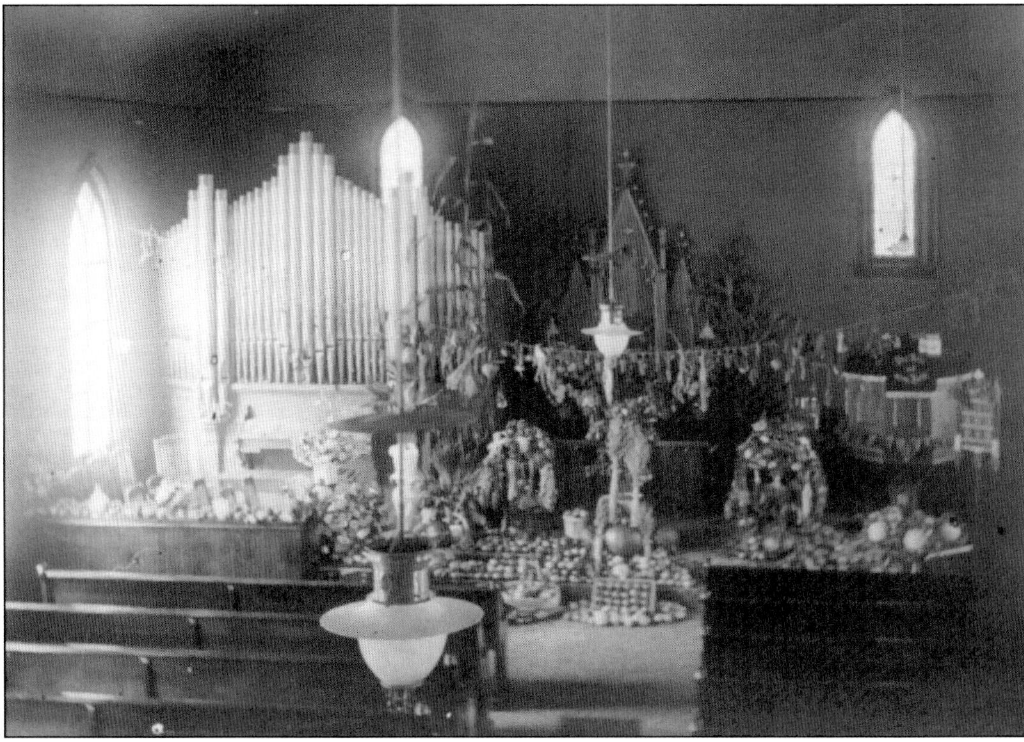

Churches have long been reflections of the communities they are a part of, and they have sought to meet the particular needs of the residents. A congregation in a rural setting will have service times that are convenient to a farmer's schedule. These congregations would often have a Harvest Sunday, when products of the harvest would be brought into the church. The produce would then be blessed, and God would be thanked for the plentiful harvest. St. Paul's Williamsville's Harvest Sunday is pictured above. The sanctuary was again photographed on an Easter Sunday (below), showcasing a vast display of Easter lilies.

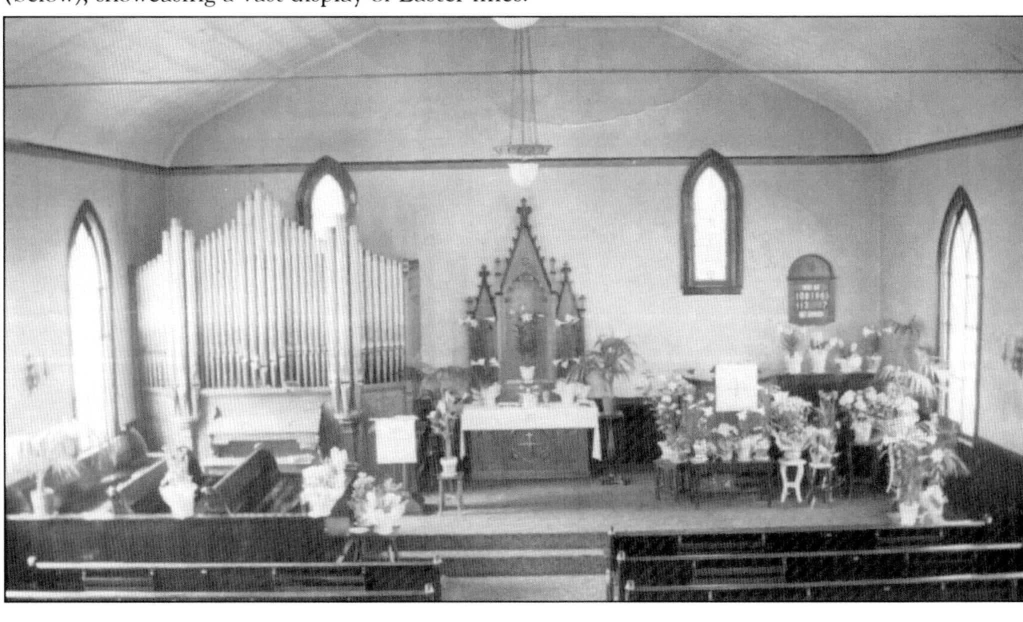

The earliest of American pastors were often called "circuit riders," a reference to the fact that most served several congregations. They would travel at regular intervals from one congregation to the next, often on horseback, quite literally in a circuit. A leader from within the congregation would lead services and tend to the church while the pastor was with another congregation. There were far more Lutheran congregations in America than Lutheran pastors. Today, congregations are sharing pastors again, not because of a shortage of pastors, but so that the cost of the pastor can be split between several congregations, helping them remain more viable. This page shows two St. John's pastors. Shown at right is Charles Volz (1857–1883); below is J.A.W. Kirsch (1896–1914).

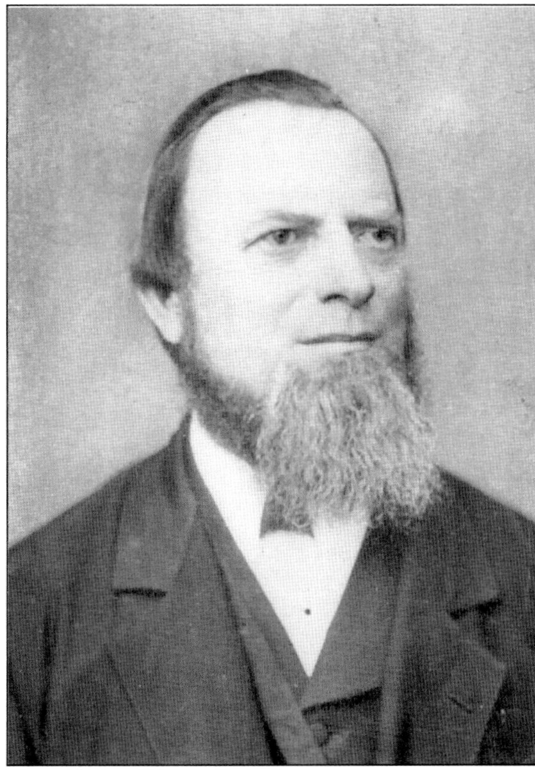

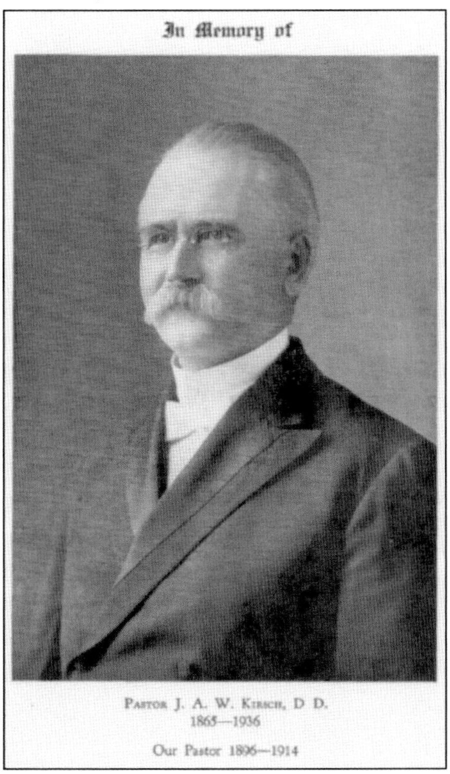

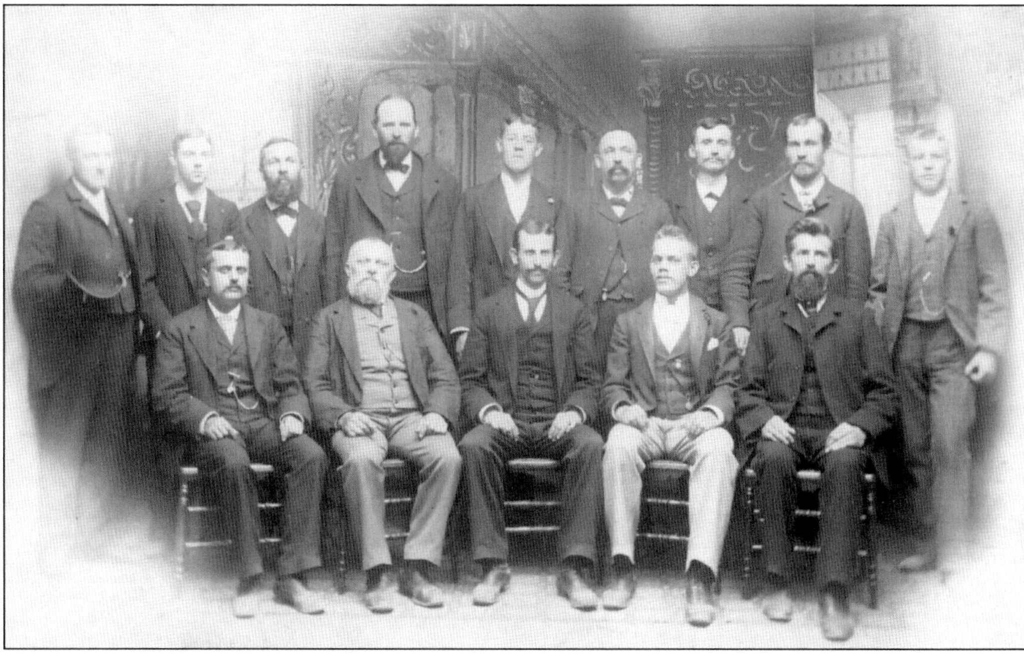

Although Buffalo Christ Church was a thriving congregation at the turn of the 20th century, as the demographics of the city began to change, it and other churches were forced to close their doors. The Buffalo Christ Church officers pose on August 4, 1891. They are, from left to right, (first row) George Flierl (president), Jacob Hamscher (vice president), Julious Villnow (recording secretary), Emil Schmelzer (corp secretary), and David Hummel (treasurer). The rest are unidentified.

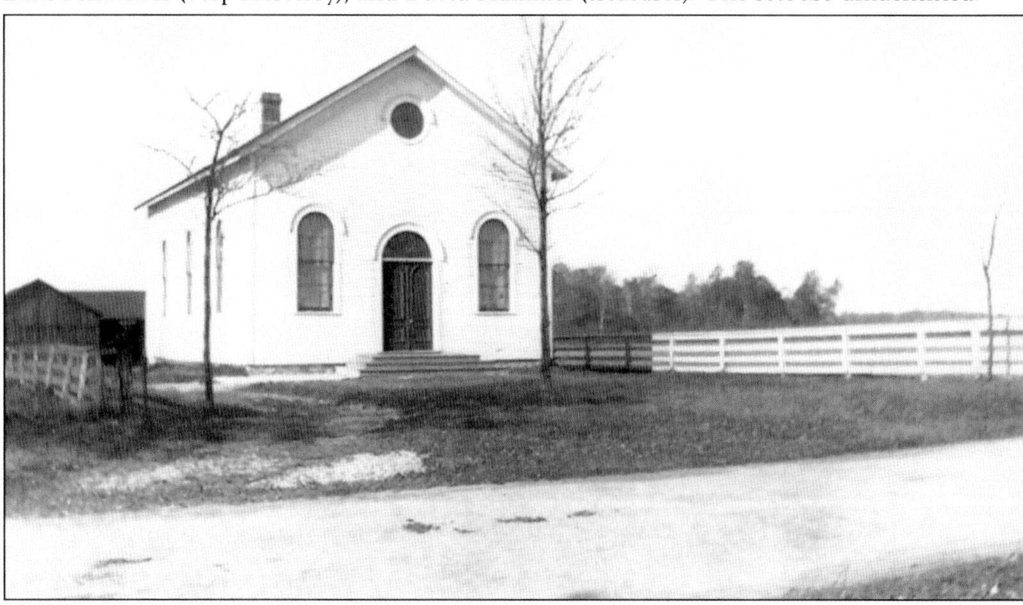

The present Trinity Evangelical Lutheran Church of South Newstead was formed on November 6, 1871, under the name German Evangelical Lutheran Church of Akron–Town of Newstead. Pastor Ernest Heydler was called as the first pastor, and he served the church from 1872 to 1873. Worship services were held every two weeks, with about 44 communing members. This is the first church building, completed in 1876.

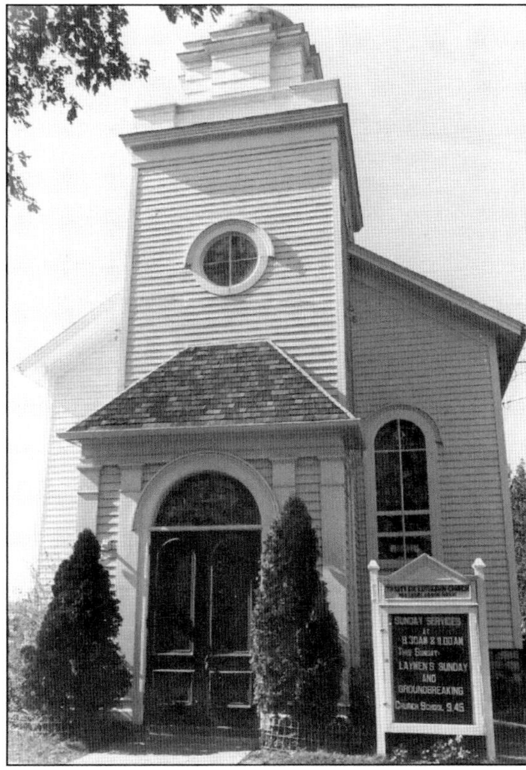

The original church building for Trinity South Newstead was dedicated in 1876. In 1931, several additions were built, including a new bell tower and entryway, both of which can be seen here. This building would continue to serve the congregation until a new church was erected and dedicated in 1969. The new church was constructed directly across the street from the original building. On the Sunday of the new church's dedication, service began in the old building. Midway through the service, the congregation walked across the street to enter their new church and finish the service in their new home.

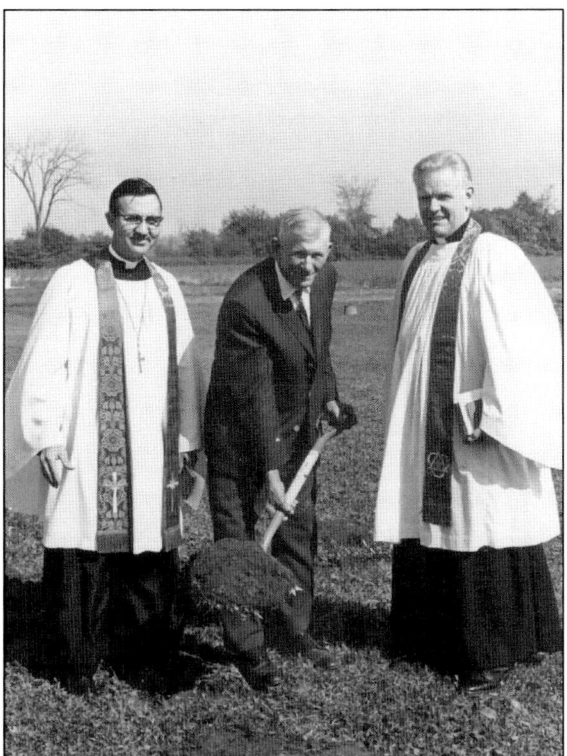

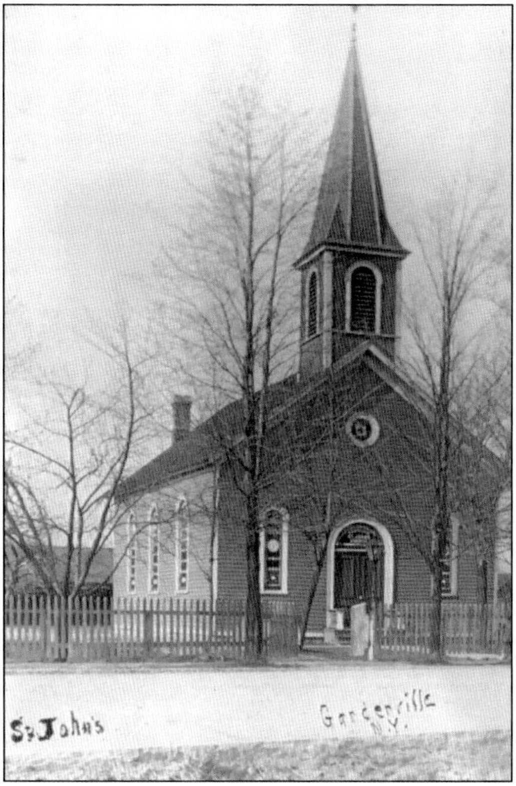

St. Johannes Evangelishe Lutheranishe Gemeinde (St. John's Lutheran Church in Gardenville) was formed by a community of German families. Like many early Lutherans, they came to America to escape religious persecution. Initially meeting in a schoolhouse, the congregation eagerly embraced its first church building (left), erected on Clinton Street in 1870. A parsonage was immediately added in 1872. The growing congregation erected a new church in 1913 (below). The old church was used for Sunday school and social activities. German remained the language of St. John's in West Seneca until the 1930s, when the transition was finally made to English. (Both, courtesy of The Traveling Picture Show.)

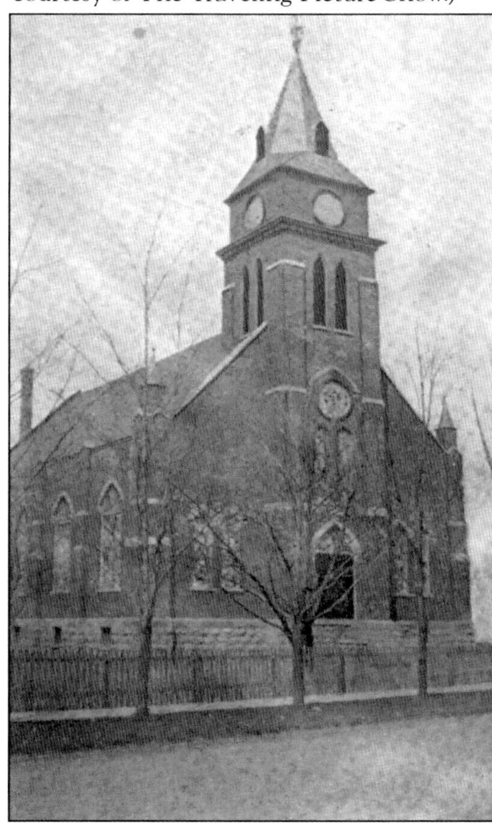

Two

Life within Church Walls

As Lutheranism moved away from being somewhat insular and decidedly German, the concept of what it meant to be a community evolved as well. Lutheran churches bonded their communities together in ways as varied as the churches themselves. The only true constant between these approaches would be the Christian faith and its Lutheran expression. With God taking a central role, Lutheran congregations began to participate in a wide array of activities. Groups were formed that were designed to appeal to particular groups of people. There were men's groups, women's groups, and youth groups, each planned and conceived to help people connect with their faith in a way that suited them. In addition, groups were formed to help conduct the business of the church, such as property committees and evangelism committees. Committees were overseen by a church council, an elected group from within the congregation tasked with helping the pastor lead and direct the church. Being a part of the church council was seen as a great responsibility, and many members of these early councils truly helped to build their church. The group whose contributions were most apparent during worship was the choir. Choirs of varying types were formed, including junior choirs for children, bell choirs, and senior choirs. Each of these groups introduced their unique talents to the service. The story of these groups and the activities they planned and participated in are the story of the community. It was life within church walls that would help define what a church was and what it would become.

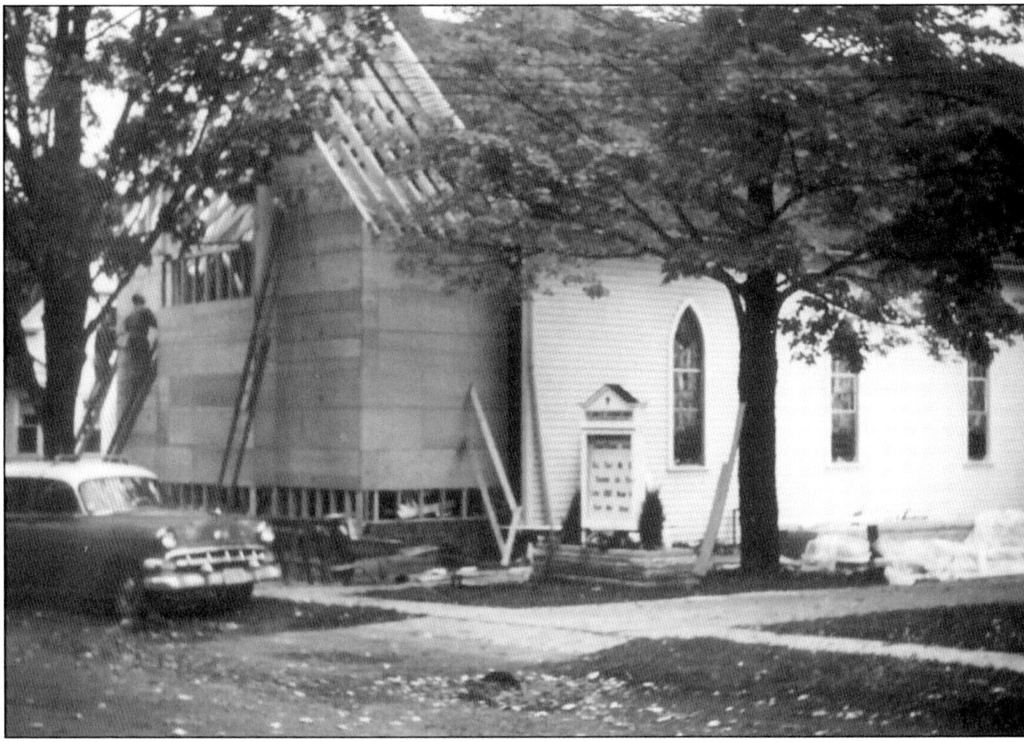

Lutheran church construction is a case of form fitting function. The distinguishing features serve particular purposes. A large central room is necessary to serve as a sanctuary, a place of worship. A large open room, often below the sanctuary, serves as a gathering area for social events and community meals. The bell tower or steeple atop the church serves as a sort of community alert system. The ringing of the bell from atop the church alerted the community to the goings-on of the church and any meetings that may be held at the church. The large and tall design of the church made its identification easy and helped people visiting the community find it. The church was often the tallest and most identifiable building in town. Pictured here is St. John's Akron.

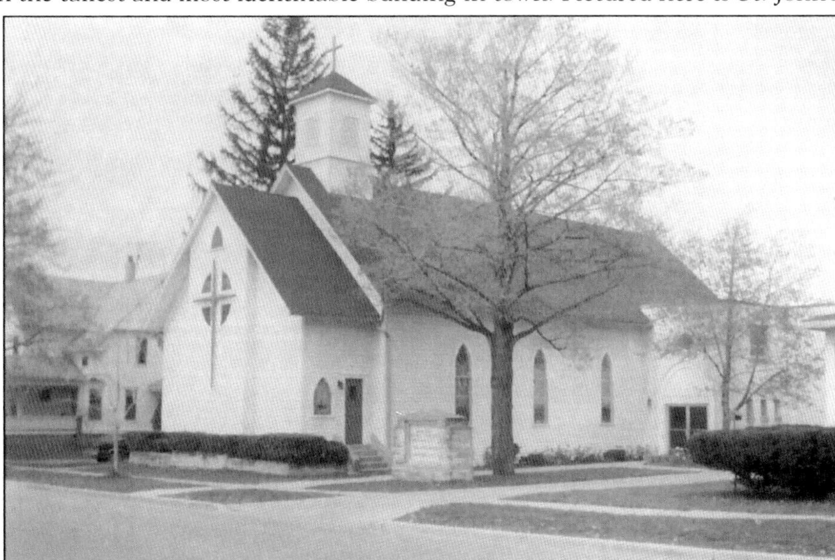

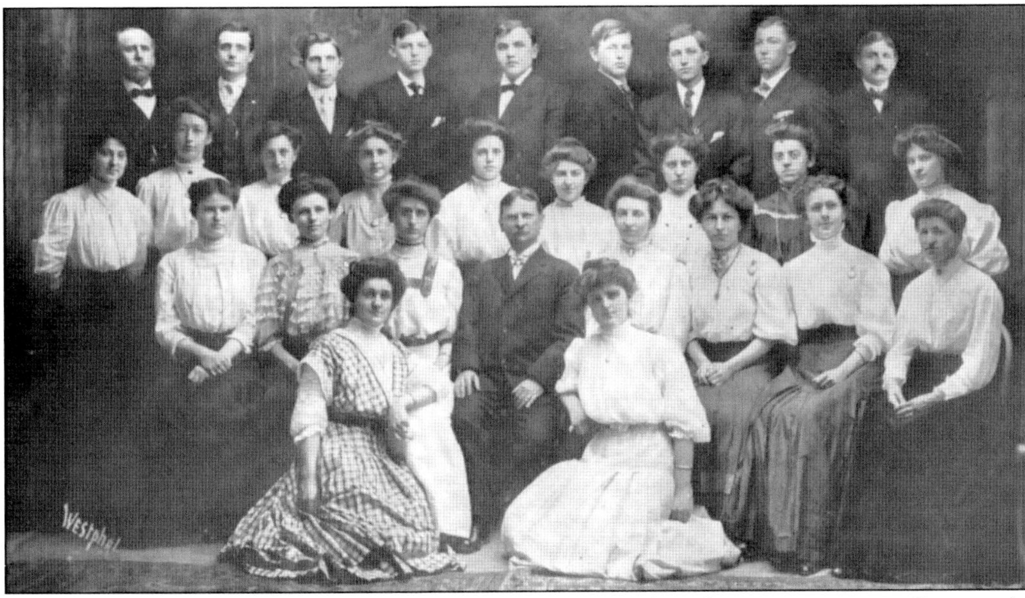

In the early years, a city congregation may have had a developed music program, reflecting the more cosmopolitan lifestyle of the congregation. A congregation in the suburbs, on the other hand, would focus on social events and activities that met the needs of the families living around the church. Pictured here is the St. Johannes Church Choir of Buffalo in 1908.

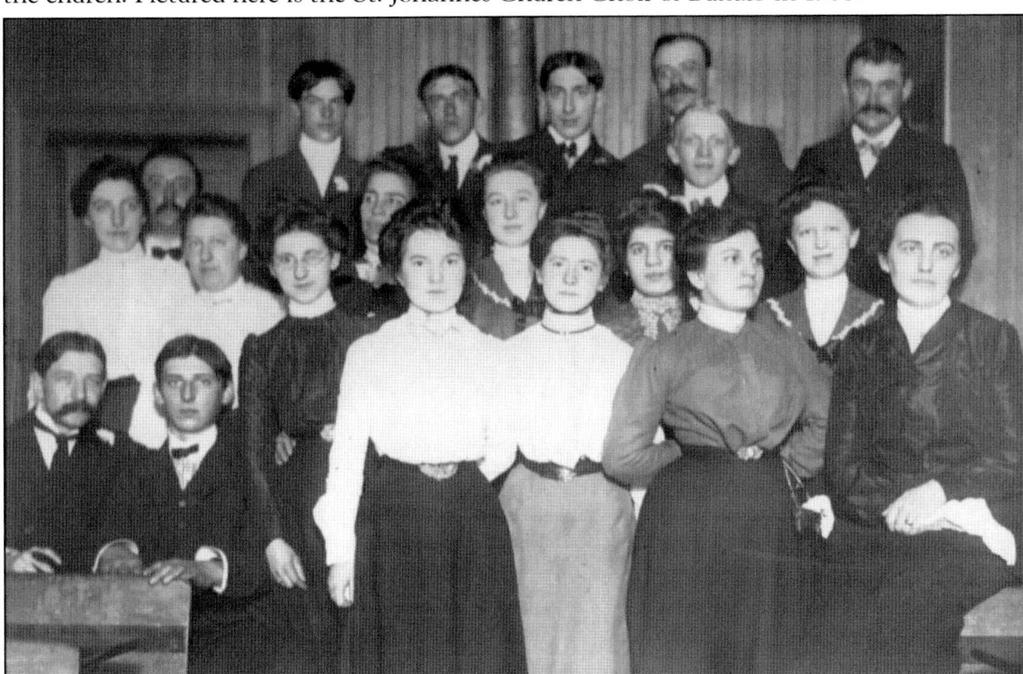

The St. Paul's Eggertsville choir is seen here in 1903. Shown here are, from left to right, (first row) a Mr. Schmidt, A. Kinderman, Kathryn Sappelt, Lydia Near, Ida Sappelt, Mrs. Martin Burke, and Mrs. Olga Schmidt; (second row) Sophia Burke, Elma Weber, Clara Wingert, Anna Webert, Elizabeth Wingert, and Katie Weber; (third row) Reverend Burke, Adolph Burke, Joe Moppert, Martin Burke, organist William Burmeister, and Charles Siegel.

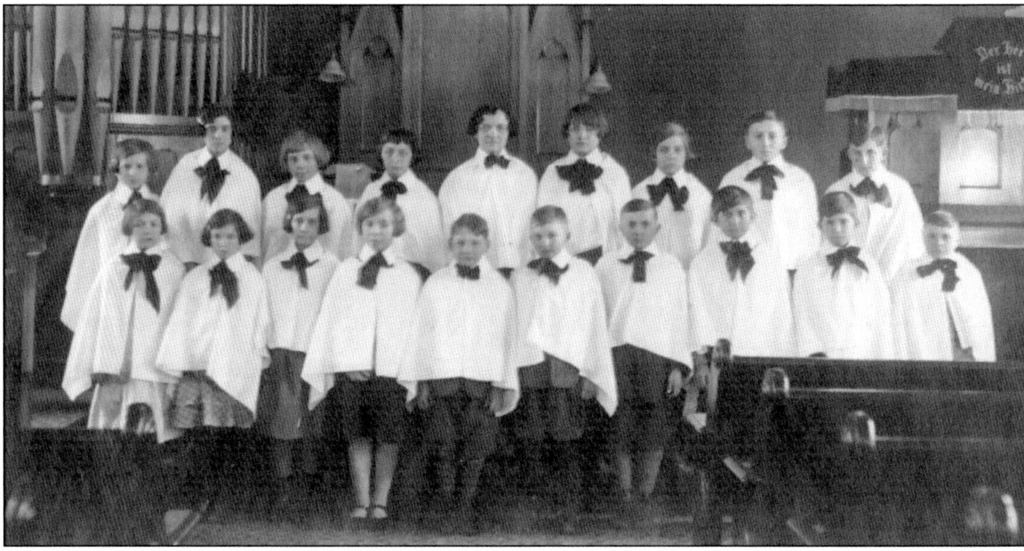

Engaging the youth and keeping them involved though adulthood has always been a priority of the Lutheran Church. Seen here is an early-1920s youth choir from St. Paul's Church in Williamsville. Cora Gramm (second row, center) served as choir director. The efforts certainly worked for Dorothy Landel Shaver (first row, second from left), an active member of this congregation for 95 years.

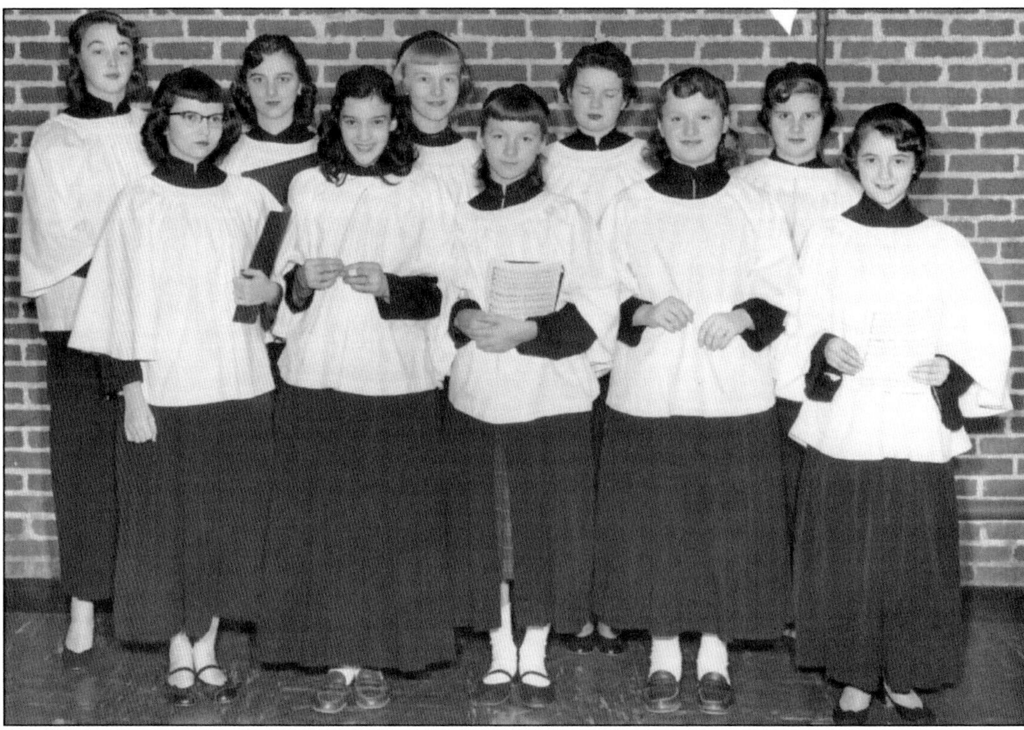

A children's choir has been a long-standing tradition for Lutheran youth. In the early years, only the affluent city congregations offered this activity. Today, however, it is a widespread and celebrated tradition. Pictured is the children's choir of Parkside Lutheran Church on Easter, April 10, 1955. Members included Patricia Allein, Barbara Schlitzer, Gretchen Dunden, Judy Eppers, Karen Olstad, Nancy Allein, and others.

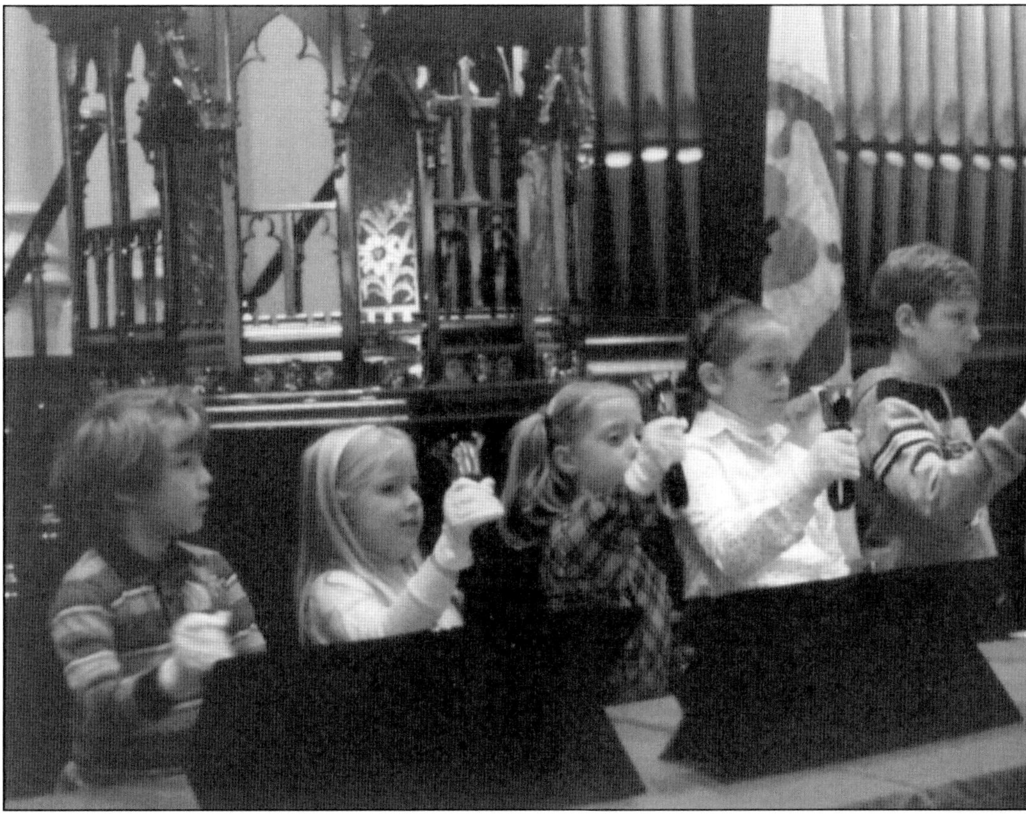

In medieval times, Christians traveled through Europe, ringing bells to spread the word of the risen Christ. Although handbells have been in existence since the 17th century, the tradition of ringing handbells in church did not come to America until the early 1900s. Since then, a handbell choir has been a valued Lutheran tradition for young and old alike. Pictured here are some Holy Trinity youth ringers in 1982.

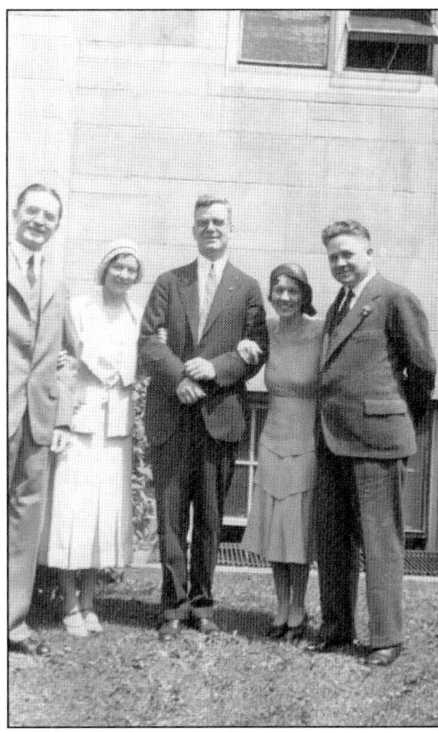

Music has been an integral part of the Lutheran Church since its inception. This image of the Parkside Quartet was given to retired pastor Fleck in Boston in 1981, when he hired a moving company and serendipitously met Larry Dryer, son of the group's tenor. Pictured is the quartet in 1933. Members are, from left to right, Thomas Woodruff (baritone), Geraldine Ayers (contralto), Harry Whitney (organist), Helen Minchen (soprano), and Elmer Dyrer (tenor).

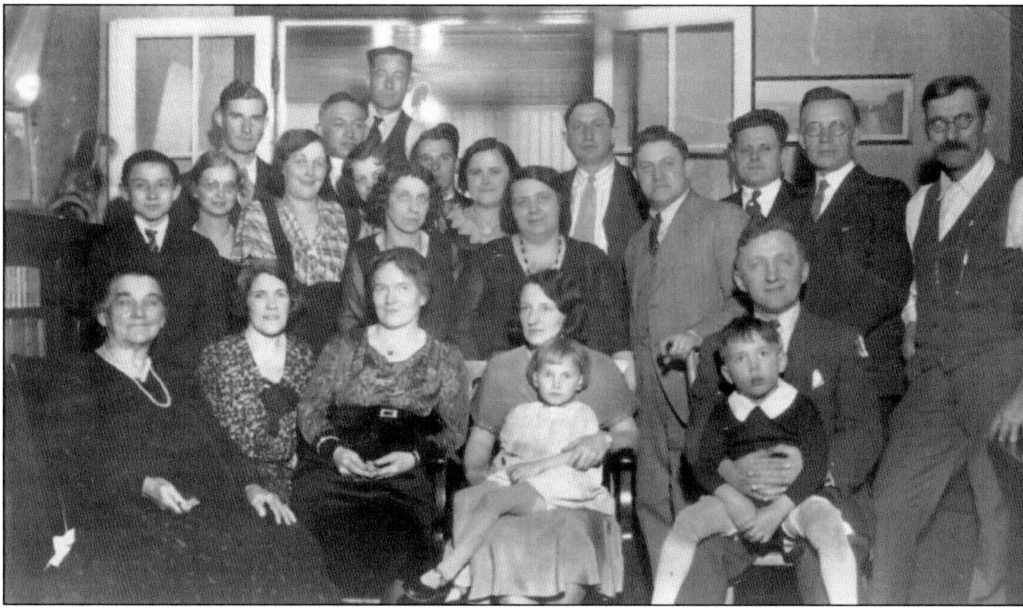

The 1933 choir of St. Paul's Lutheran Church in Eggertsville included, from left to right, (first row) a Mrs. Merrill, Jesse Schott, Mary Popper, and Emelia Merrill and Charles Schott, both holding children; (second row, in no particular order) Robert Dehn, Nora Holzel, Margaret Merrill, Mary Dearlove, Estella Allenbach, Ralph Thurnhurr, Florence Graf, Elise Den, Arthur Popper, and three unidentified; (third row) Albert Hornung, George Koch, and Charles Allenbach; (fourth row) Chester Smith.

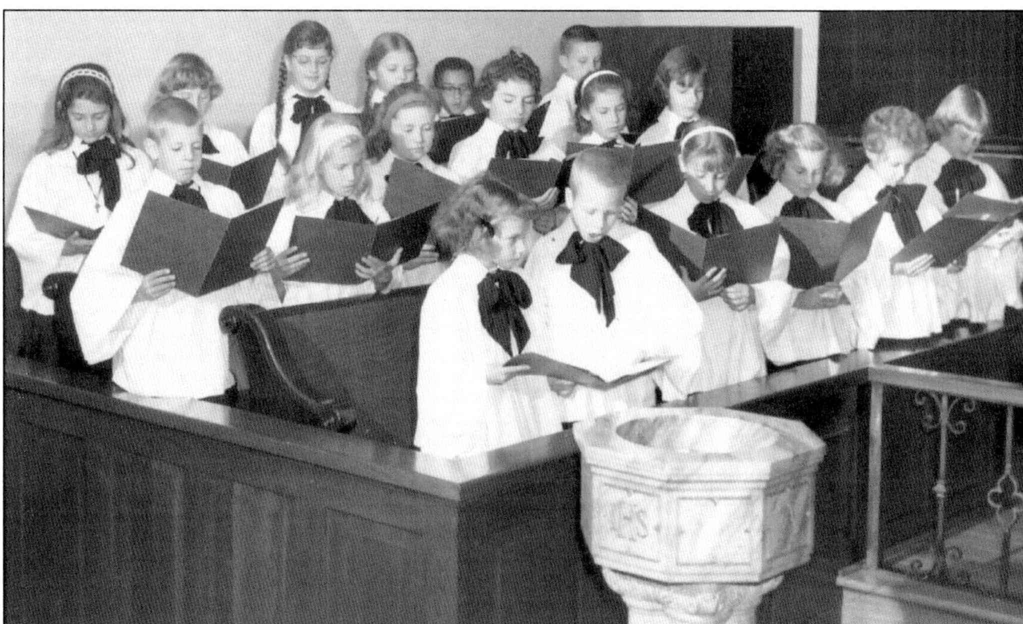

Each robe worn by those participating in church services has its own name and function. Here, the youth choir at St. Paul's Eggertsville is wearing a black cassock covered by a white surplice, a traditional dress for Lutheran choirs. The combination of these two vestments has been common in churches for hundreds of years.

One of the highlights of St. Paul's in Eggertsville's 120th anniversary celebration in 1947 was the installation of a new Moller pipe organ. Although it has undergone a few updates and modifications, including being rebuilt in 1973 by the Delaware Organ Company, this Moller organ serves the congregation of St. Paul's to this day.

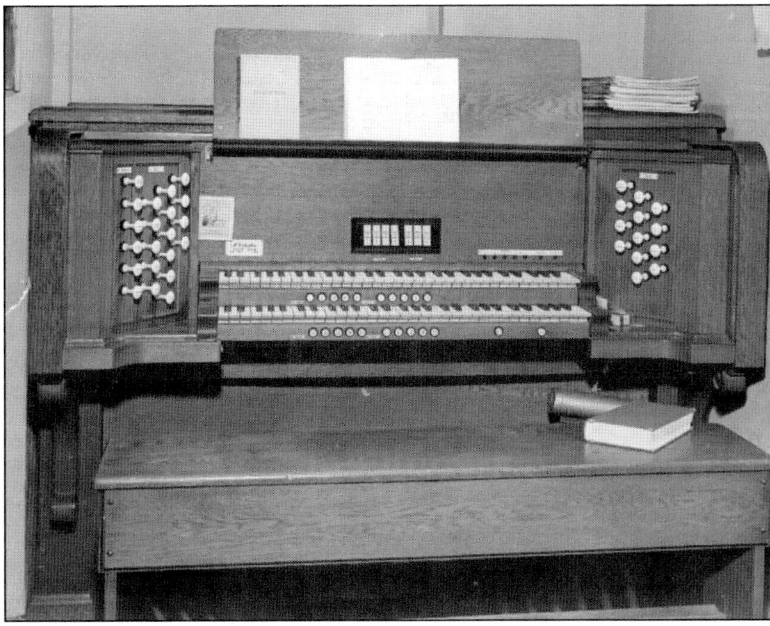

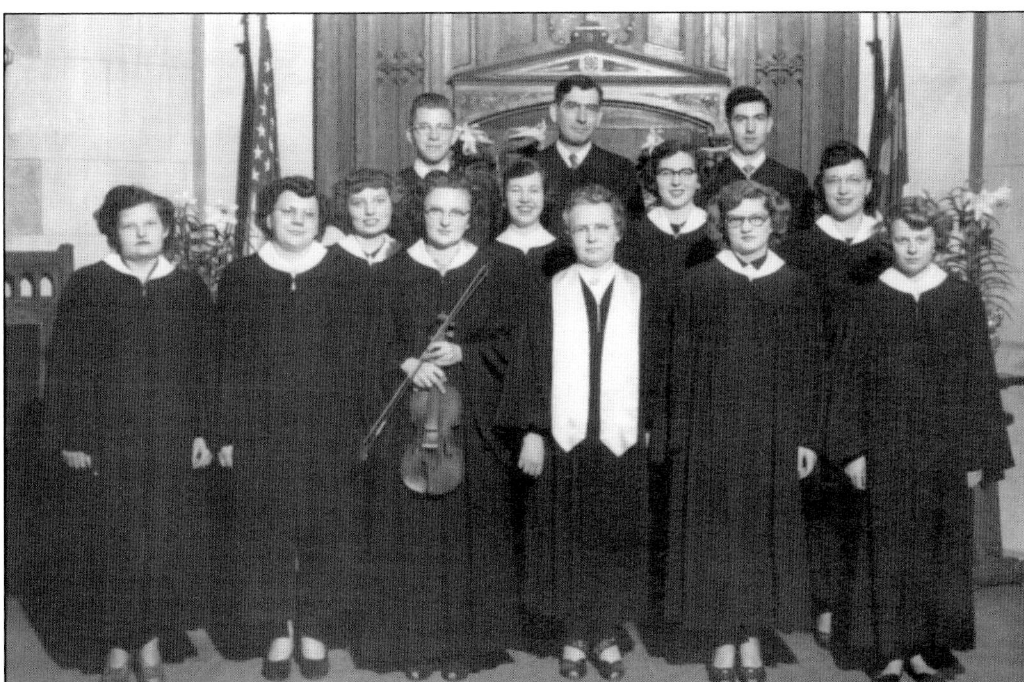

Easter is a time of grand celebration, meant to emulate the joy experienced at the resurrection of Jesus. Lilies decorate churches as a symbol of new life, and choirs often perform their most vibrant anthems. The St. John's Akron choir (pictured) included a violin for its special Easter music.

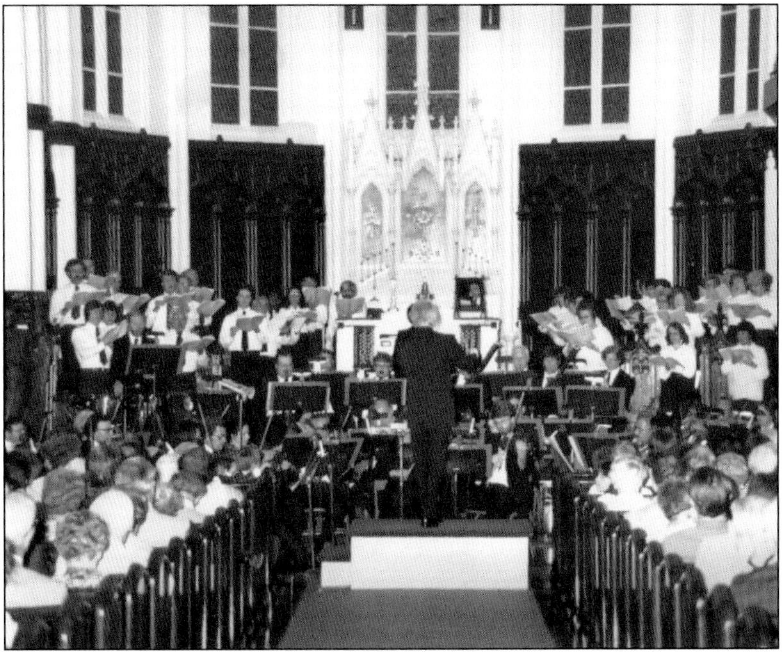

Holy Trinity has long been known for its powerful music program. In 1979, the same year Holy Trinity celebrated its 100th anniversary, choirmaster James Bigham's concert choir performed with the Buffalo Philharmonic Orchestra, conducted by Peter Perret. It was during this same year that the congregation honored Pastor Matthew Winters for the 25th anniversary of his ordination.

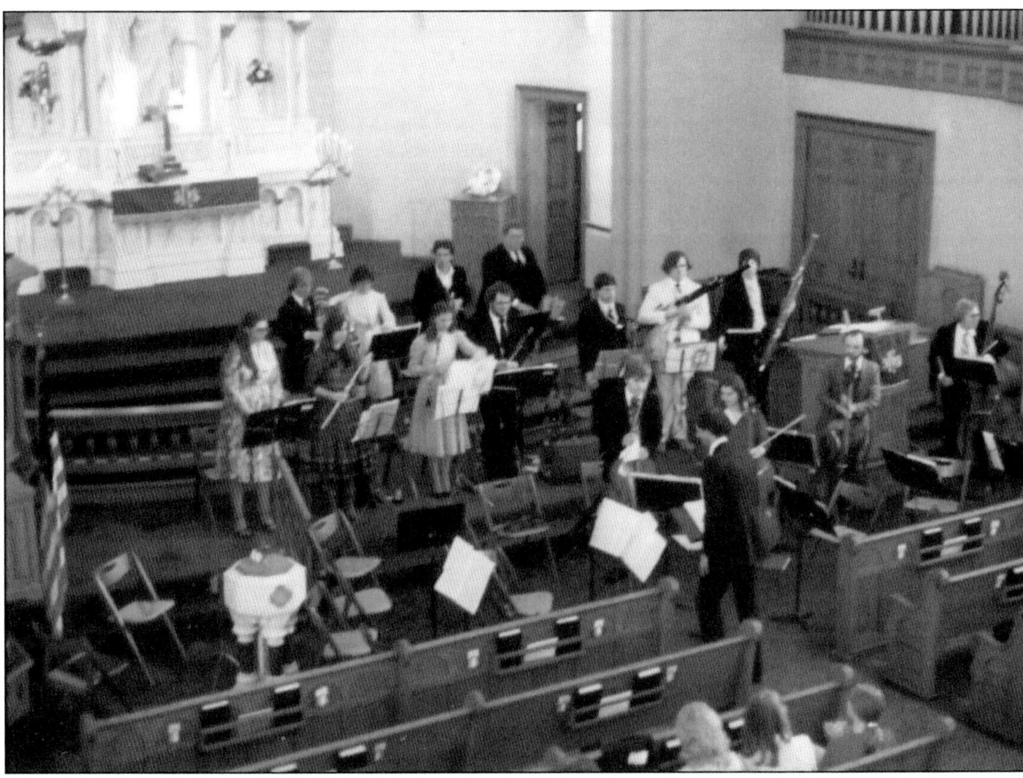

Music continued to be monumental at Holy Trinity in 1981. The University of Buffalo Philharmonic Orchestra performed in the main church. During this same year, a handbell choir was formed. This is also when the first tour of the Margaret L. Wendt Memorial Organ occurred. Music helped to celebrate the 50th anniversary of Dr. Ralph Loew's ordination this same year.

Many Lutheran churches are home to a pipe organ. Organ music is commonly associated with churches these days, but in the past, the pipe organ was the popular instrument of the day. Organ music could also be heard in theaters, concert halls, and in silent-movie cinemas. The pipe organ was quite a technological achievement. As used in churches, organs provided the widest array of musical styles and sounds without employing an entire orchestra. In Lutheran churches, the organ is also a reminder of German heritage, since several of the most accomplished composers of organ music, including Bach and Handel, were German. In these photographs, St. John's organ is being serviced by Koch Organ Company.

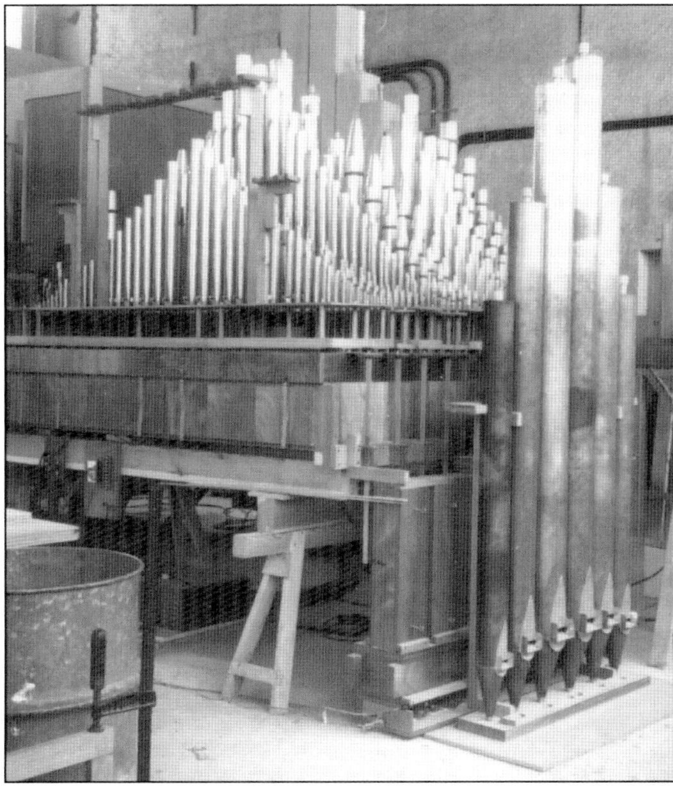

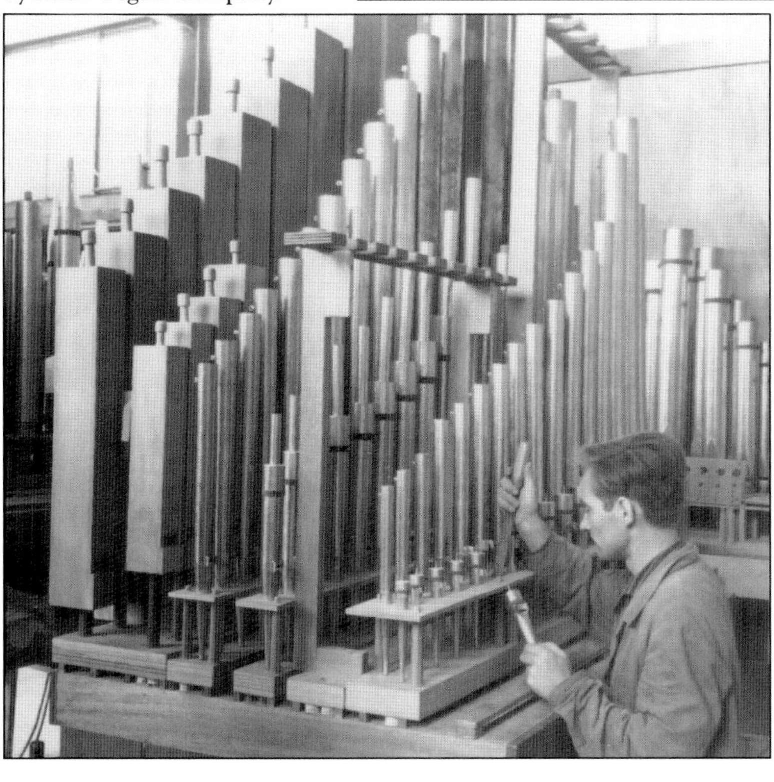

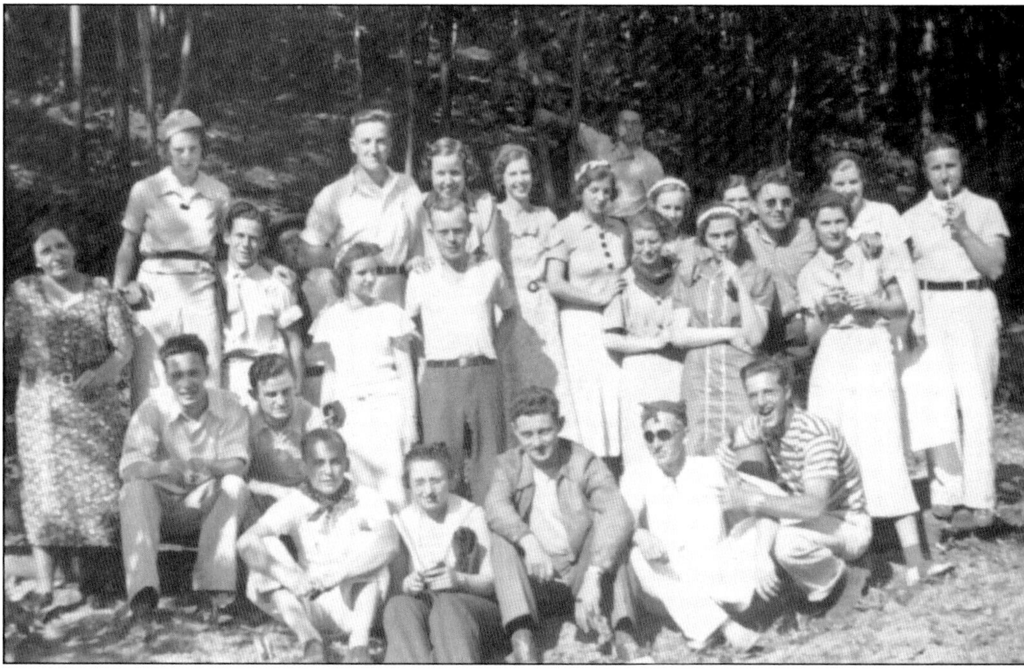

Social outings and activities have been a central part of Lutheran life since the denomination's earliest days. Martin Luther was known to regularly invite people to his talks about theology and the church. At these gatherings, Luther and his guests would share in food and fun as well, and the gatherings were noted for being a raucous good time. Perhaps this was spurred on by the fact that Luther's wife, Katie, had a beer brewery in the family home and guests were treated to their freshest brews. These gatherings became known as "Luther's table talks." Events like potlucks, picnics, and socials have always dotted church calendars. Shown on this page is the St. Paul's Williamsville Fellowship Club at the Young People's Picnic of 1937 (above) and at Chestnut Ridge Park in September 1940 (below).

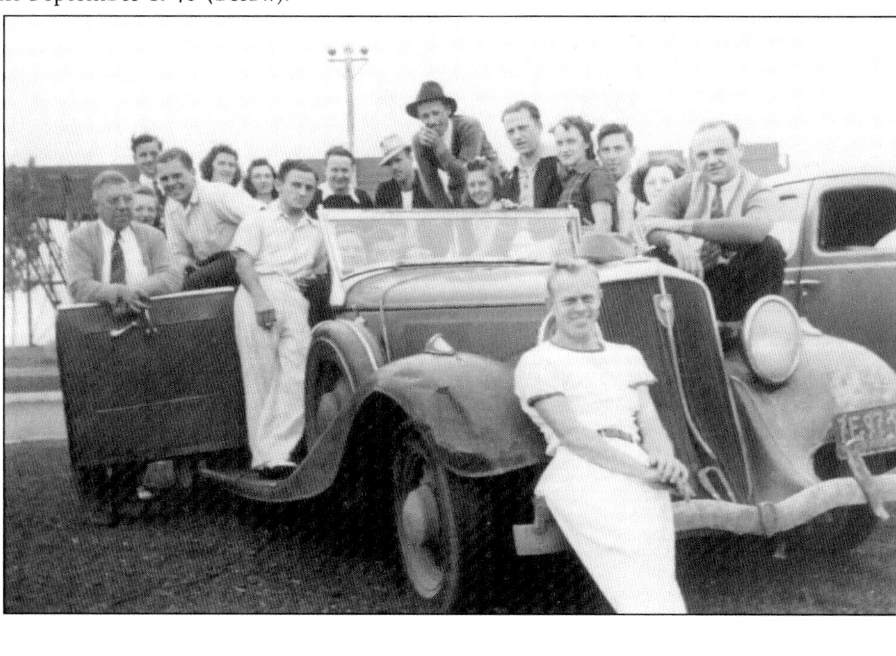

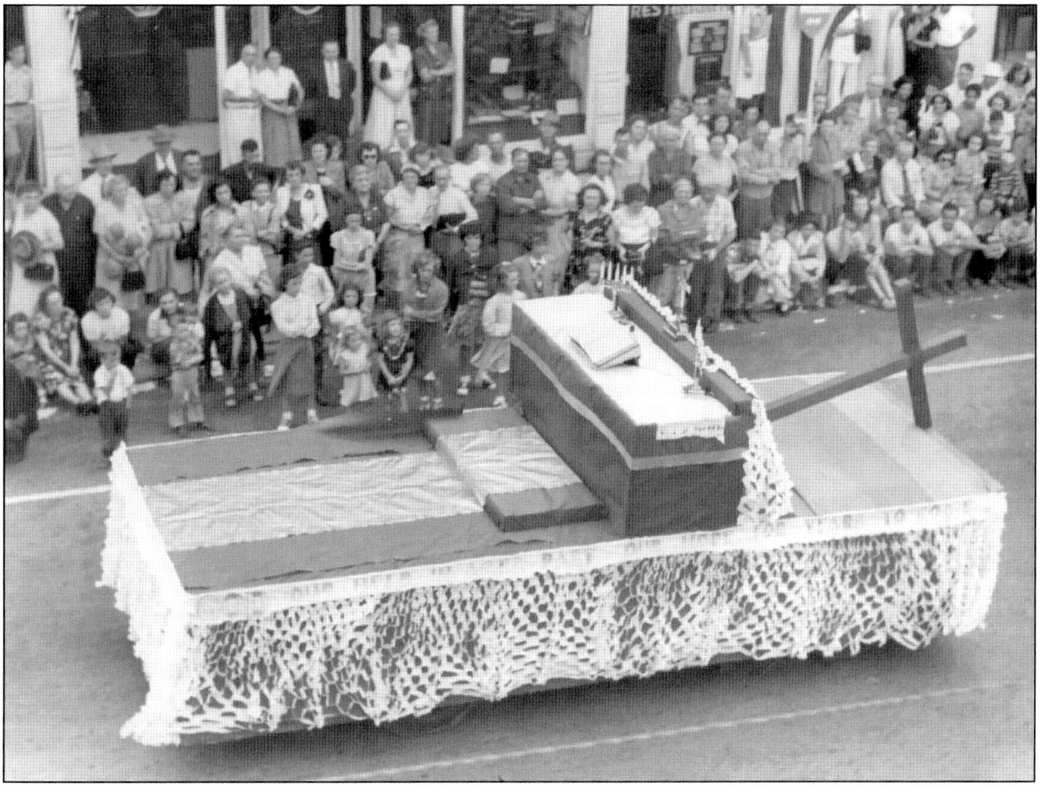

Small communities often have a several churches representing a variety of denominations. During the height of Christendom, each of these churches had its own activities, strengths, and focuses. So churches strived to exhibit to the broader community their identifying hallmarks. One way to do so was through participation in community events, including parades. Here, St. John's Akron prepared two floats for a community parade. The above photograph shows the church's focus on worship, with the cross of Christ leading the way, followed by a replica of the congregation's altar. The float shown below emphasizes the church's focus on its youth by showing the youth choir and Sunday school members.

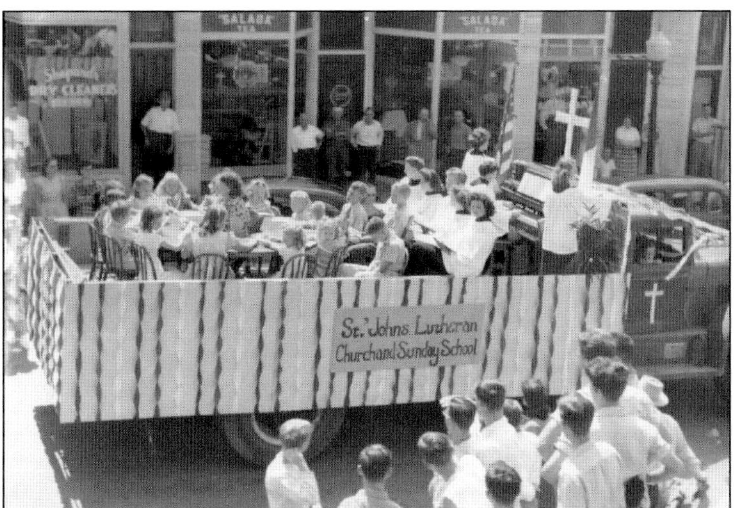

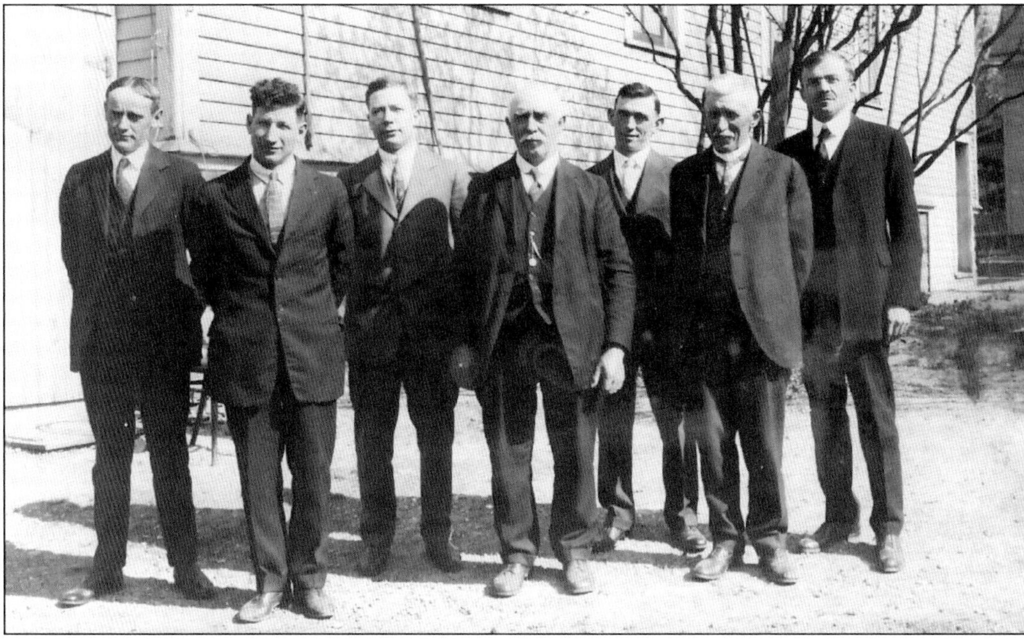

The Roaring Twenties was a very prosperous time for Lutheran churches in Western New York. Congregations were bolstered by wealthy members, and children born after the war filled the Sunday schools. Pictured here is the church council of St. Paul's in Williamsville in the late 1920s. The members include, from left to right, David Gramm, Henry Hanel, Lawrence Landel, August Kleast, Charles Landel, William Bartlett, and Rev. Bartholomew Henry Schleifer.

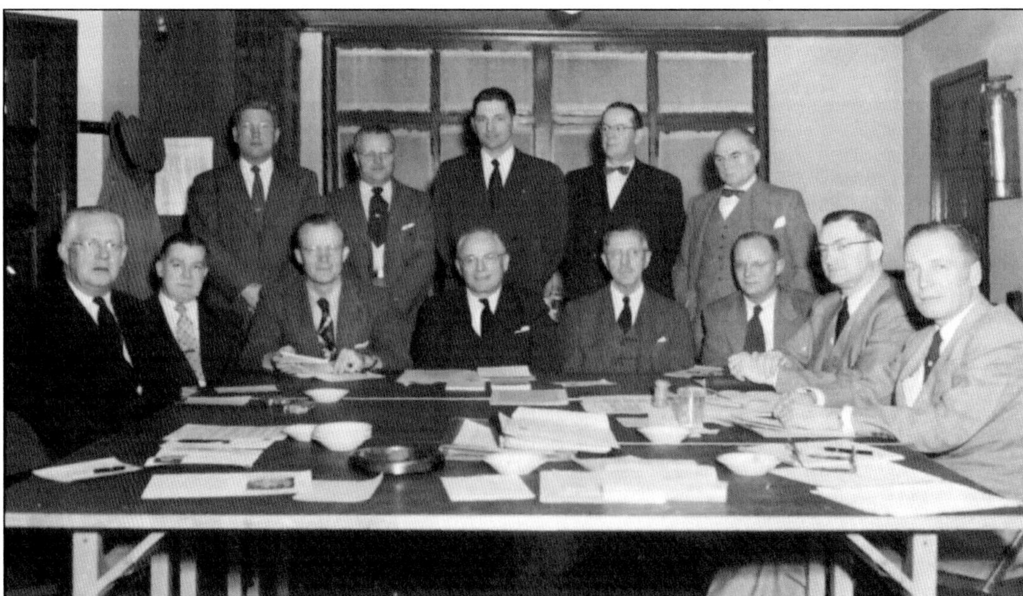

The church council has remained a very important part of the Lutheran Church infrastructure. A council seat is typically an elected position, and many early councils were responsible for building and creating the personality of their new church. The council also typically oversaw many subcommittees, ranging from maintenance to evangelism. Seen here is the Parkside council during the tenure of Pastor John Fleck.

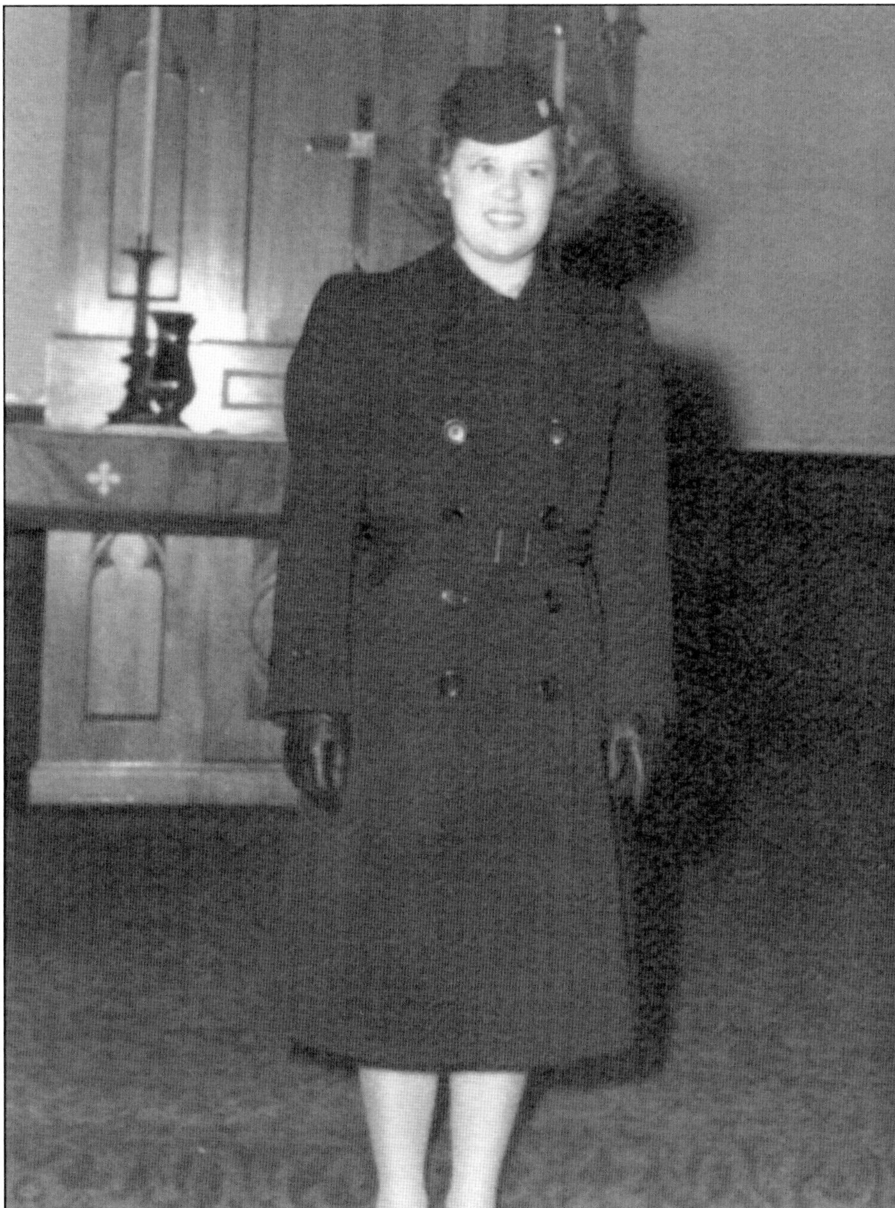

The period surrounding World War II was especially challenging for Lutheran churches, as individual congregations struggled to strike a balance between their German roots and their American loyalties. Particularly difficult was reconciling their faith with the knowledge that Adolph Hitler was using Martin Luther's writings to advance his Nazi propaganda. For many congregations, distancing themselves from Hitler's shadow meant discontinuing what remained of their nearly obsolete German-language services. While most churches had abandoned the German language during World War I, pockets of German speakers remained, and they did not choose to abandon the language entirely until war struck again. Meanwhile, Lutherans all over Western New York joined the war effort. With her husband already serving overseas, Eva Freeburg Paulson decided to serve her country in the US Coast Guard. A lifetime member of St. Paul's Lutheran Church in Williamsville, she is pictured here at St. Paul's during a visit home.

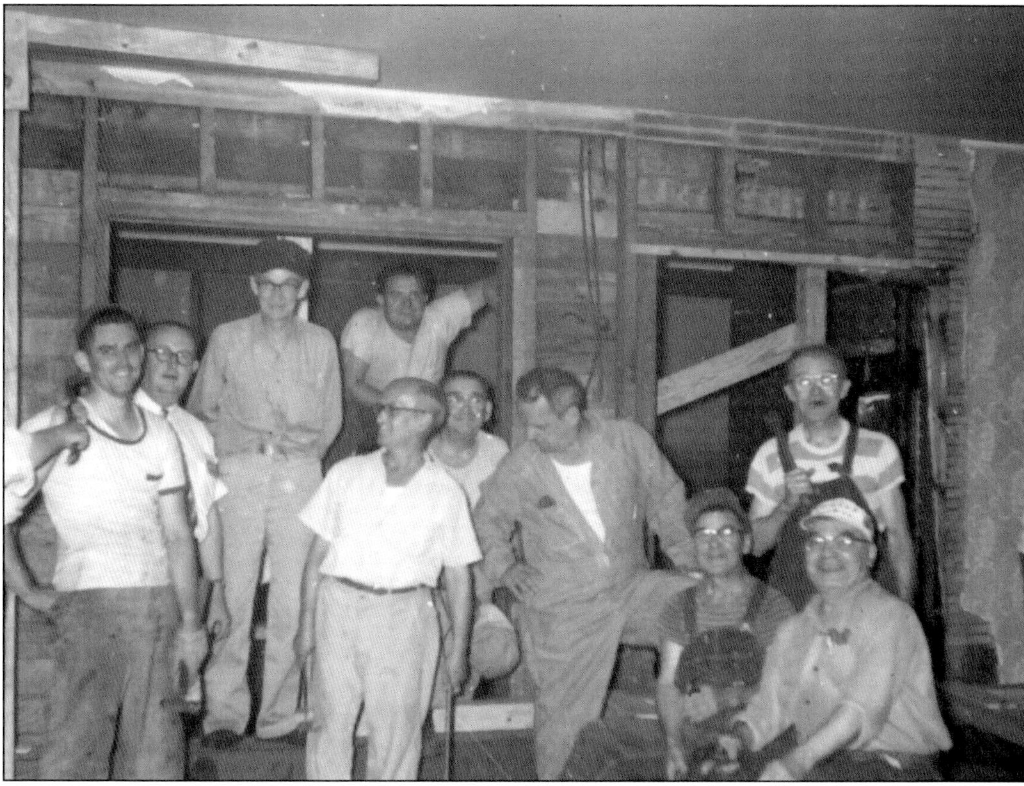

One of the timeless challenges of the Lutheran Church has been keeping men actively involved in church-related activities. Throughout history, women have been more apt than men to attend Bible-study groups as well as various social groups. One method has been to engage men in physical activities, such as maintenance and construction. Many pastors feel that there is no greater avenue to a man's thoughts than through a paintbrush. Pictured above are some very engaged and happy workers at St. John's. Below, members of St. Paul's in Eggertsville enjoy a meal together after a hard day's work in 1957.

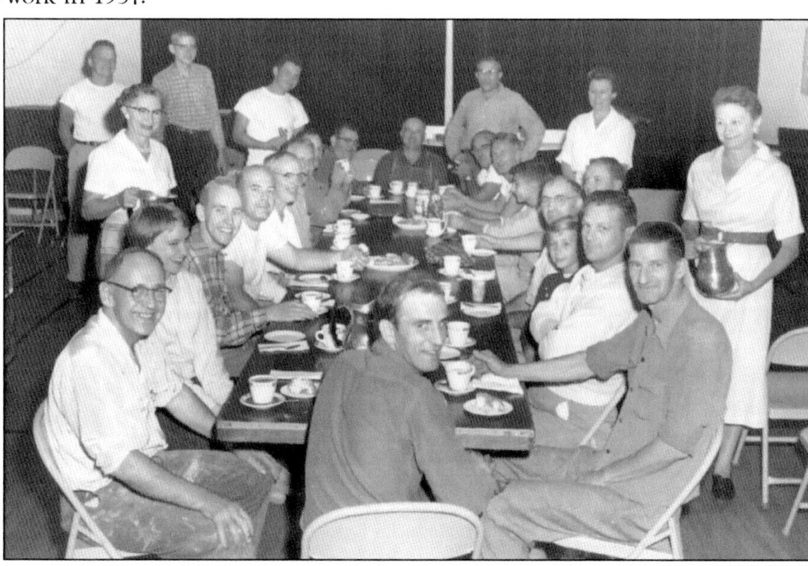

Following World War II, the United States experienced a period known as the baby boom. During this period, from the late 1940s to the early 1960s, churches, like the nation, experienced tremendous growth. St. Paul's in Williamsville, as well as most churches across the region, suddenly found their facilities lacking in space. Between 1949 and 1956, St. Paul's funded three additions to its building to accommodate its growing Sunday school. Pictured is the 1956 expansion, which necessitated the demolition of an adjacent parsonage. The property pictured to the left of the construction site in the photograph at right would be purchased three years later, and the house and garage were torn down. The lot was turned into a yard that is still enjoyed today.

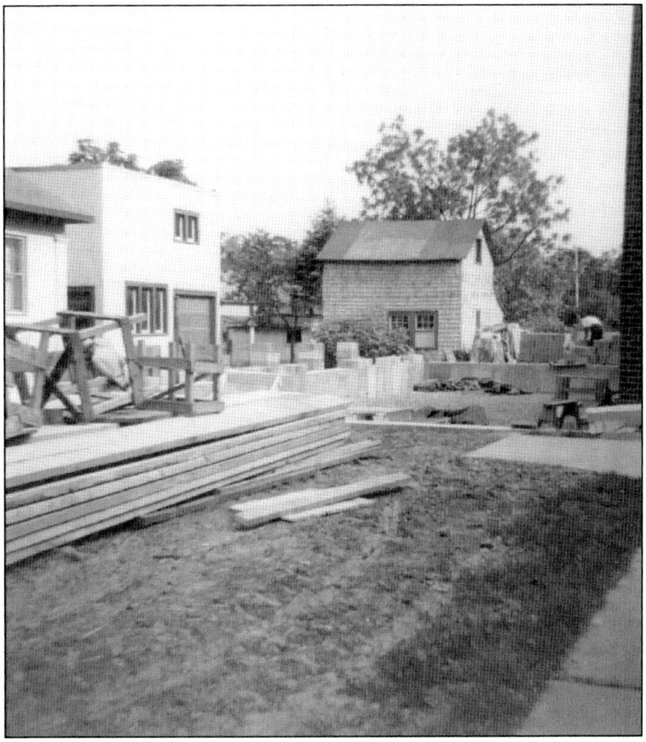

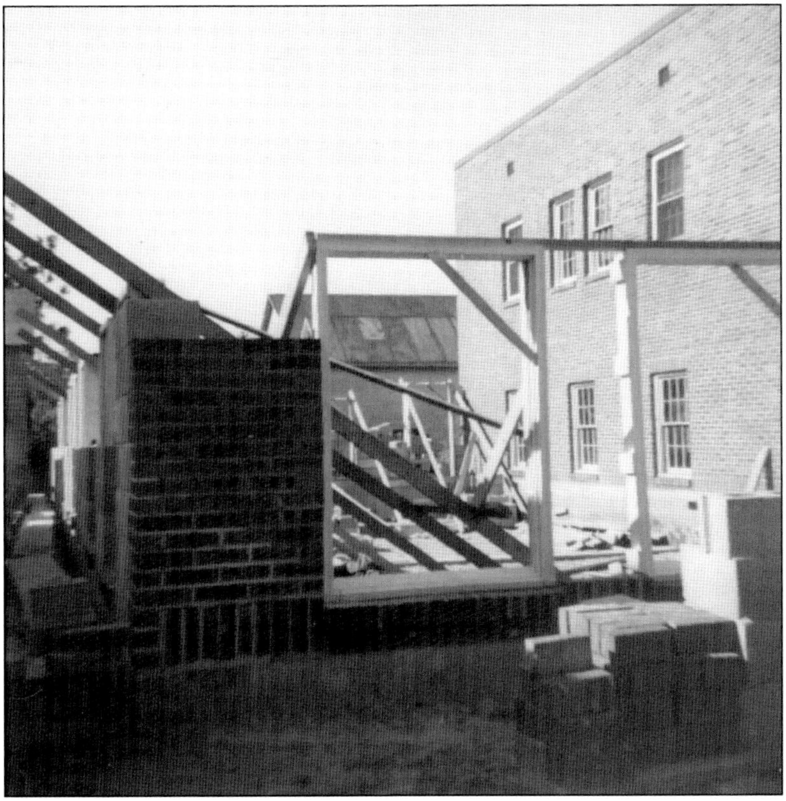

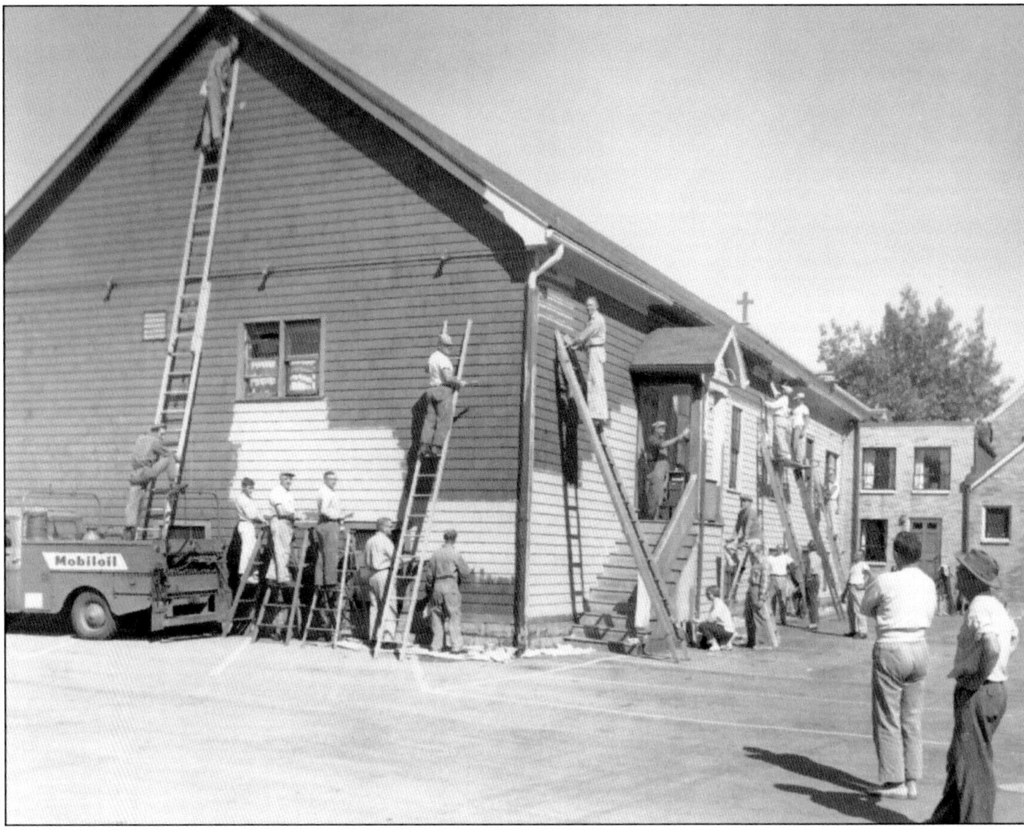

Many churches underwent construction projects following World War II. The baby boom gave rise to a growth in church membership, and churches expanded or erected entirely new buildings as a result. Looking at a particular construction project can reveal the church's focus of ministry at the time. If a church built a Sunday school wing, its focus was likely on Christian education. If it constructed a gymnasium, it probably targeted youth, providing them a place to play and explore their faith. If a social hall was constructed, the church was likely focused on providing a place for the community to gather. Churches knew that by enhancing their buildings, they could improve opportunities to share their faith. The above photograph depicts the 1957 construction at St. Paul's Eggertsville. Shown below is a blessing prior to 1957 construction at Holy Trinity.

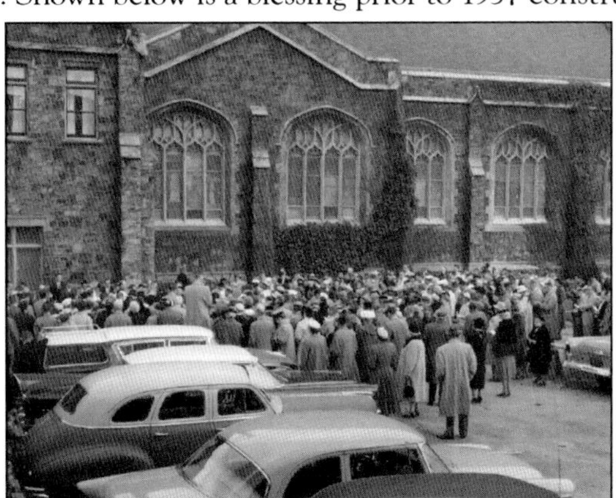

In the past, moving a building from one location to another was common practice. With limited materials, machinery, and manpower, transporting a structure was often a more cost-effective method than knocking it down or building a new one from scratch. This page shows two photographs of the parsonage of St. Paul's Lutheran Church in Eggertsville en route to its new location. It was decided to move the building after its location was deemed unsuitable due to its proximity to a widening Main Street and an expanding church. Not wishing to lose the structure completely, the council decided to move it to a more suitable location.

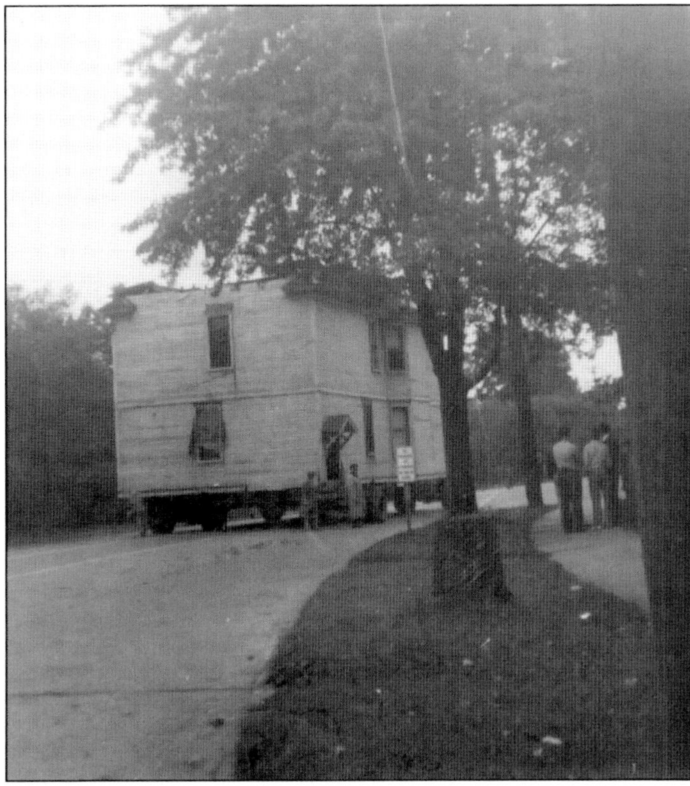

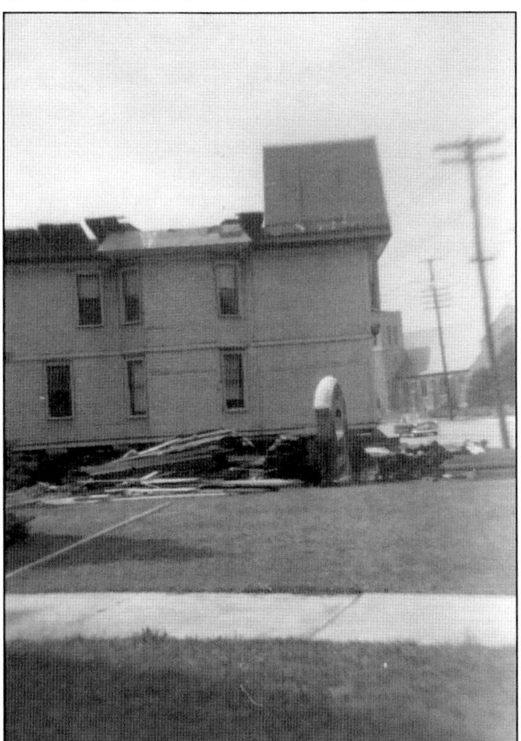

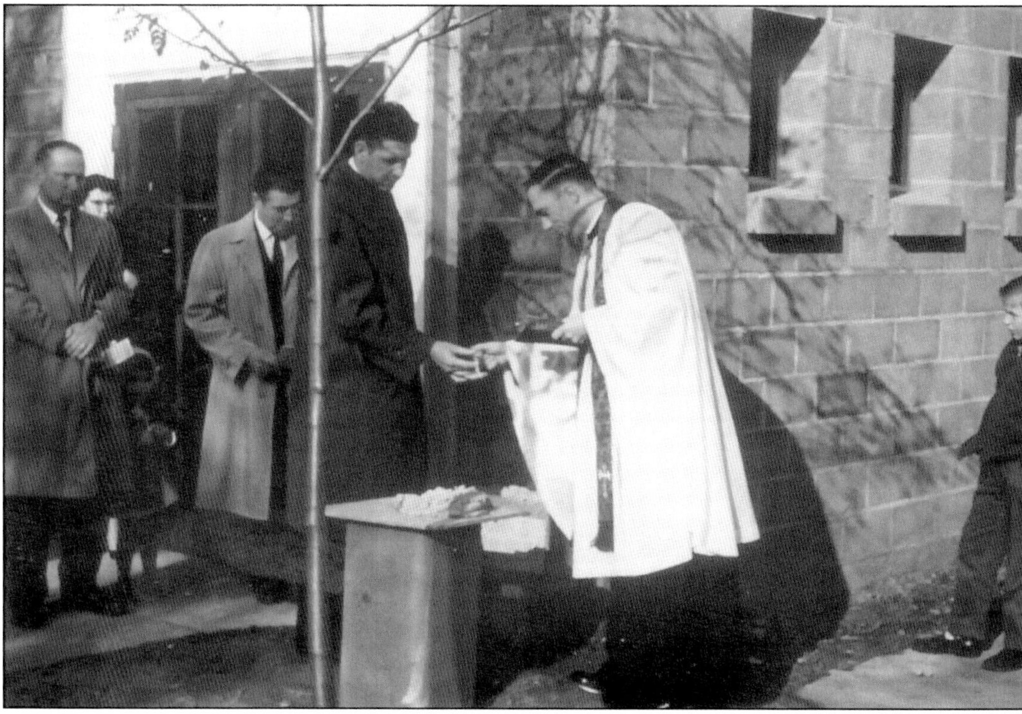

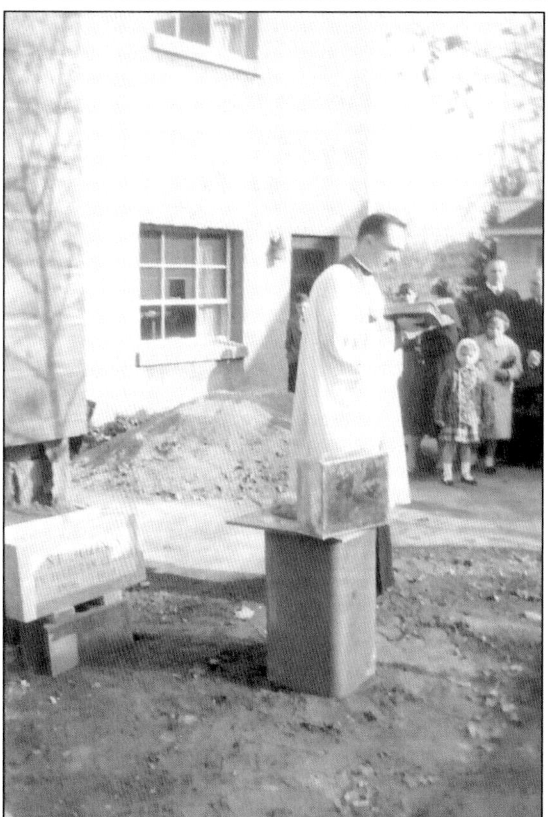

Building projects are difficult tasks for congregations. Most often, such projects are funded by financial contributions from within the congregation, funds that are given in addition to the weekly offering. Because of this, congregations need to find appropriate ways to celebrate such accomplishments. St. John's Akron chose to add an additional cornerstone when it built a social hall and new classrooms in 1959. Laying a second cornerstone is a way of connecting those who supported the new construction with those who came before them and funded the initial construction. The time capsule that was placed within the cornerstone was retrieved and opened years later, when St. John's Akron began worshiping jointly with Trinity South Newstead.

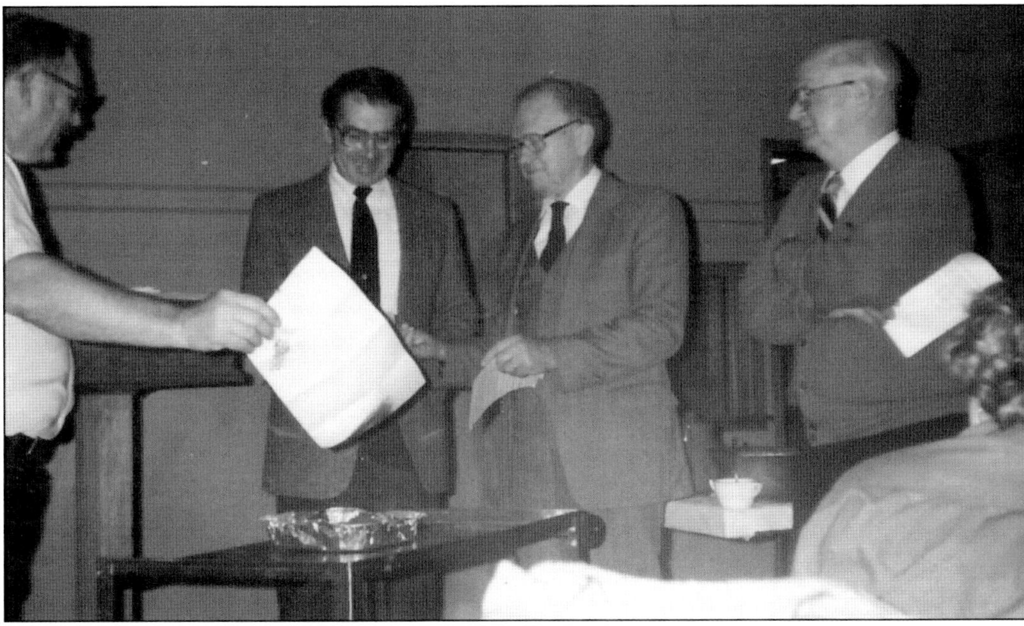

Churches often take on financial debt in order to complete a construction project. The members of the congregation agree to help pay that debt as well as support the rest of the congregation's ministries and costs. There is a great satisfaction and sense of accomplishment when that debt has been paid off, feelings expressed symbolically in the "burning of the mortgage." This photograph was taken at St. John's Akron on November 29, 1987.

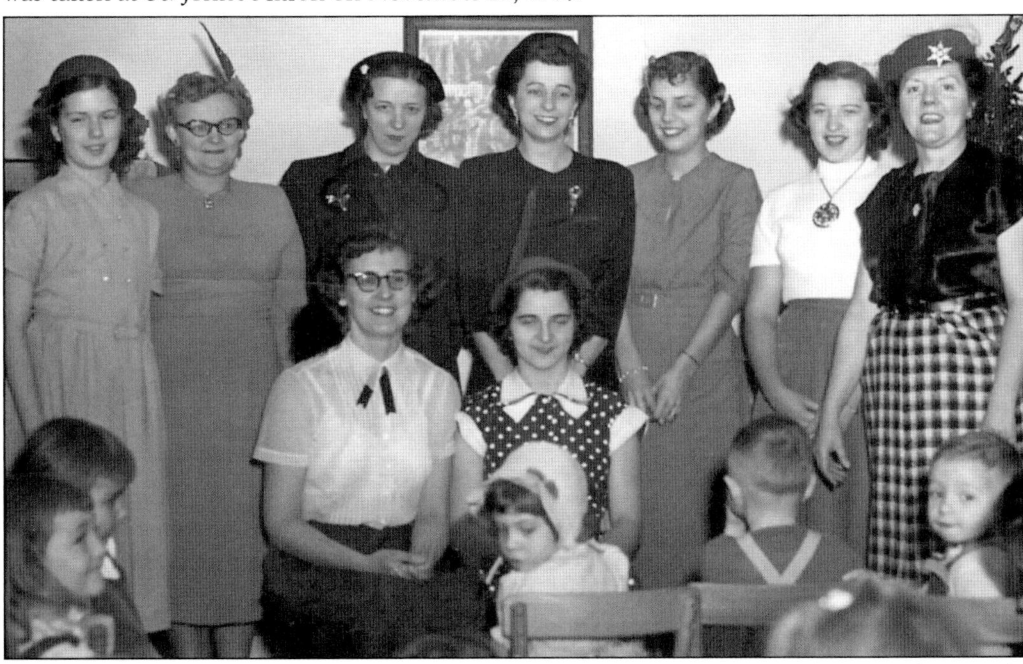

Happy to have more classroom space, the Sunday school staff of 1952, including Arlene Muhr, Donna Welton, Gerry Gelinas, Lois Idzak, and Rita Klein, take a break from their teaching duties to pose for a photograph. The following year, four more classrooms, a kitchenette, a furnace room, and a lavatory were also be completed.

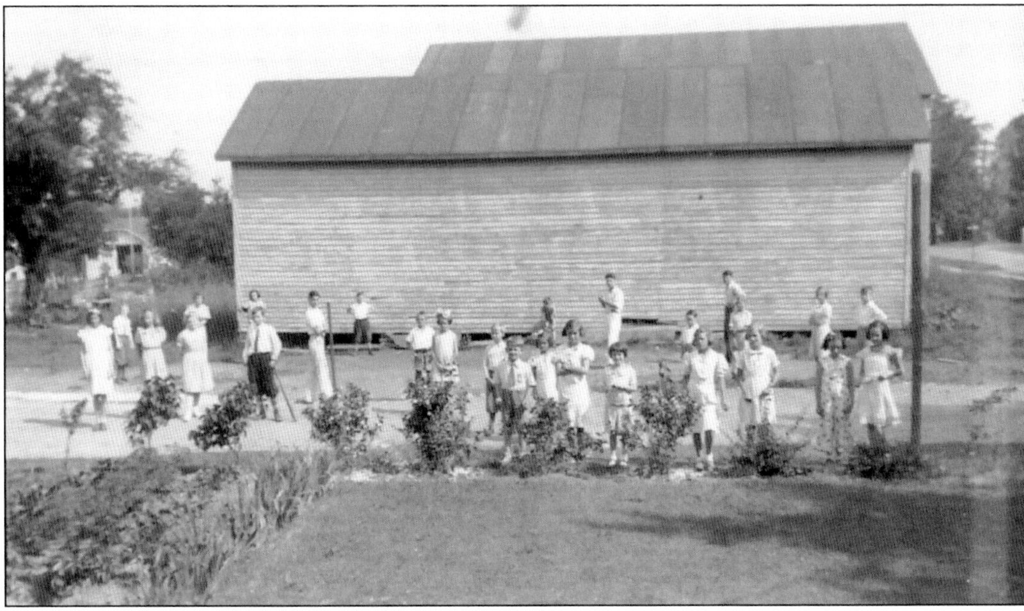

In the summer months, area churches began to offer Vacation Bible School for the youth of the congregation. This afforded children a chance to balance their religious education with some well-needed summertime fun. The above photograph shows the 1934 Bible school class of St. Paul's Lutheran Church in Williamsville enjoying a break with a game of stickball. This garden and adjacent barn, once occupied by Chalmers Gelatin Corporation, would eventually be torn down to make room for the church's parking lot. Below, youth are pictured around 1935 enjoying the sunshine in the yard between the church and parsonage. In 1956, this yard and the parsonage would be sacrificed to build a much-needed addition to the Sunday school.

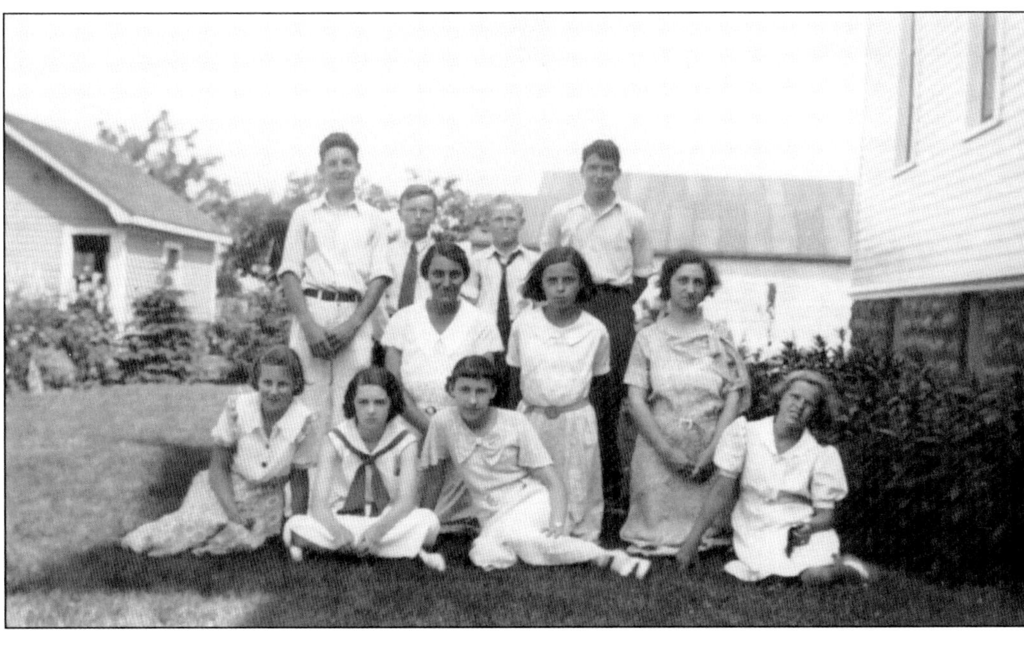

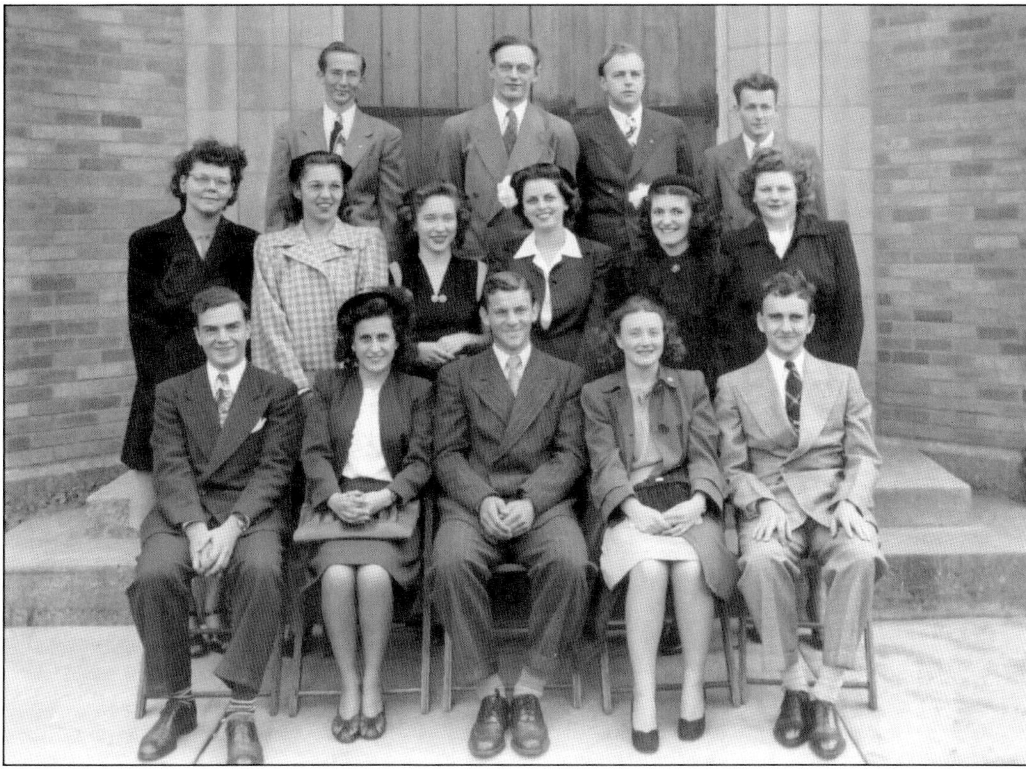

The Reverend George A. Martin accepted a call to St. Paul's Evangelical Lutheran Church in Eggertsville on October 24, 1942. He served until his sudden death in the summer of 1952. One of the highlights of Pastor Martin's tenure occurred in 1947, when St. Paul's celebrated its 120th anniversary. The event was commemorated by a number of events as well as the publication of an anniversary booklet. The booklet contained a history of the congregation, compiled by Willard Dixon, as well as current and historical photographs. The above photograph depicts the Young People's Luther League of 1947. The photograph below showcases the sweet faces of the 1947 St. Paul's Sunday school.

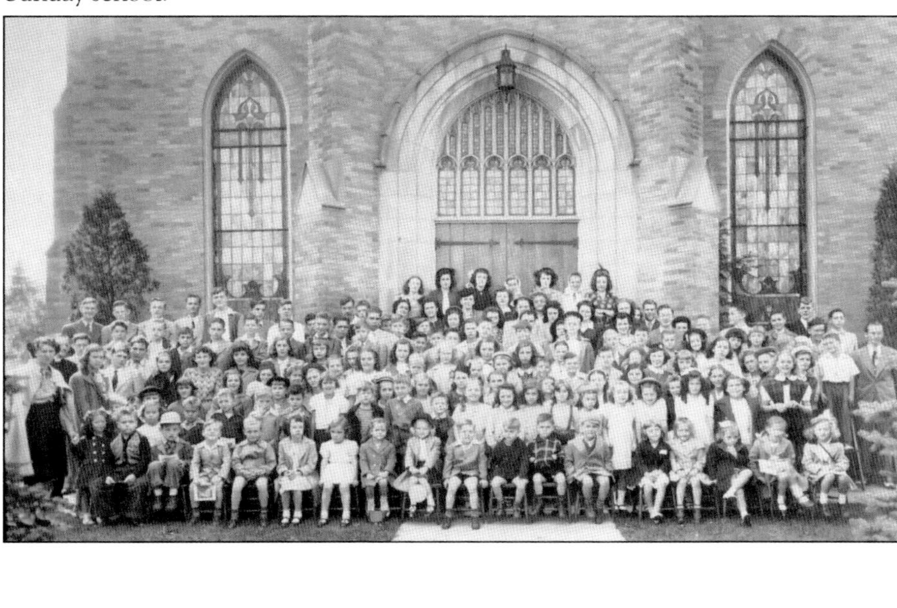

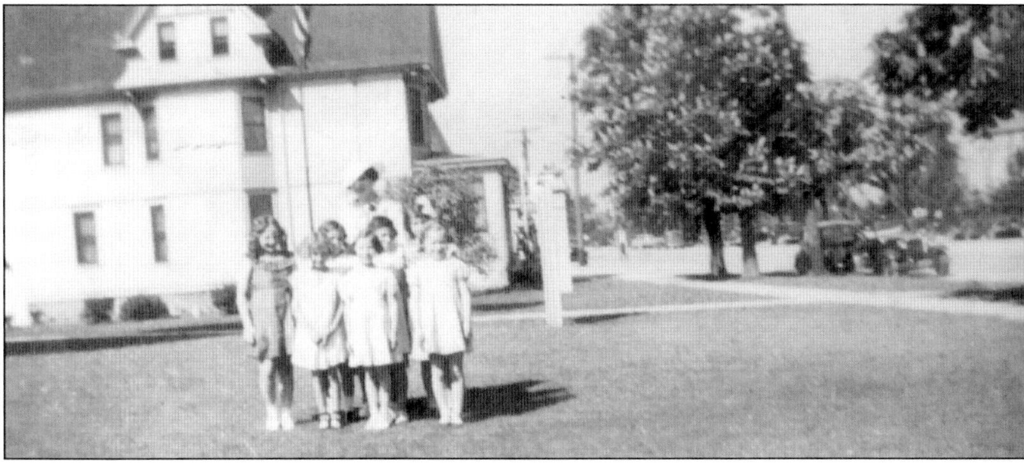

The Reverend Gustav K. Huf came to St. Paul's in Eggertsville in 1932. During his tenure, the 1872 constitution was translated from German, abrogated, and a new constitution was adopted according to the model of the United Lutheran Church in America. He also organized the first Luther League. This Sunday school class poses on the church's front lawn in 1938. The photograph is looking west down Main Street.

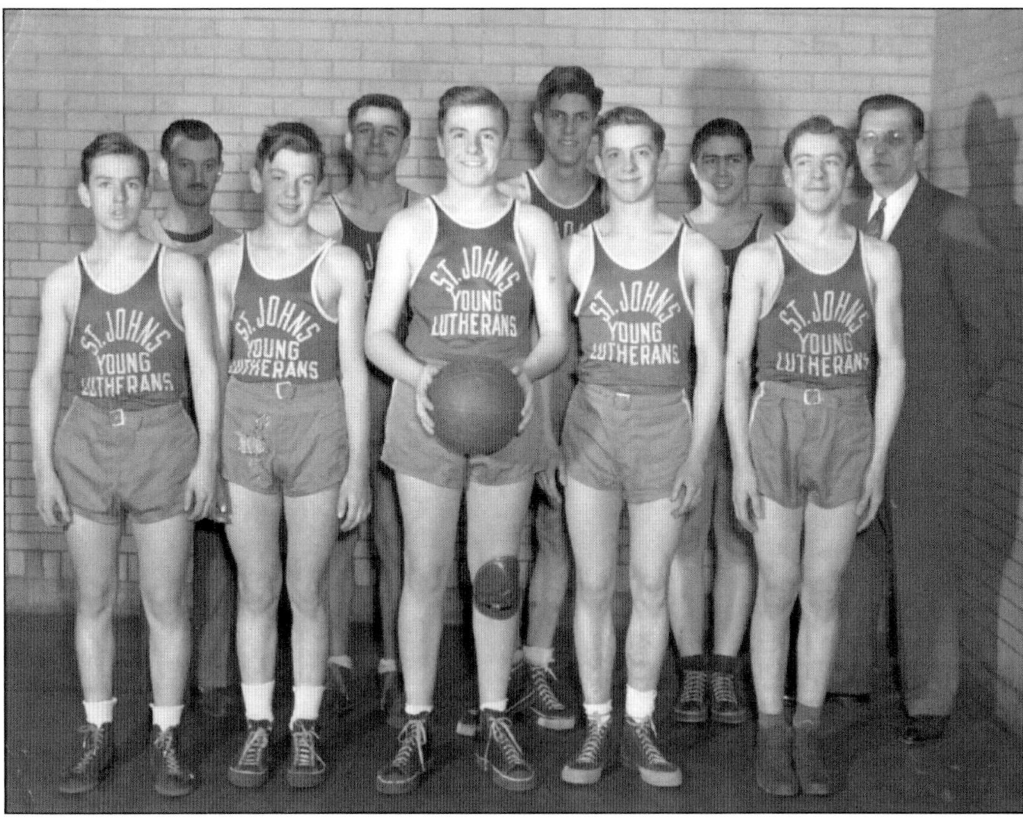

Churches sought nontraditional ways to connect with their youth. Athletics and team sports have often been identified as successful avenues to make such connections. St. John's found success with its basketball team. Playing competitively against other churches, the St. John's Young Lutherans traveled as far as the Midwest for competitions.

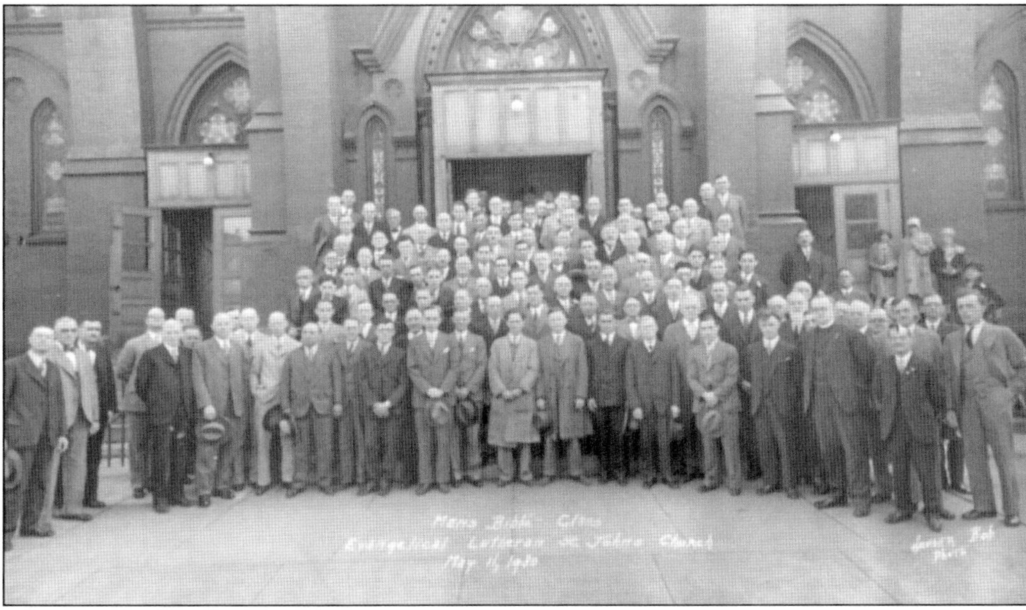

Study of the Bible is a central part of Lutheran life. Lutherans strive to understand the Bible as a way of growing in their faith and understanding who God is and what God is doing in the world. Study groups have been a central part of Lutheran congregations in Western New York. Men's groups, women's groups, and youth groups have provided opportunities for study and devotion. These groups often gathered at social events or other activities, taking time out for a moment of Bible study. The more groups or gatherings a church had, the more opportunities congregants had to enjoy a social time together as well as a moment of study. Pictured are the St. John's Men's Bible Class on May 11, 1930 (above), and the 1955 Parkside Sunday school (below).

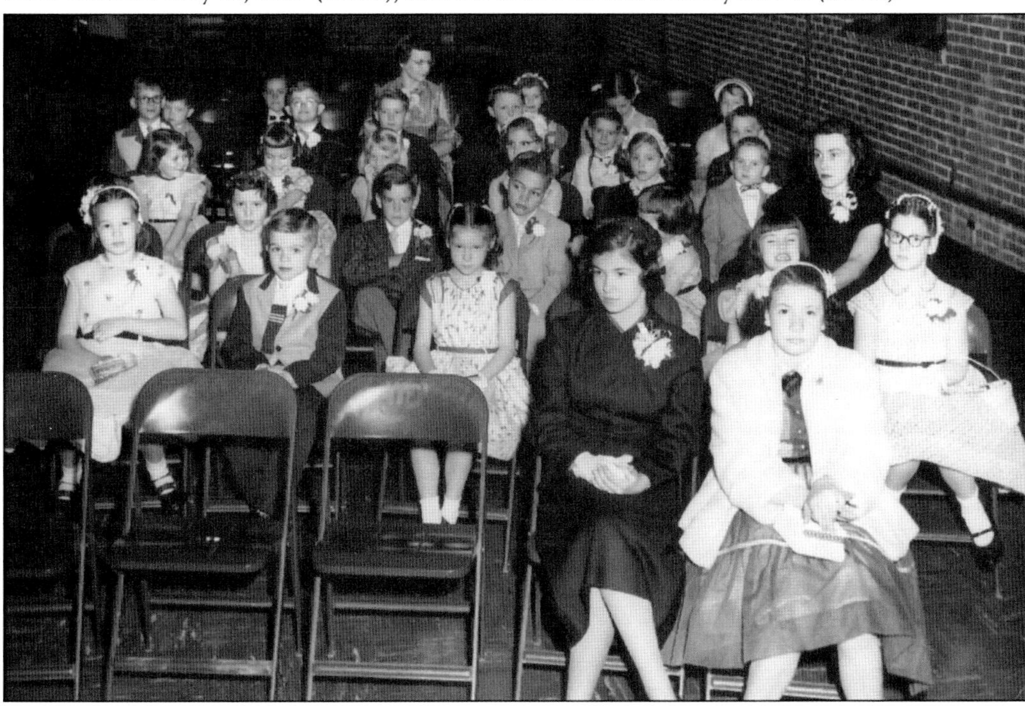

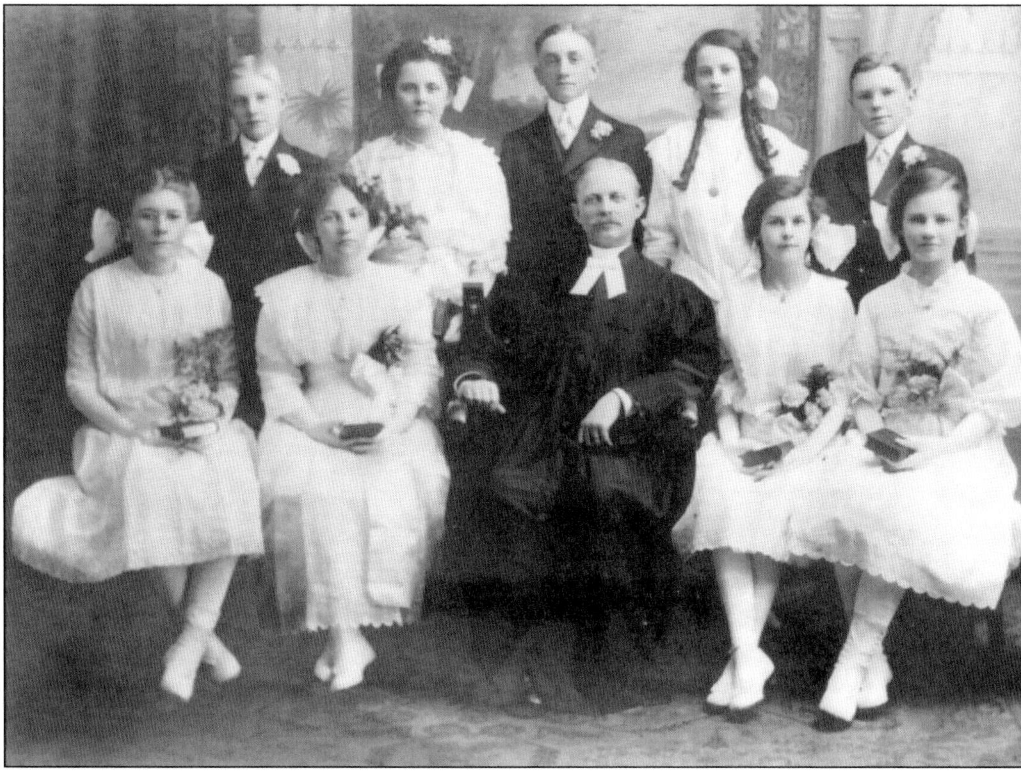

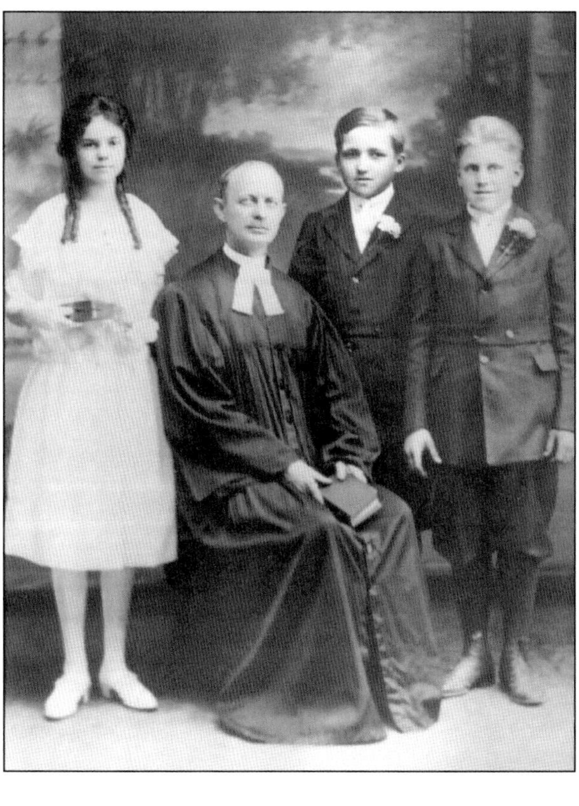

The Reverend John Hartman served St. Paul's from 1910 to 1925. Under his guidance, the music program continued to grow. In 1910, the Young People's Society of St. Paul's raised $950 and purchased the first pipe organ to be used in the sanctuary of the church. Unfortunately, the size of the organ necessitated a slight remodeling of the altar area. Nevertheless, this organ was finally dedicated on February 11, 1911. The first choir was also established about this time. Pictured above is Reverend Hartman (first row, center) with the confirmation class of 1915, including Florence Dalzour, Lauretta Fries, Madelin Fries, Florence Gross, Charles Hartmann, Johannes Hartmann, Otto Minholn, Edna Morningstar, and Ruth Schoelles. Shown at left is the confirmation class of 1922, including, from left to right, Dorothy Gruinn, Reverend Hartman, Floyd Klein, and Earl Meyer.

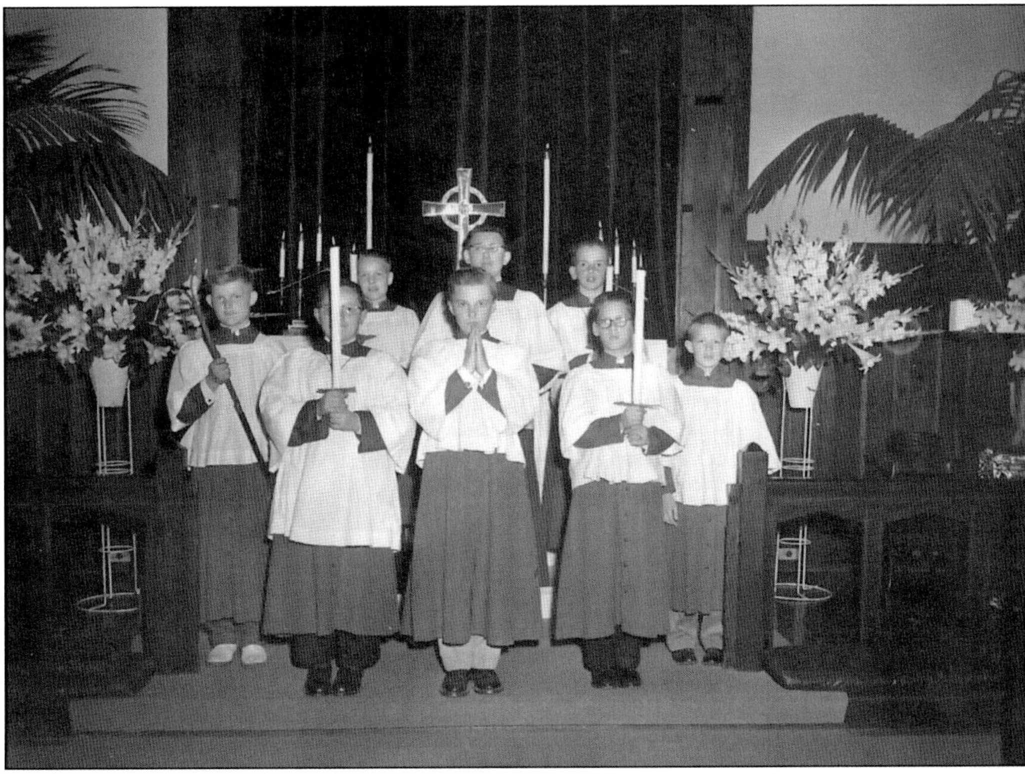

Acting as an acolyte has long been a rite of passage for Lutheran youth. In addition to candle lighting, an acolyte can fill other important roles, such as crucifer, communion assistant, and worship assistant. Although this practice was initially limited to boys, girls began to fill these roles as well. Pictured here are the acolytes of Parkside Lutheran Church on Easter, 1938.

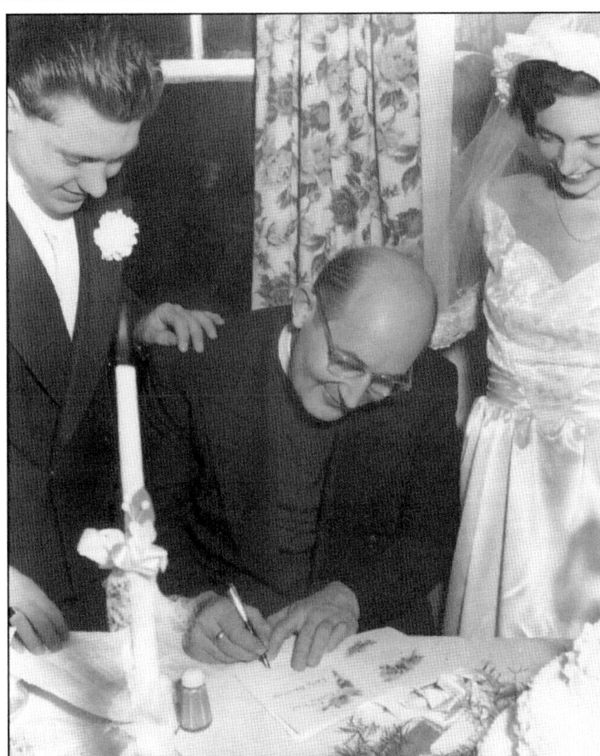

The Reverend Charles Julius Menge was called to St. Paul's in Williamsville in 1933. In 1971, he was named pastor emeritus and remained in that capacity until 1977. Pastor Menge is shown signing the marriage certificate of the authors' parents/grandparents, Lois Landel and Robert Fiddler, who were married at St. Paul's on February 16, 1951. (Courtesy of Lois Fiddler.)

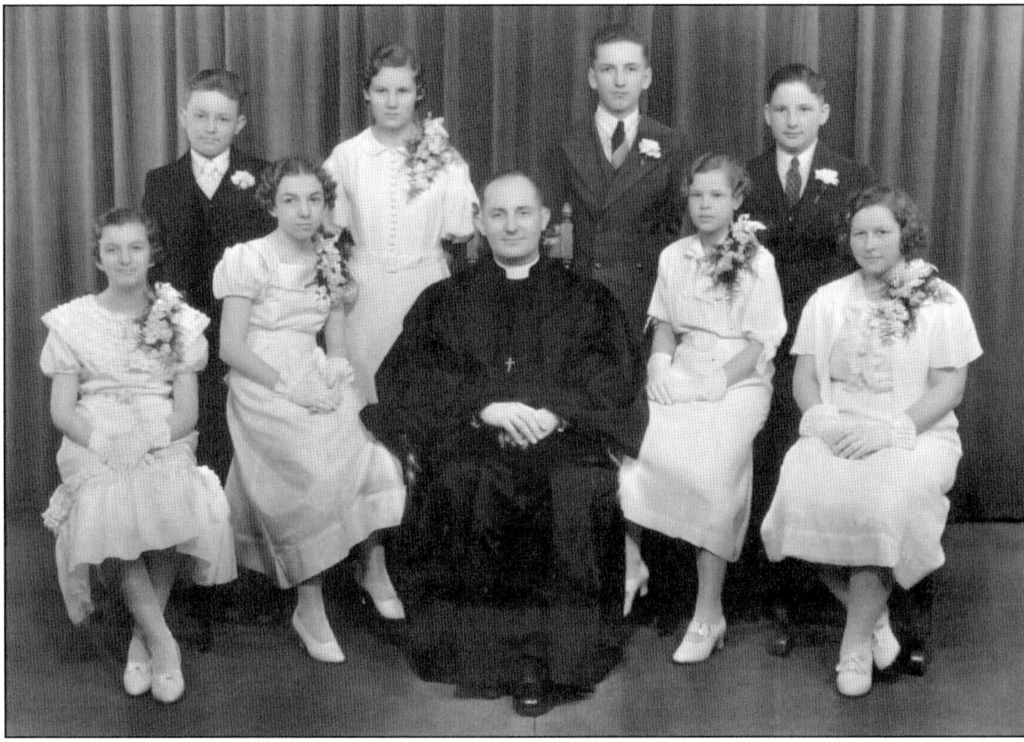

When the Reverend Charles Julius Menge arrived at St. Paul's Williamsville in 1933, he inherited an operating budget of $2,538. During his 44-year tenure, Pastor Menge oversaw a radical remodel of the inside of the church and two generous additions to the building and Sunday school. In the summer of 1955, the original glass windows were also removed and replaced with stained glass donated by individual members. Pastor Menge is pictured above with the confirmation class of 1936, including Lee Gilbert, Edna (Poss) Kress, Marjorie (Landel) McKeegan, Eva (Freeburg) Paulson, Harry Poss, Marjorie (Sagerman) Redding, Frederick Sagerman, and Dorothy (Peterson) Stein. He is seen below with the confirmation class of 1939, which included June Cahalaw, Edwin Jones, Norman Jones, James Kaeppel, Ethel Kirsch, David Minick, Elmer Ostwald, Warren Reifsteck, Allan Roeser, and Elmer Sagerman.

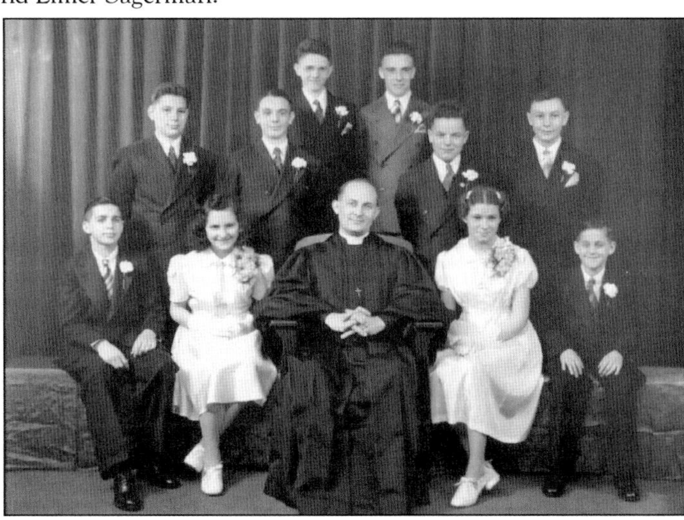

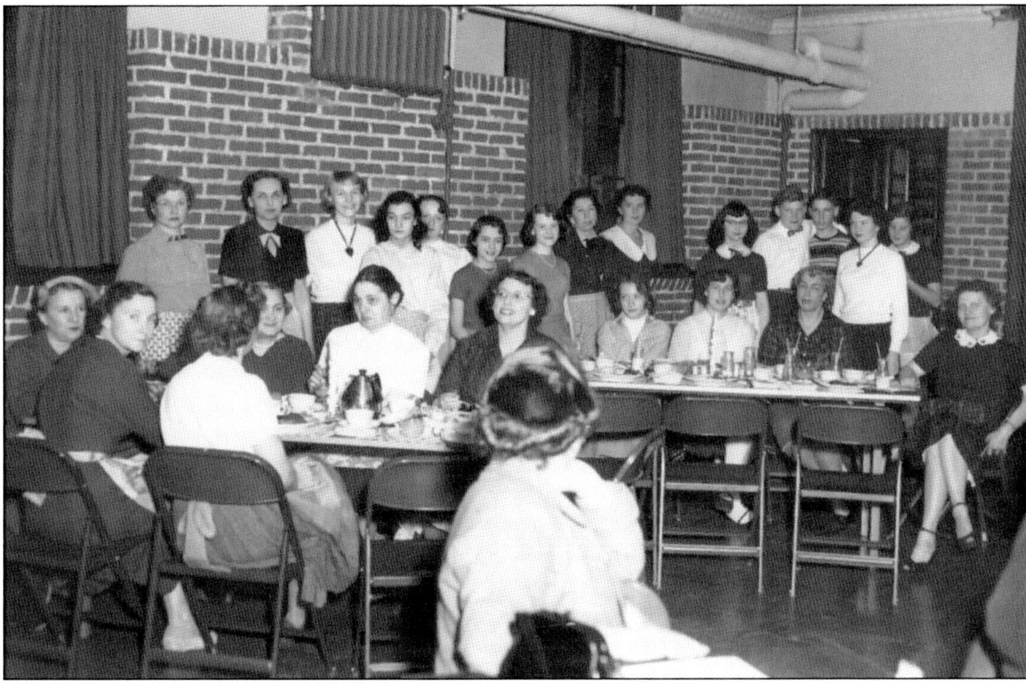

Parkside Lutheran Church celebrated its 25th anniversary in May 1938 with a vast array of festivities. On May 8, guest preacher the Reverend Henry J. Pflum, minister of Holy Trinity Lutheran Church, Buffalo, presided over a service entitled "The Silversmith's Dream." A historical pageant written by Parkside member Carl A. Arneson was held on May 13. The pageant consisted of 60 members of the church and told the story of the preceding 25 years. It also offered predictions for the next 25 years. On May 15, the culminating service, entitled "To Heights Unimagined," was held with guest preacher Rev. J. Sahner Blank. Following the service, a banquet was held in the parish hall. Howard Chapel, the speaker, is shown standing in the photograph below.

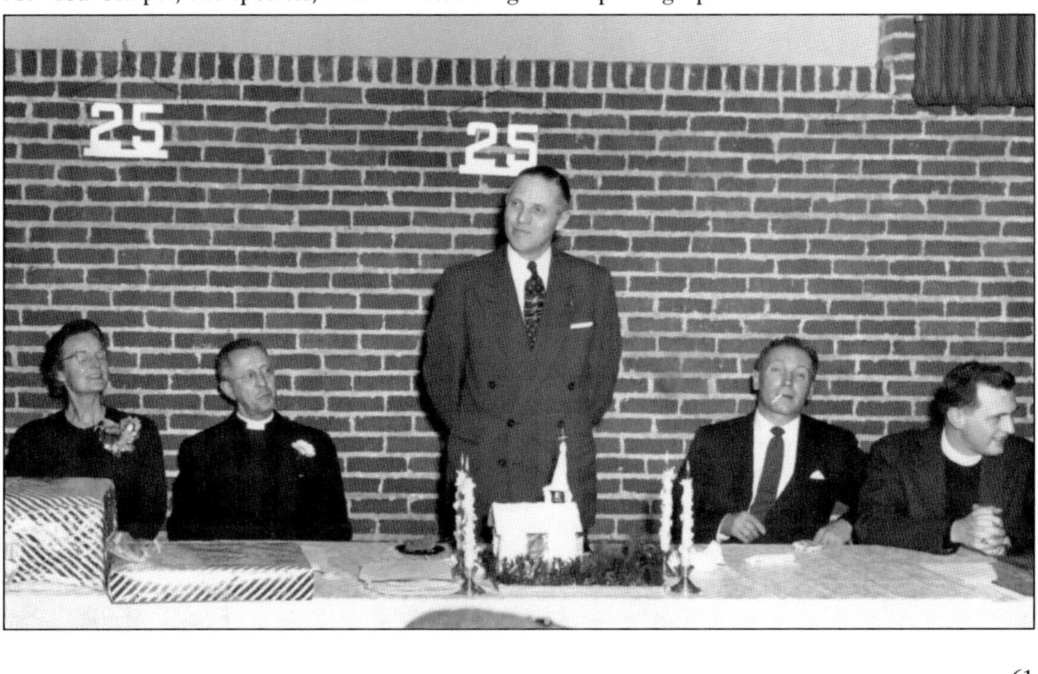

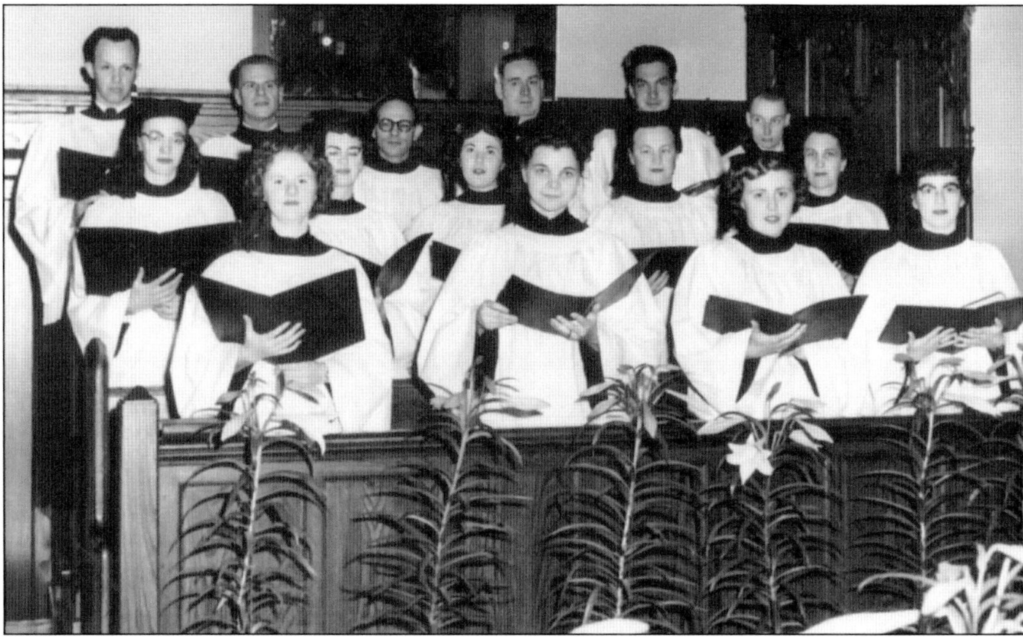

Historically, music has been woven throughout Lutheran Church services, and this was never more apparent than on holidays. "Silent Night" was traditionally sung by candlelight on Christmas Eve, and "Jesus Christ Is Risen Today" was sung at sunrise on Easter. Pictured is the Parkside Choir on Easter morning, April 10, 1955.

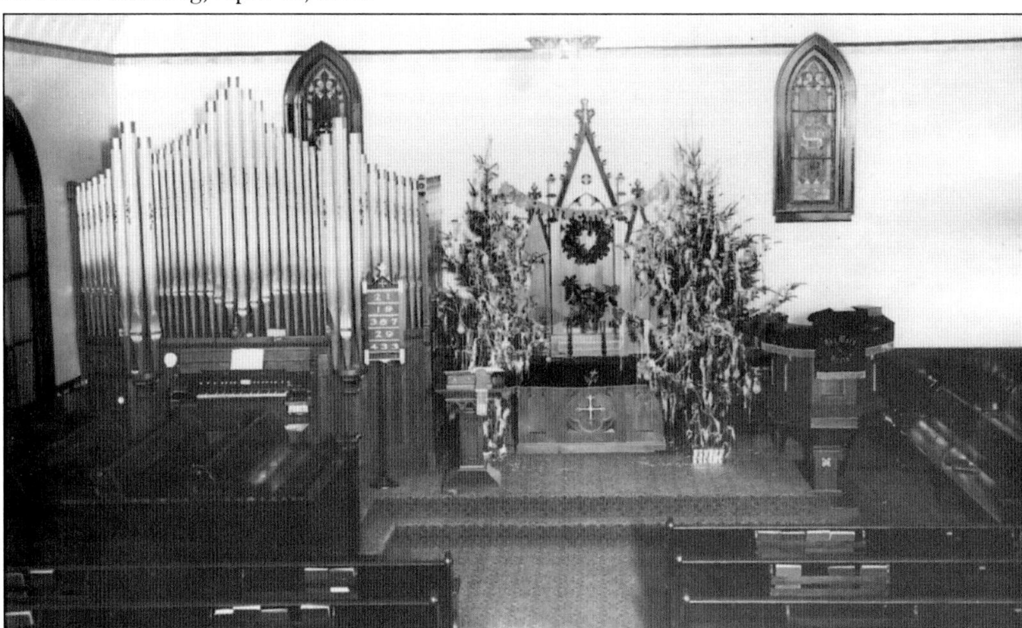

Despite the stock market crash that occurred just two months prior, St. Paul's in Williamsville was extravagantly decorated for Christmas, 1929. A wreath was hung from the altar, and a pair of generously tinseled trees flanked each side. A "Merry Christmas" sign was also draped between the trees, a subtle reminder that, regardless of challenges existing outside its walls, the church would remain a place of comfort for parishioners.

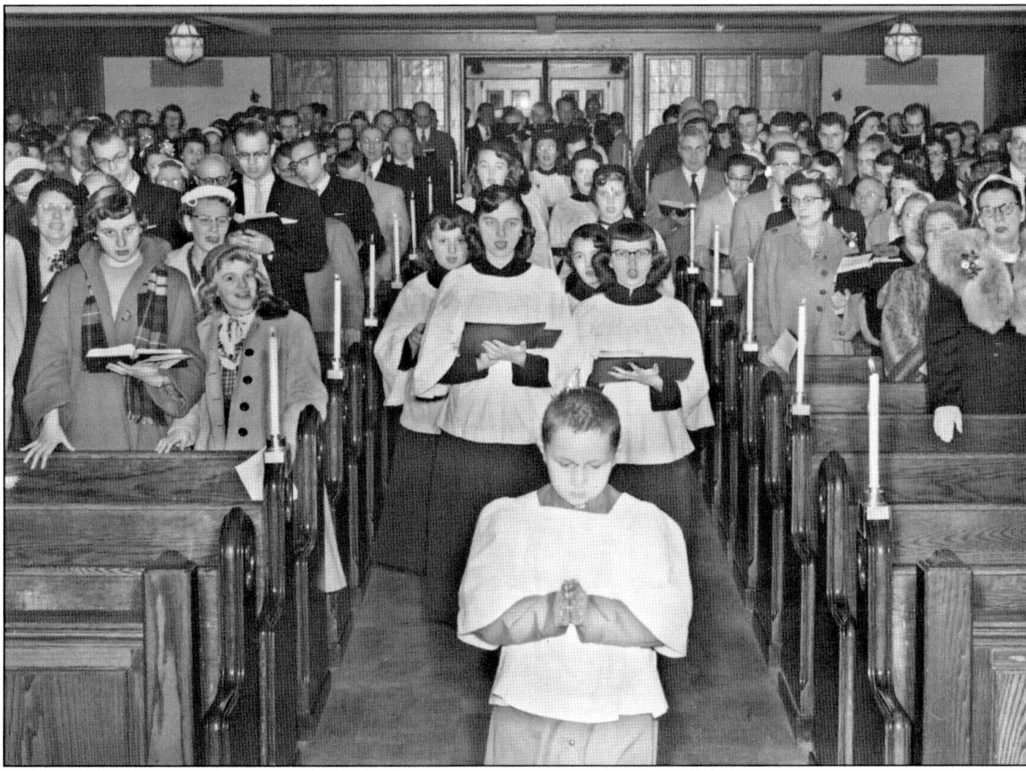

Germany is credited with starting the tradition of the Christmas tree. When the first Lutherans immigrated to America, they brought their rituals with them. Traditional trees were lit with candles, as were the churches in which they stood. This custom of lit candles is evident in this image from Parkside on Christmas Eve, 1955.

Like the Christmas tree, many popular Christmas carols also have German origins. "Silent Night" ("Stille Nacht, Heilige Nacht"), "O Christmas Tree" ("O Tannenbaum") and "Still, Still, Still" originated in Germany. They have been translated into English to appeal to a wider audience. Pictured here is carol singing on Christmas Eve 1978 at Parkside.

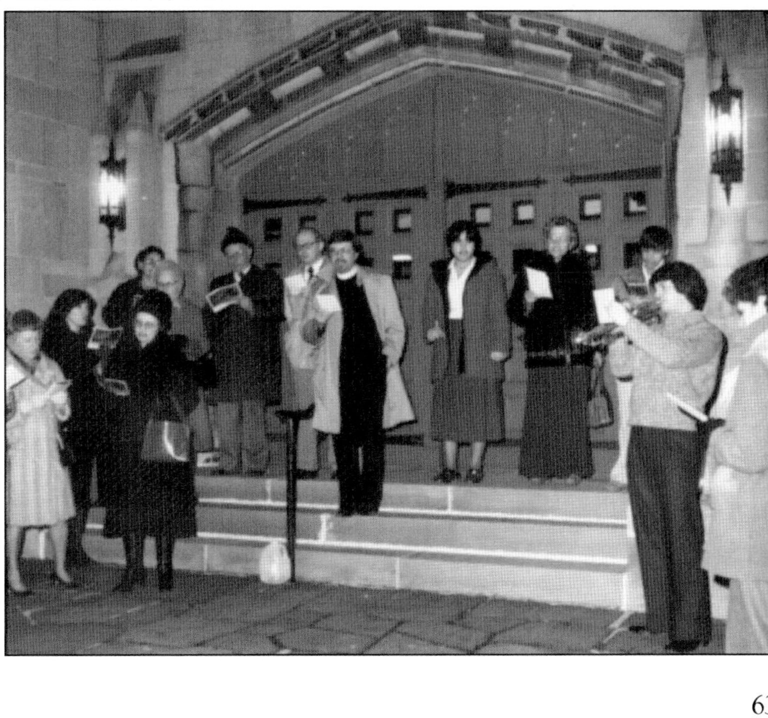

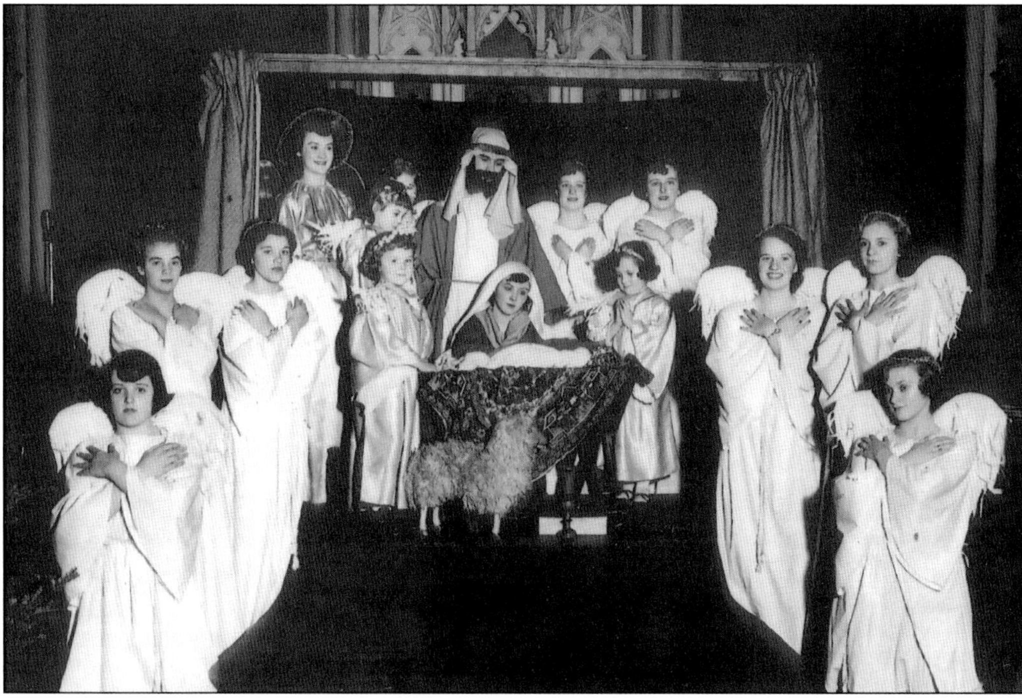

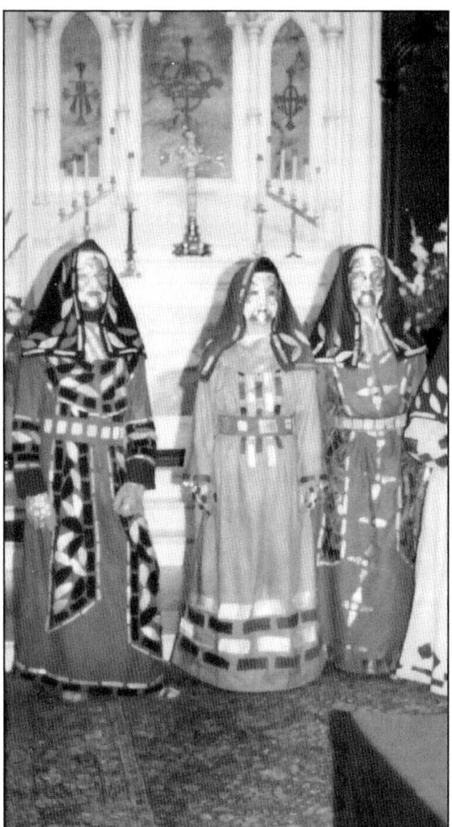

The Christian message has not changed; people are justified by the grace of God through faith. What has changed, however, is society and culture. Consequently, the manner in which Lutherans preach and teach the unchanging Gospel message has had to adapt through the ages. Pictured here are two very different ways of sharing the Gospel message. Shown above is a traditional Christmas pageant. Shown at left is a much different expression of a Christmas pageant, influenced by expanding cultural experiences. Both share the story of Jesus's birth and are likely to connect with different people. These pageants were performed at Holy Trinity Lutheran Church.

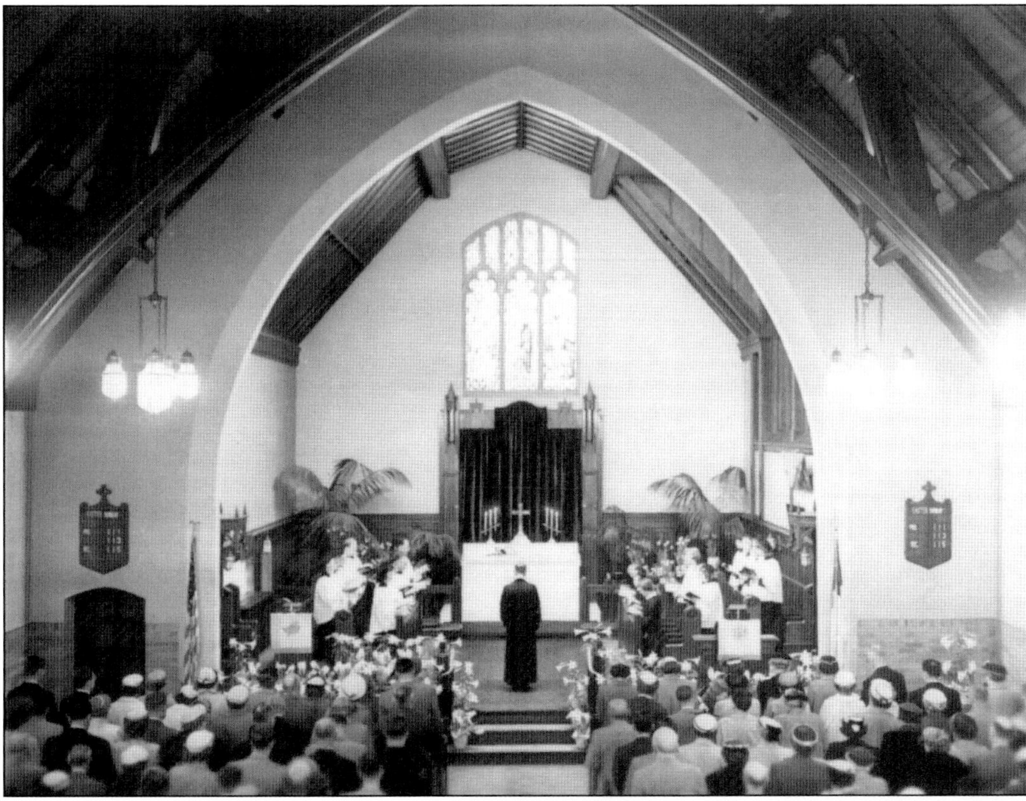

The celebration of the resurrection of Jesus, Easter, is understood to be the most important day of the church calendar. Traditionally, it was the best-attended service and contained the most pomp and ceremony. The congregation stood shoulder to shoulder in the pews, and the sanctuary was decorated extensively. Over the years, however, Christmas and the secular celebrations surrounding it became the most noted event in the church year. Easter remains of vital importance to the church, but it has slipped in the popular consciousness. Shown above is the 1938 Easter service at Parkside Lutheran Church. At right, the choir leads the recessional after the service.

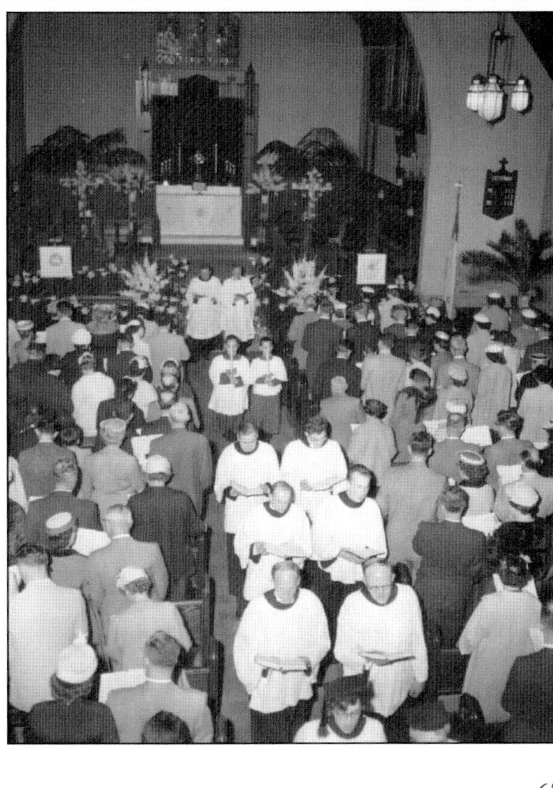

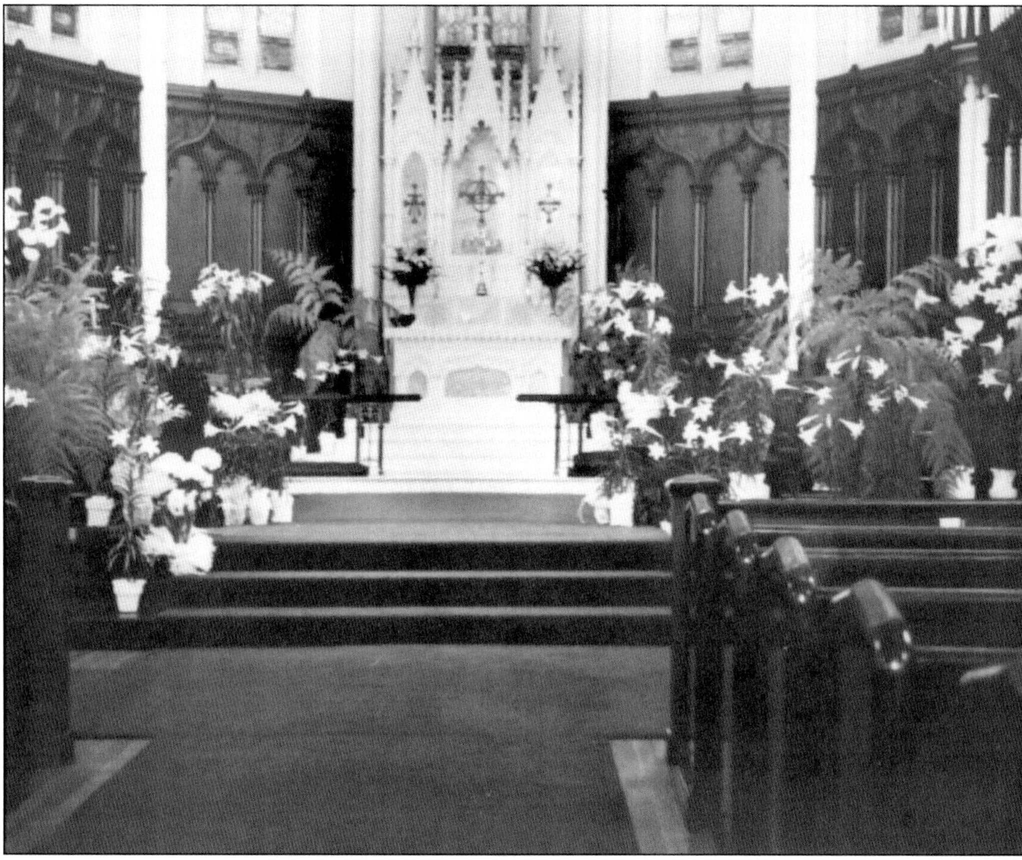

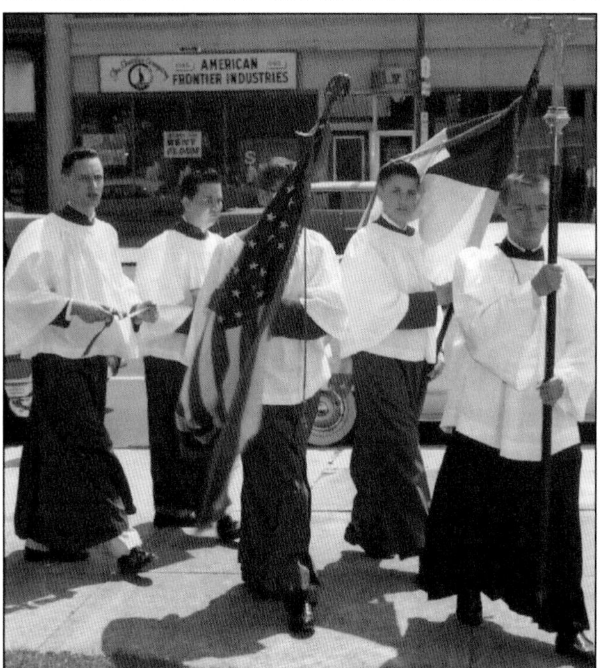

Easter at Holy Trinity has always been full of spiritual ceremony. Whether it be attending daily Lenten devotions at breakfast time or worshipping during the special services of Holy Week, Holy Trinity provides many opportunities for reflection during this solemn season. For years, Holy Trinity held a sunrise service. During that time, it was a special treat to go to the early service and then have breakfast at Your Host restaurant. Getting a special corsage to wear was also part of some Easter memories at Holy Trinity. Choir members will remember arriving at church by 6:00 a.m. to enjoy a big Easter breakfast before performing in the many services that day. The altar boys added to the pomp and circumstance of the day.

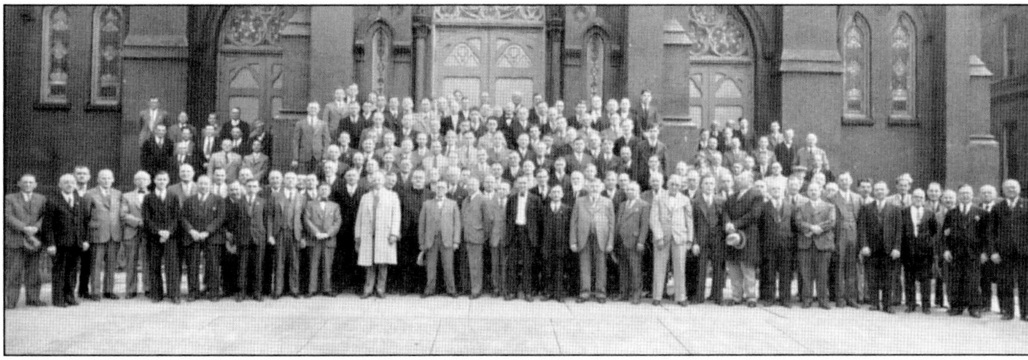

The Men's Bible Class of Holy Trinity took part in the Laymen's Missionary Movement, which swept across the nation in 1909. This local group of parishioners provided support to Rev. C.F. Kuder as a missionary to India. This is one of many examples of church members working beyond the walls of Holy Trinity. Pictured here is the Men's Bible Study Banquet of 1910.

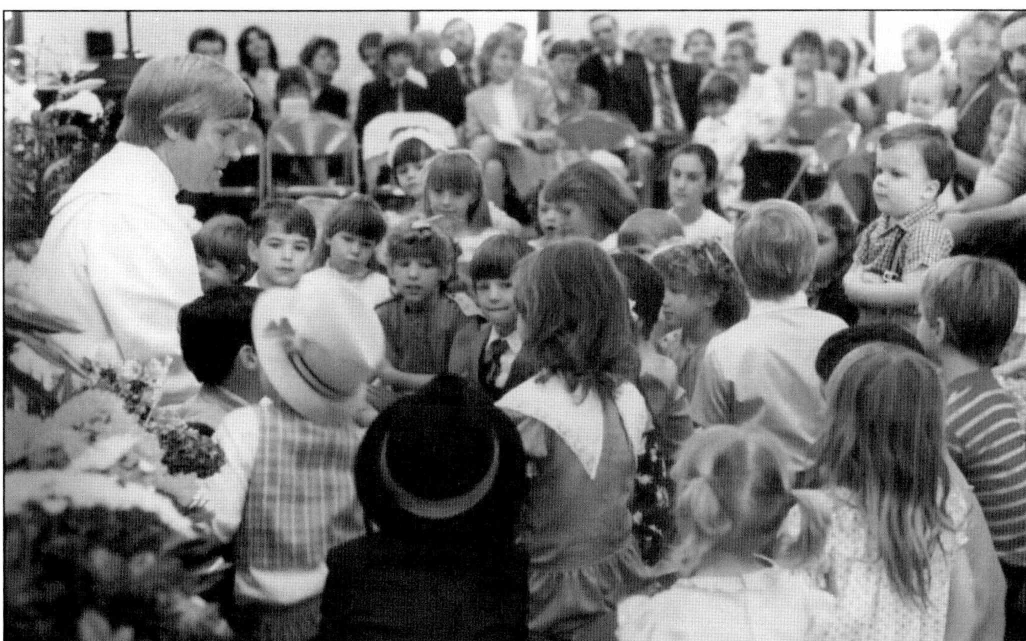

Lutheran services often contain a children's sermon. The pastor or another church leader will call the children to the front and teach them the daily lesson in a way appropriate for their developmental stage. Often including images, props, and a lot of energy, many find the children's sermon to be a highlight of the service. Here, Pastor Dean Hunneshagen delivers an Easter children's sermon at Lord of Life.

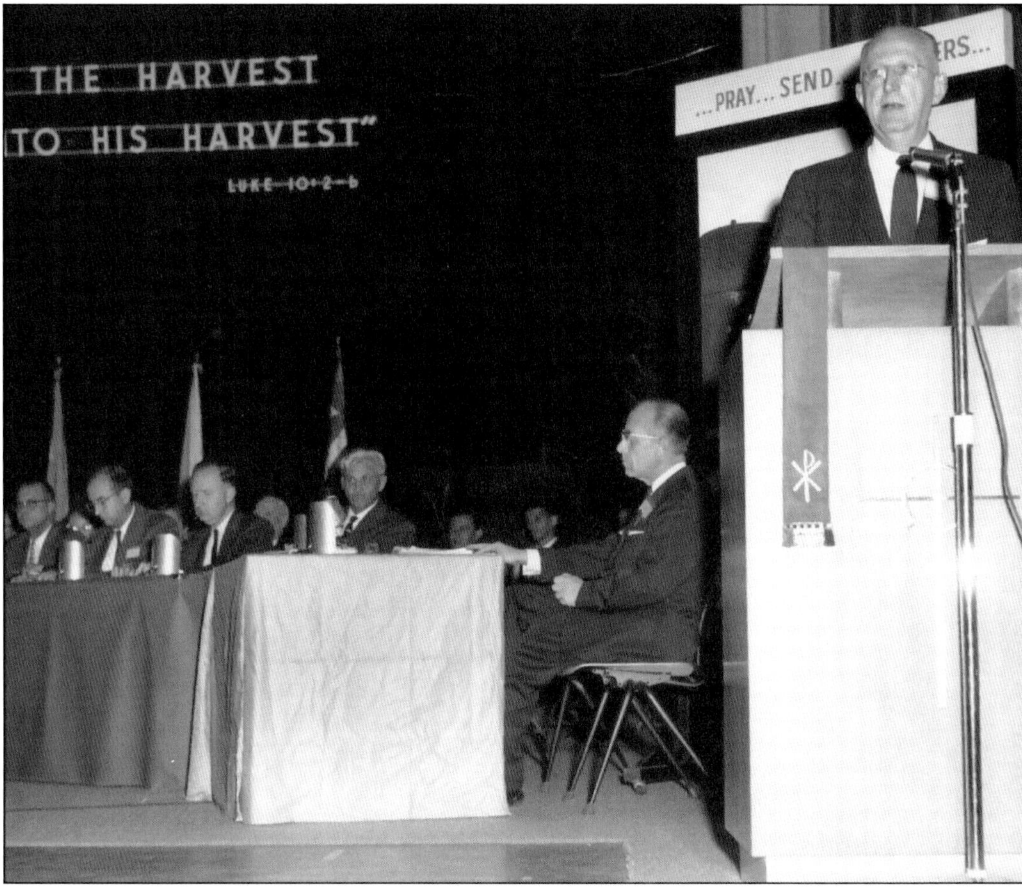

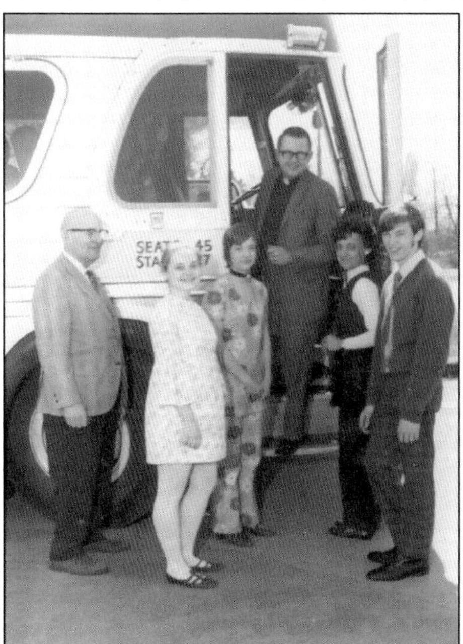

There have been many governing bodies with which area Lutheran churches have been affiliated. The largest have been the Lutheran Church of America (LCA), the American Lutheran Church (ALC), and the Lutheran Church–Missouri Synod (LCMS). In 1988, the LCA and ALC merged to form the Evangelical Lutheran Church of America (ELCA), which remains the largest organization of Lutherans. Pictured here is a 1956 LCA gathering, with Dr. Ralph Loew presiding.

When automobiles made traveling a great distance easier, the family vacation was born. The church, which often operates similarly to a family, has engaged in its fair share of travel as well. Lutherans of Western New York have traveled together frequently, to camps, gatherings, and retreats, often as far away as the Midwest. These parishioners from St. John's Akron are preparing for a retreat.

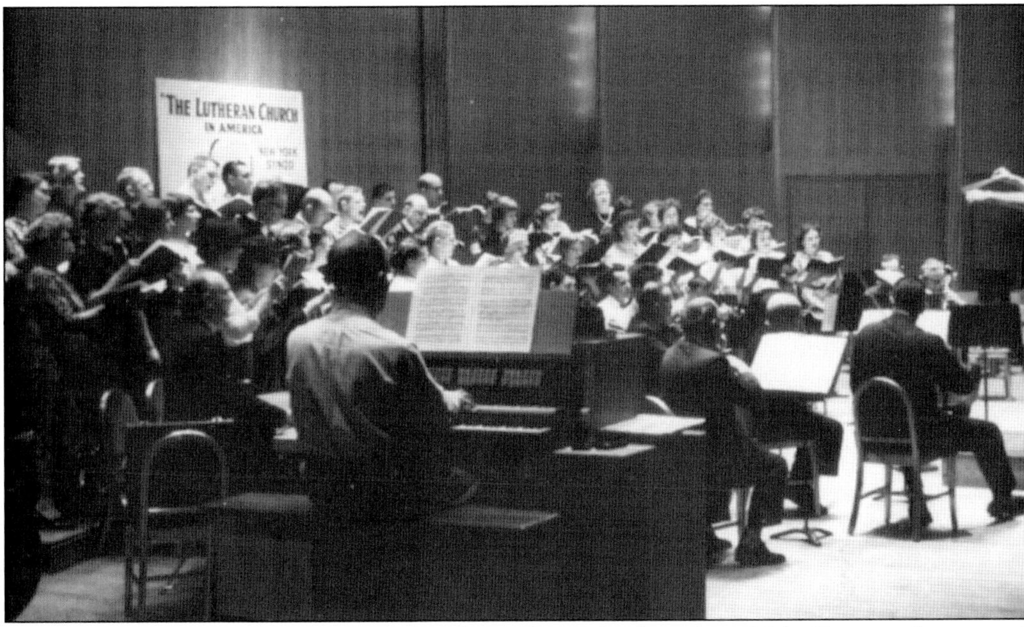

Seen here in Kleinhans Music Hall, members of a 1970s choir from Holy Trinity rehearse with members of the Buffalo Philharmonic Orchestra for an upcoming performance. The banner to the rear advertises the Lutheran Church in America (LCA) New York Synod, which became part of the ELCA in 1988.

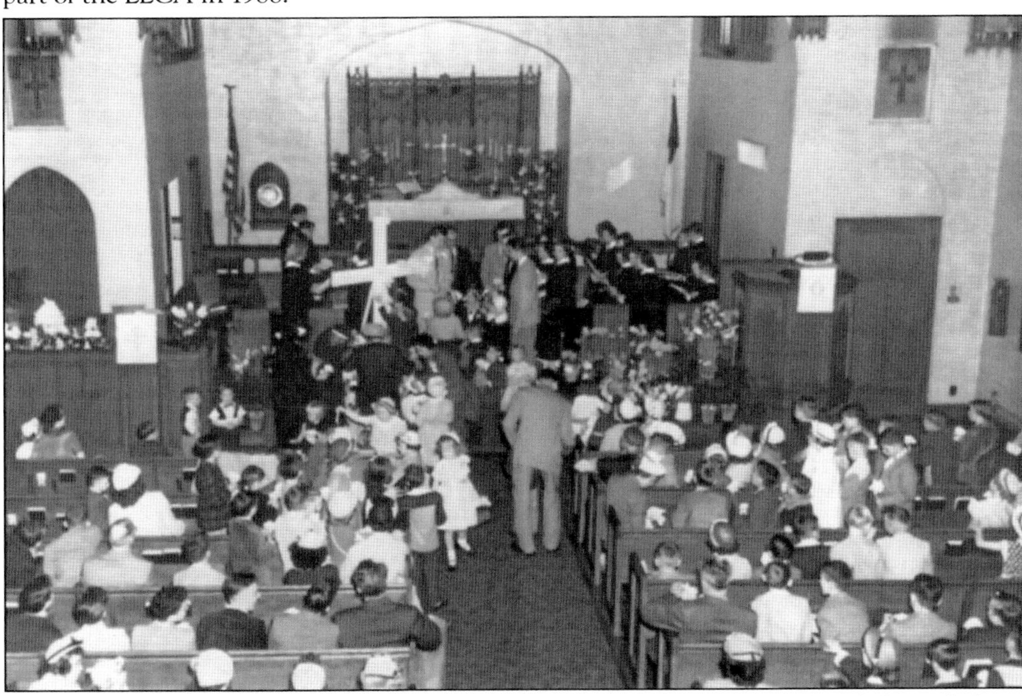

While churches of other denominations began placing the choir in a "choir loft," or balcony, Lutheran churches preferred their choirs to be seated in the front of the church. This allowed the choir to remain an integral part of the service and for parishioners to enjoy a balcony view. This photograph was taken from the balcony at Parkside Lutheran.

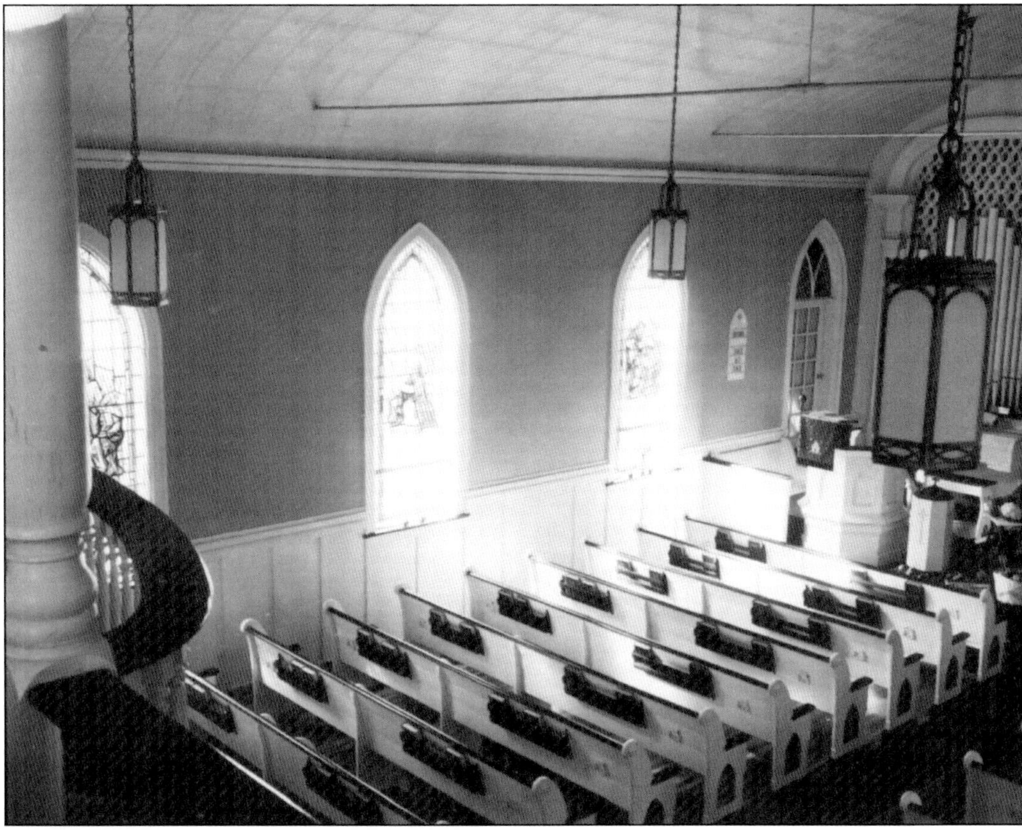

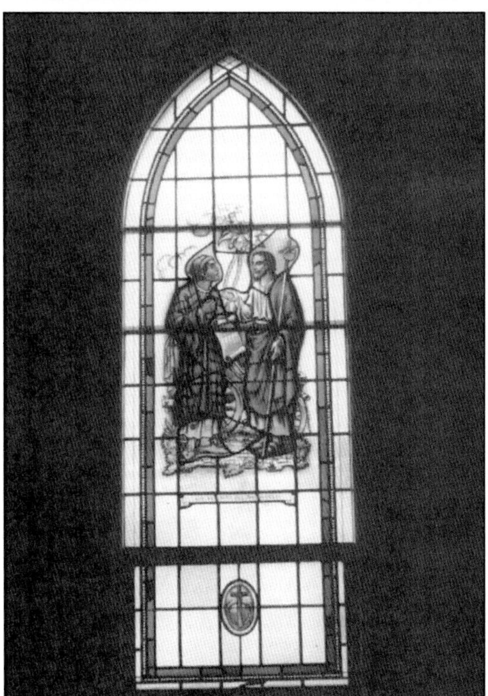

Among the most distinct features of a church building are the stained-glass windows. Windows of varying colors laid out in a mosaic design and held together by a framework of lead are ubiquitous elements of most Lutheran churches. Many older churches have windows that illustrate a scene from the Bible or depict an image or symbol of the church. This was originally a tool of instruction. In a time when many were illiterate, stained-glass windows helped to teach lessons and stories from the Bible. As this function became less necessary, churches chose to continue using stained-glass windows for ascetic reasons. Shown on this page are the new stained-glass windows of St. Paul's Williamsville on Harvest Sunday, 1955.

Three

Faces of Lutheranism

Regardless of the decade, one thing has remained true about the Lutheran Church in Western New York. At the foundation of every successful congregation is the same unit: the family. At its birth, the Lutheran Church was glued together by families of common language and descent. As congregations aged and their children took over, the church became a place to bond a current family as well as to remember family members that had passed. For many congregations, family roots run deep, and going to church can become as much about tradition as it is about worship. This chapter celebrates the individuals and families that the Western New York congregations were built upon. From the wealthy Buffalo businessmen of Holy Trinity to the humble country farmers of Trinity South Newstead, these faces are the church's most valuable history. They are its family tree.

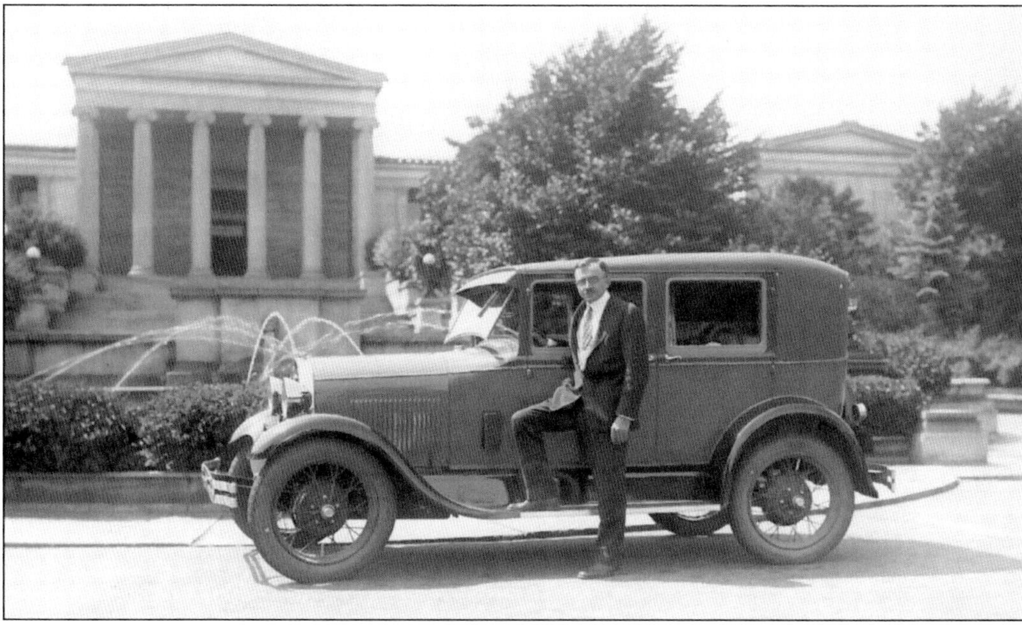

The Reverend Bartholomew Henry Schleifer served St. Paul's Lutheran Church in Williamsville from 1925 to 1932. He is seen in the above photograph, posing in front of the Albright Knox Art Gallery, and below inside the church. Although English and German had both been spoken at St. Paul's since 1907, under Pastor Schleifer's guidance, St. Paul's officially abandoned the German language and conducted all services in English. More important, Pastor Schleifer bore the difficult task of leading his congregation through the economic shift following the stock market crash of 1929. Suddenly, a once-affluent congregation saw many members affected by the Great Depression. Although jobs were scarce, homes were lost, and lives were turned upside down, the bell of St. Paul's continued to ring every Sunday, reminding the community that their church, their pastor, and their congregation would not falter.

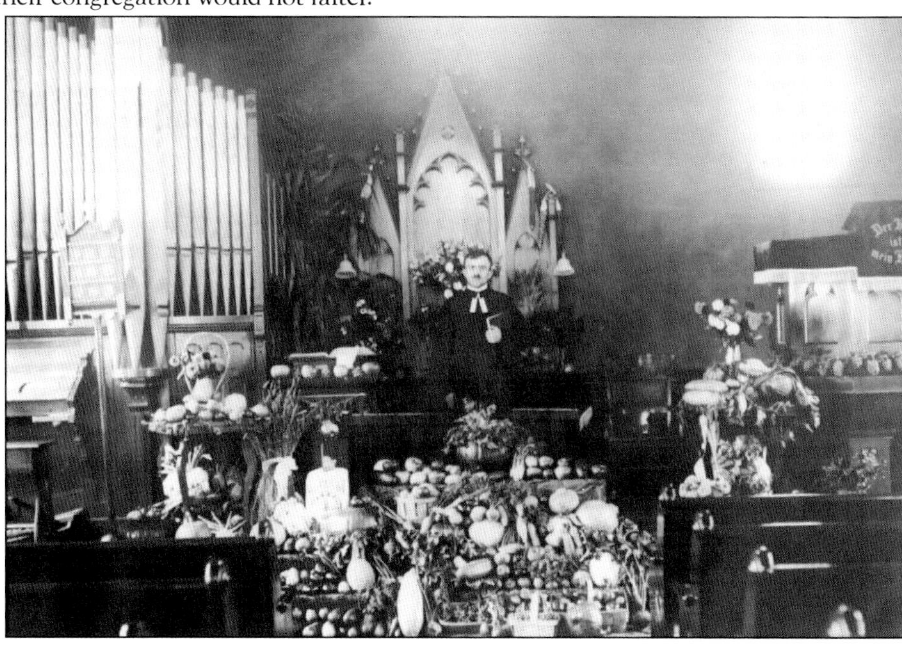

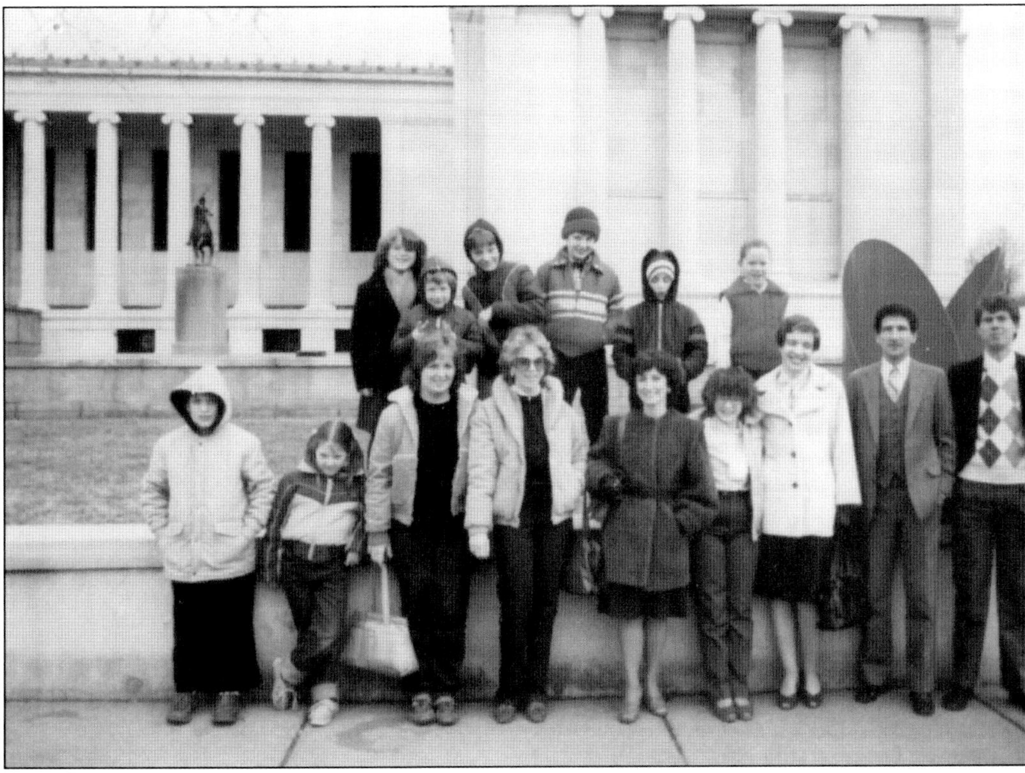

The lore of the Albright Knox Art Gallery has been long-standing in Western New York. More than 70 years after Pastor Schleifer posed in front of the gallery, the youth of Holy Trinity traced his footsteps with a field trip of their own. Shown in the 1980s, this group of Lutheran youth enjoyed a day of fine art and fellowship.

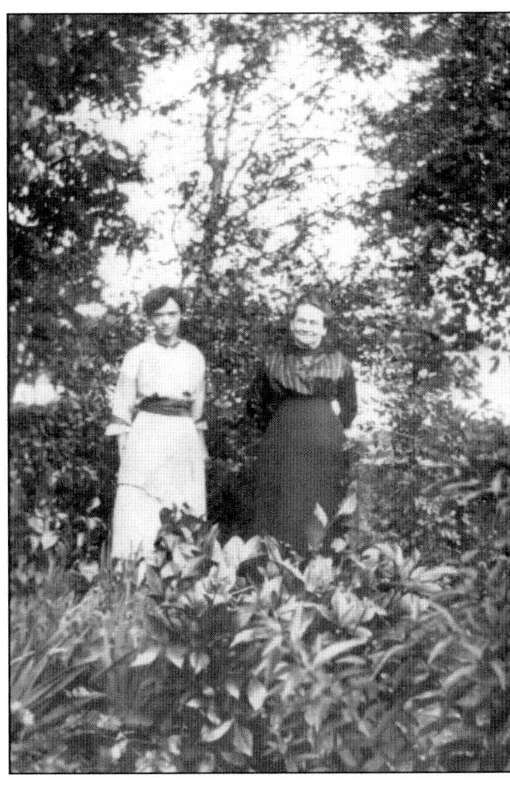

Without the ease of quick and reliable transportation, a family move often meant a change in church congregation. Although Julianna Knoche Landel (left) was raised and married in the German Evangelical Church in Tonawanda, when she and her husband, Fred, moved to Clarence, their affiliation shifted to St. Paul's Lutheran Church in Williamsville. Their daughter Cora Landel Gramm (right) went on to become St. Paul's choir director. (Courtesy of Julianna Woite.)

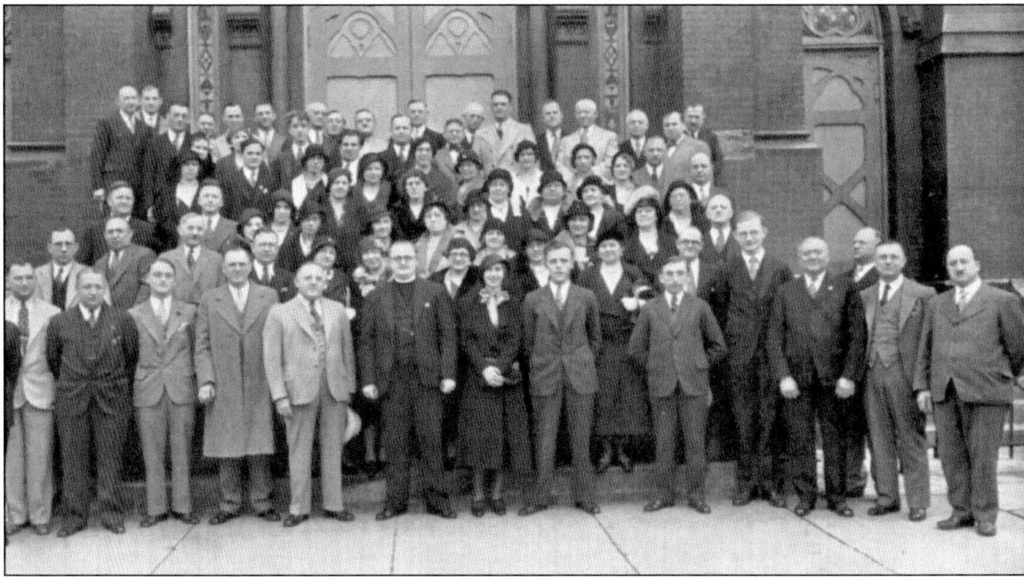

In 1908, St. John's Church of Buffalo celebrated its 75th anniversary. According to a publication from its centennial celebration in 1933, "June seventh, 1908, was another great occasion when the seventy-fifth anniversary of the organization of St. John's was fittingly celebrated. Two thousand commemoration booklets were printed and distributed. There are still a great number of these booklets to be found in Buffalo homes, and should be kept as valuable souvenirs." These commemoration booklets sported a blue paper cover and were printed entirely in German. Entitled "1833–1908—Ev. Luth. St. Johannes Gemeninde, Buffalo, N.Y.", these 14-page booklets contained the program for the service as well as a mixture of current and historical photographs. Taken from the booklet, the above image depicts the Centennial Committee of St. John's and below are the "Officials of the Bibelklaffevereins." (Both, Bible Gaping Club.)

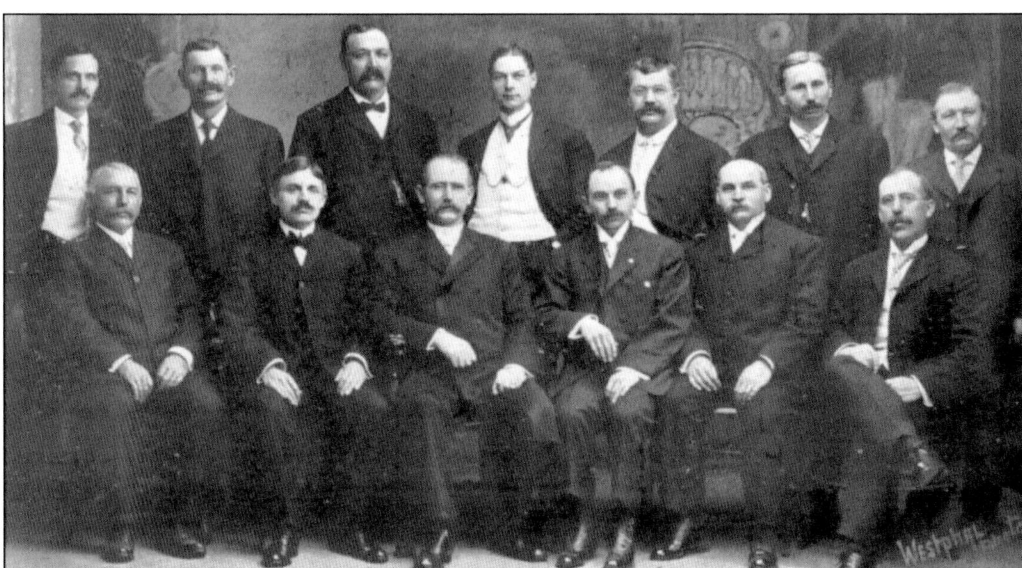

In 1929, the United States, which had enjoyed great prosperity, was on the brink of the Great Depression. This is the 1929 confirmation class from St. John's in Akron. Shown are, from left to right, (first row) Helen Everett, George Everett, Alma Granke, the Reverend Louise Hever, Dorothy Schultz, Chester Granke, and Hilda Linderman; (second row) August Drachenberg, William David, Delmer Berghorn, Elmer Graf, Harvey Brucker, and Daniel Finger.

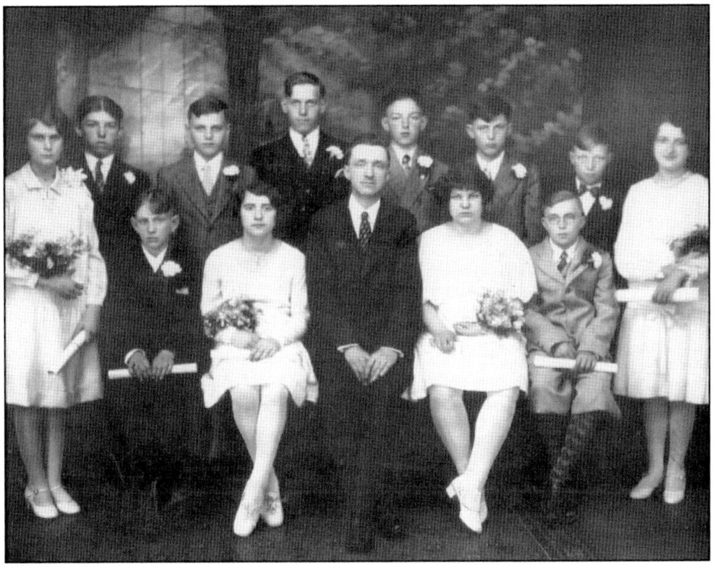

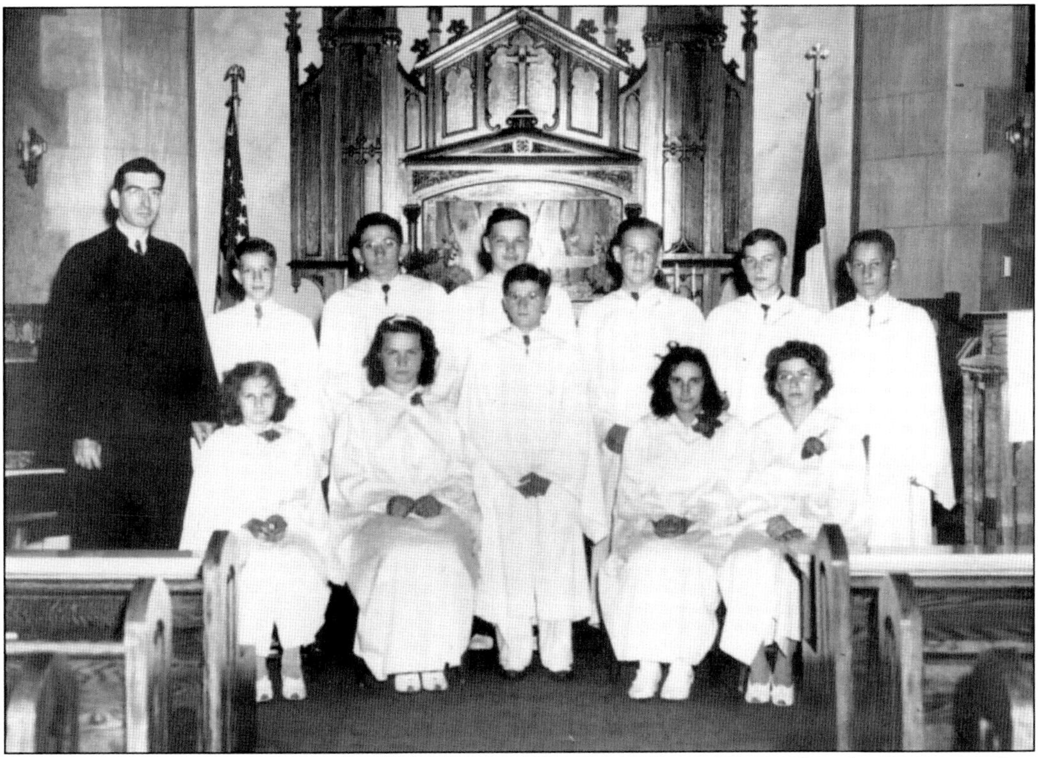

With the United States in the midst of World War II, area Lutheran churches continued to carve a unique identity, separate from their German roots. Despite the war, St. John's in Akron celebrated the confirmation class of 1943. Shown here are, from left to right, (first row) Marjory Aylsworth, Doris Witt, Charles Ellis, Thelma Stage, and Betty Graser; (second row) the Reverend Robert Winters, Louis Kietzman, Donald Lotz, Fredrick Aylsworth, Melvin Nice, Richard Renn, and Herbert Roggen.

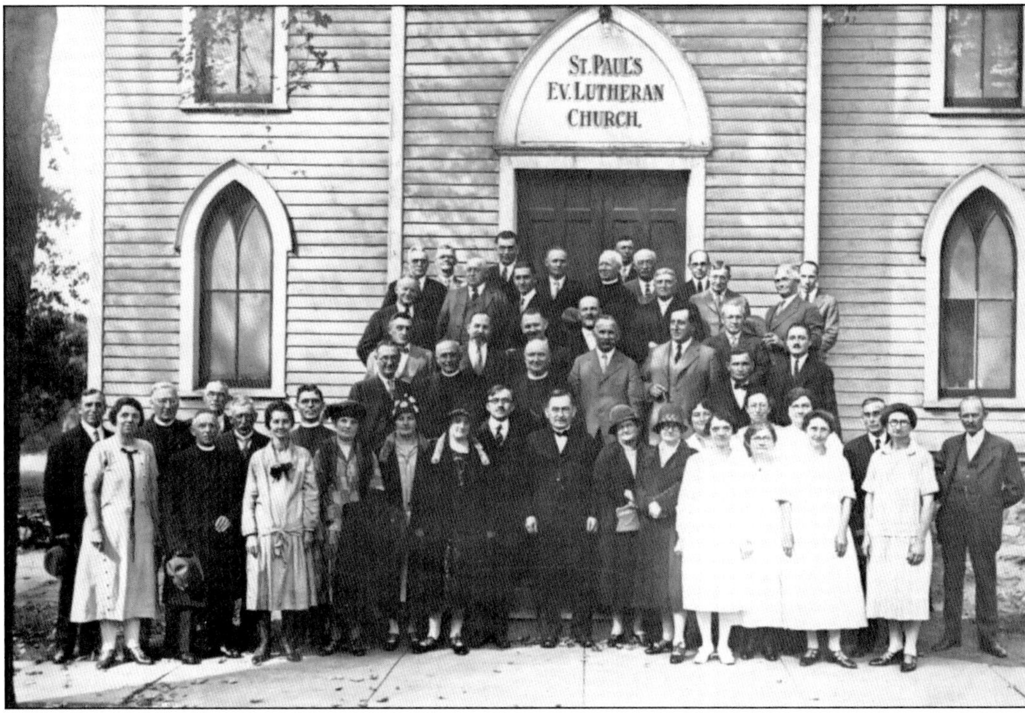

For much of its early life, the church was at the center of a community's social circle. Citizens of this age worked long hours, usually six days a week, and had little time for recreation. By observing the tradition of rest on "the seventh day," early citizens enjoyed a much-needed break from their demanding lifestyles. Furthermore, with only rudimentary means of communication, townsfolk found themselves isolated from their friends and neighbors for most of the week. Whereas people of the 21st century can receive a message by email or text in a matter of seconds, our forefathers received messages by letter or postcard in a matter of days. For these reasons, Sundays were a chance to reconnect and catch up on the affairs of the previous week. For most folks, coming to church on Sunday was as much about the worship service as it was about the fellowship. Pictured here are the congregations of St. Paul's Lutheran Church in Williamsville in the 1920s (above) and the 1930s (below).

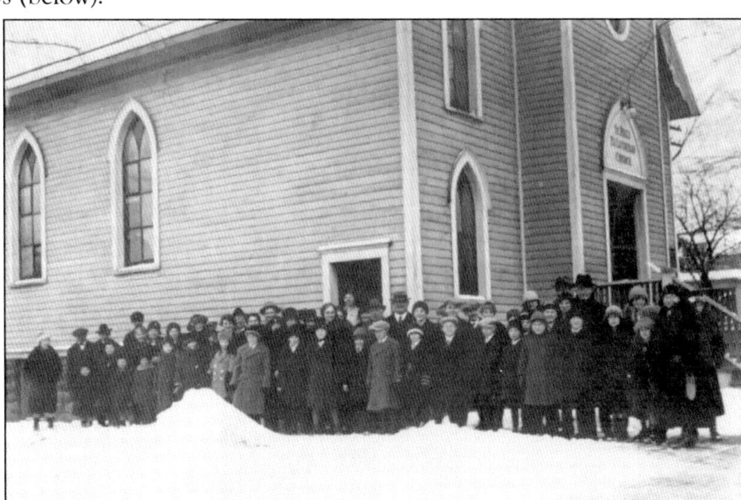

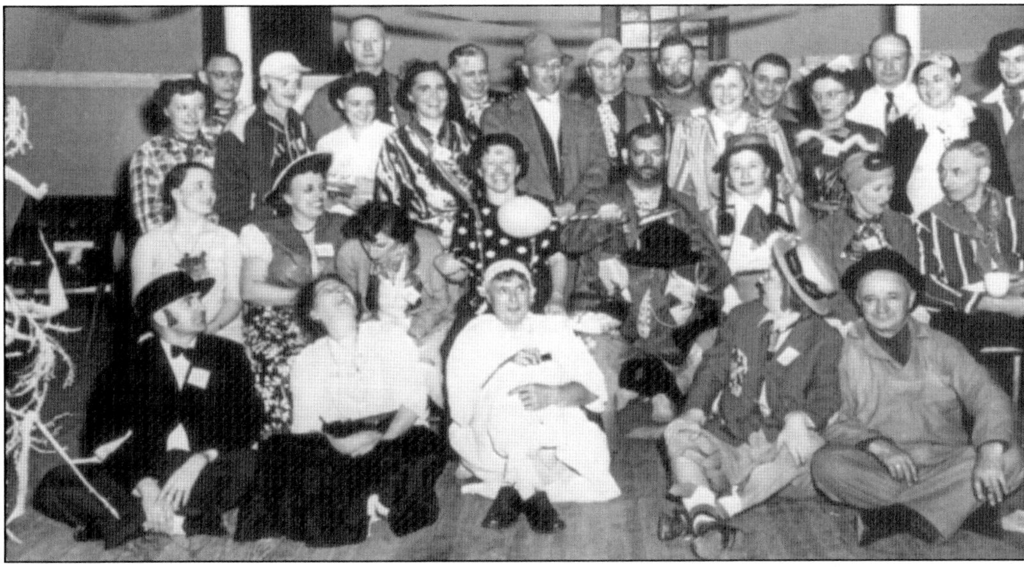

Although church social events have always been rooted in faith, this does not preclude the reality that many were also filled with a healthy dose of silly fun. It is safe to assume that a look into any church's archives will produce evidence of such times of goofiness. In Lutheran churches, social groups and congregational outings have been ways to strengthen bonds and grow together in common faith. As evidenced by these incriminating photographs, left behind after a few crazy costume parties, these congregations were experts at this form of bonding.

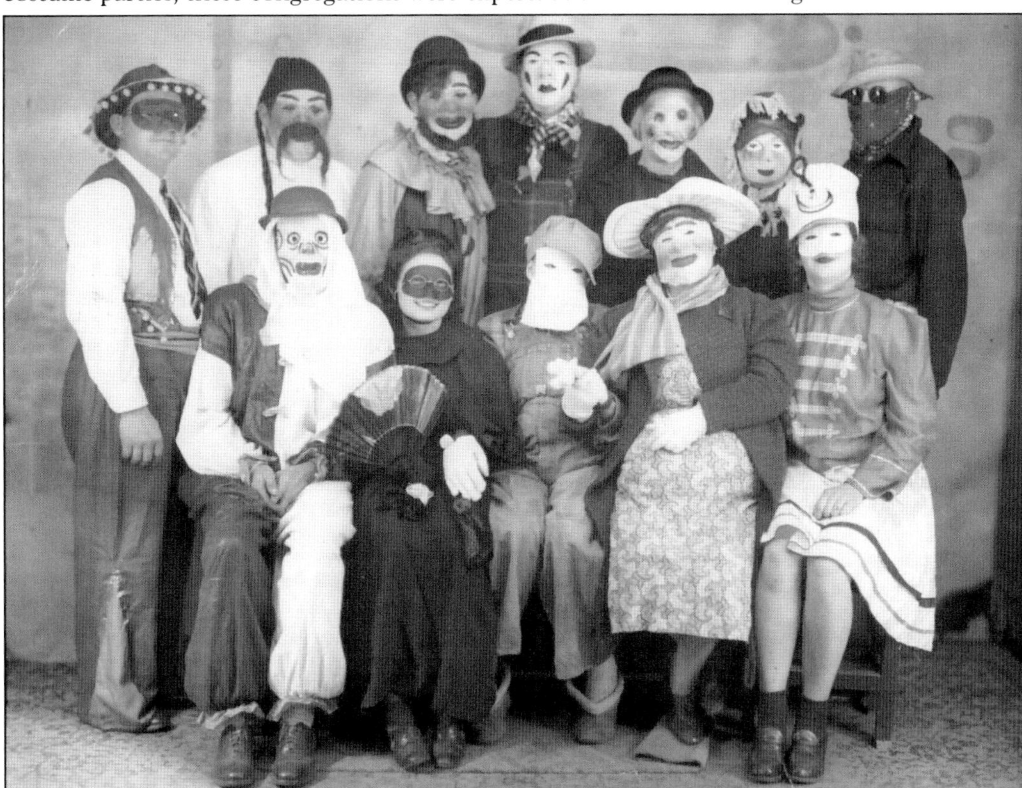

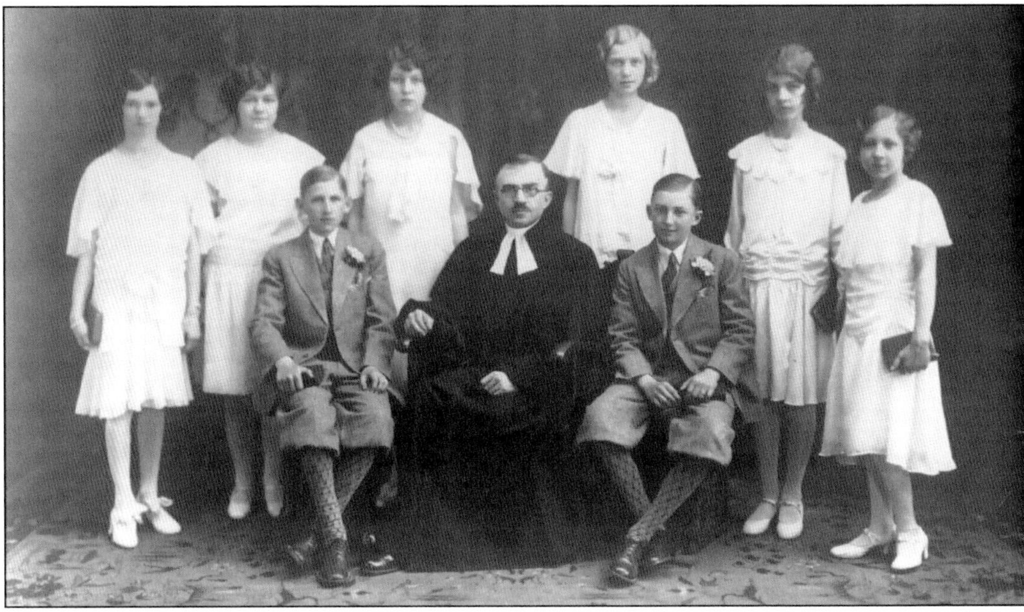

The personality of any church is a direct reflection of its members. Much like a marriage, finding the right people to fit into the right congregation can breed a lifetime of loyalty and satisfaction. St. Paul's Williamsville has been lucky to maintain relationships with many of its founding families and can boast roots six generations deep. One lifetime member was Dorothy Landel Shaver, pictured above second row, far left, and below as a newborn in 1916. She is shown above with her confirmation class of 1930. Shaver spent 95 years with St. Paul's, where she was baptized, confirmed, married, and mourned. Her daughter still sings in the choir, and her grandchildren and great-grandchildren, although out of town, still pay visits. The confirmation class of 1930 included Kathryn Grunewoald, Irma Heisen, Earl Klein, Dorothy (Landel) Shaver, Viola Spiesz, Mary Steeb, and Laura Weatherbee. (Below, courtesy of Julianna Woite.)

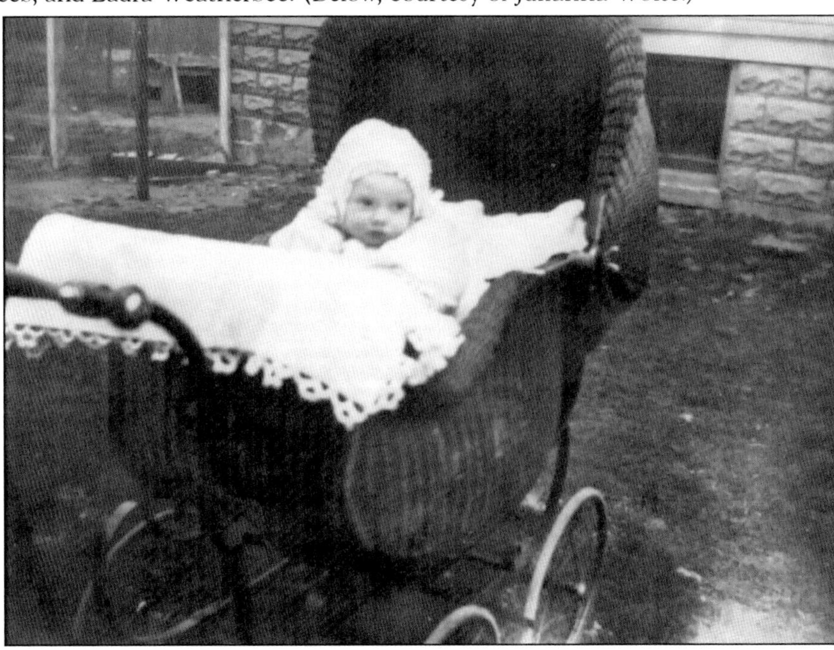

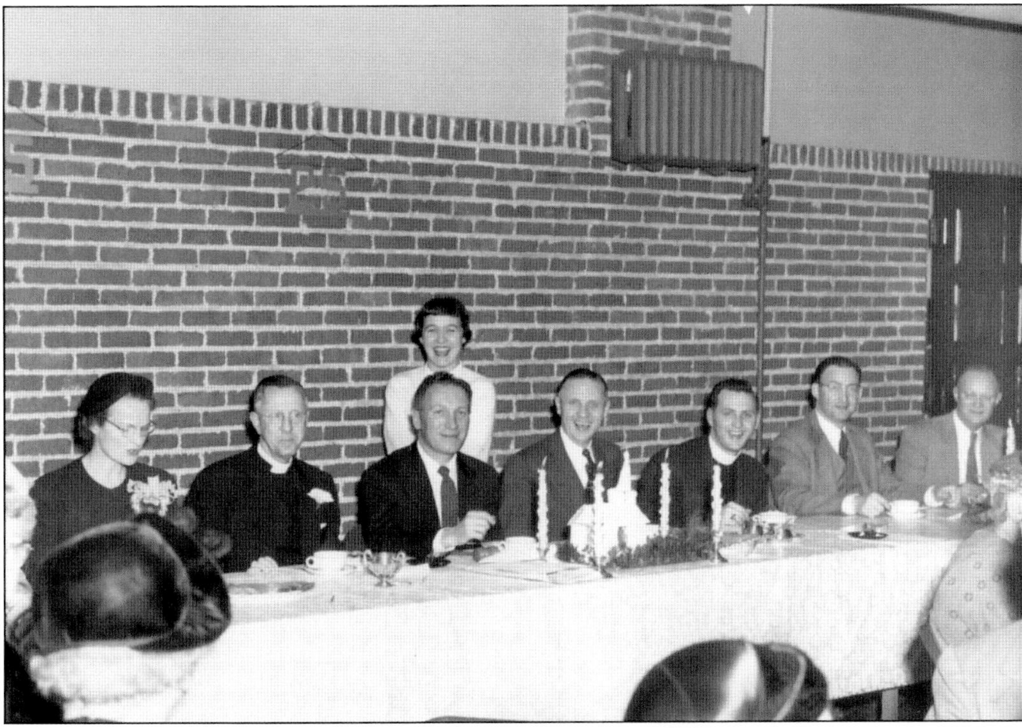

This photograph from the Parkside 25th anniversary celebration on May 15, 1938, includes Mrs. and Rev. John Fleck, seated at left. Mary Hochreiter stands at center. Also shown are George Hochreiter, Brian Snyder, Howard Chapel, and two unidentified men. In the center of the table is a cake replica of the church.

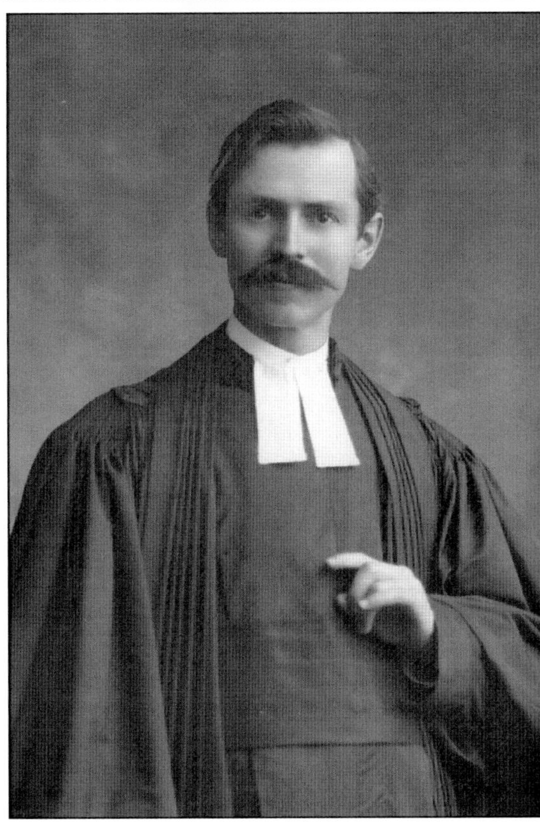

The Reverend T.W. Kretschmann, PhD, was pastor of the Church of Atonement on Eagle Street from 1898 to 1905. His many accomplishments include being prominently identified with the Lutheran City Mission Society as well as being a passionate worker with the Luther League. Most notably, however, Reverend Kretschmann was the promoter of the South Buffalo Mission, which became Grace Evangelical Lutheran Church in 1905.

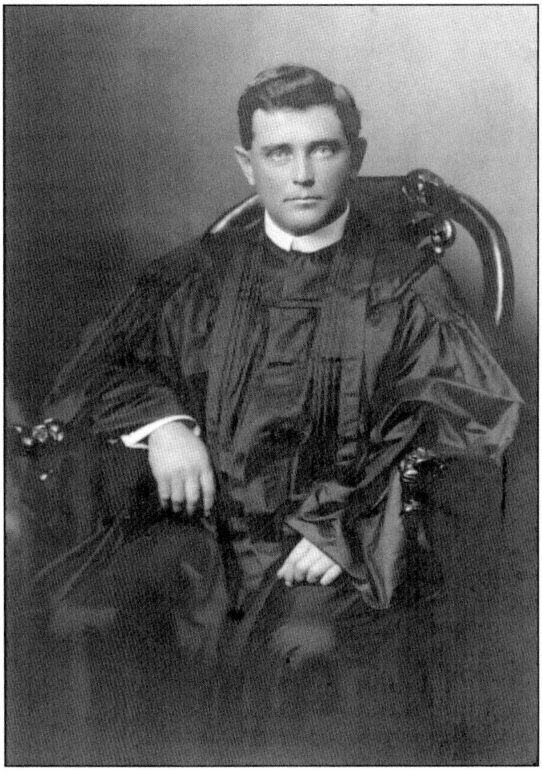

In 1906, the Reverend Peter Altpeter succeeded Dr. Kretschmann as pastor of the Church of Atonement, where he remained for 14 years. Prior to becoming a pastor, Altpeter worked for seven years in the sheet-iron and copper trade, studying machinery in his spare hours. Hearing his calling, however, he graduated from Thiel College in 1892 and promptly entered the Lutheran Theological Seminary in Philadelphia, graduating in 1895.

A service of installation was held at Parkside Lutheran Church for Kenneth Christian Heuermann on July 25, 1954. Pastor Heuermann was joined by Assistant Pastor Vernon F. Squire as successors to the ironically popular Pastor Dr. Fleck. Heuermann is shown presiding over Easter services on April 10, 1955.

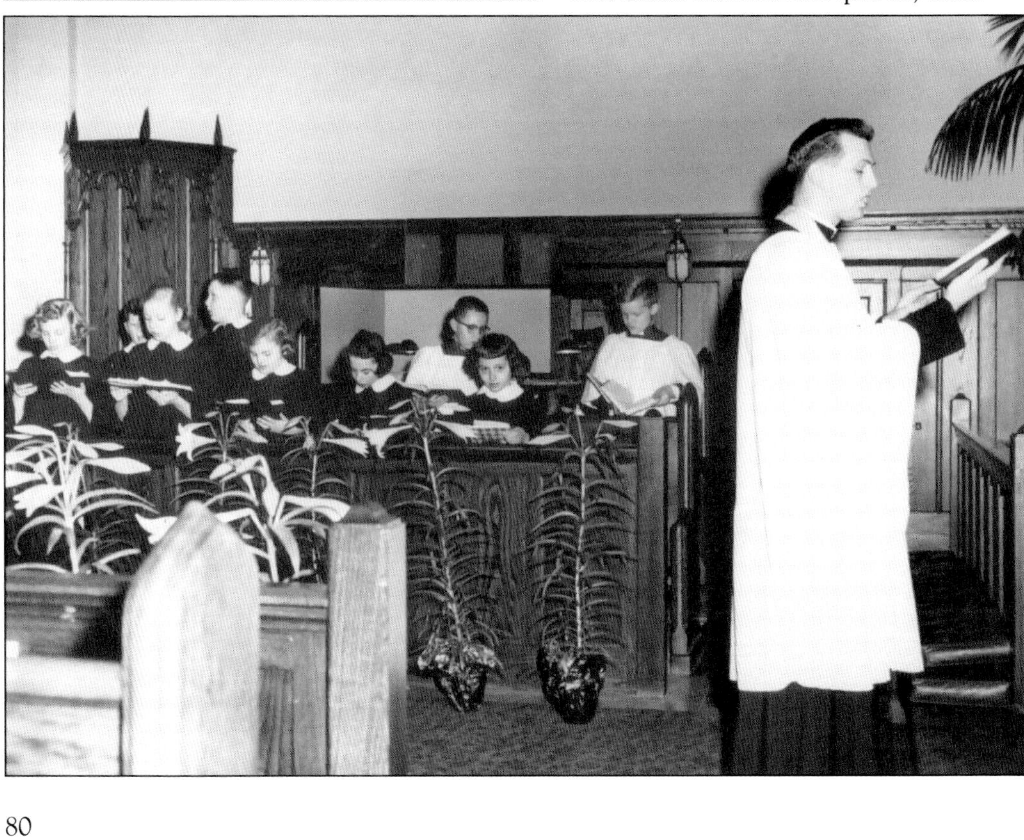

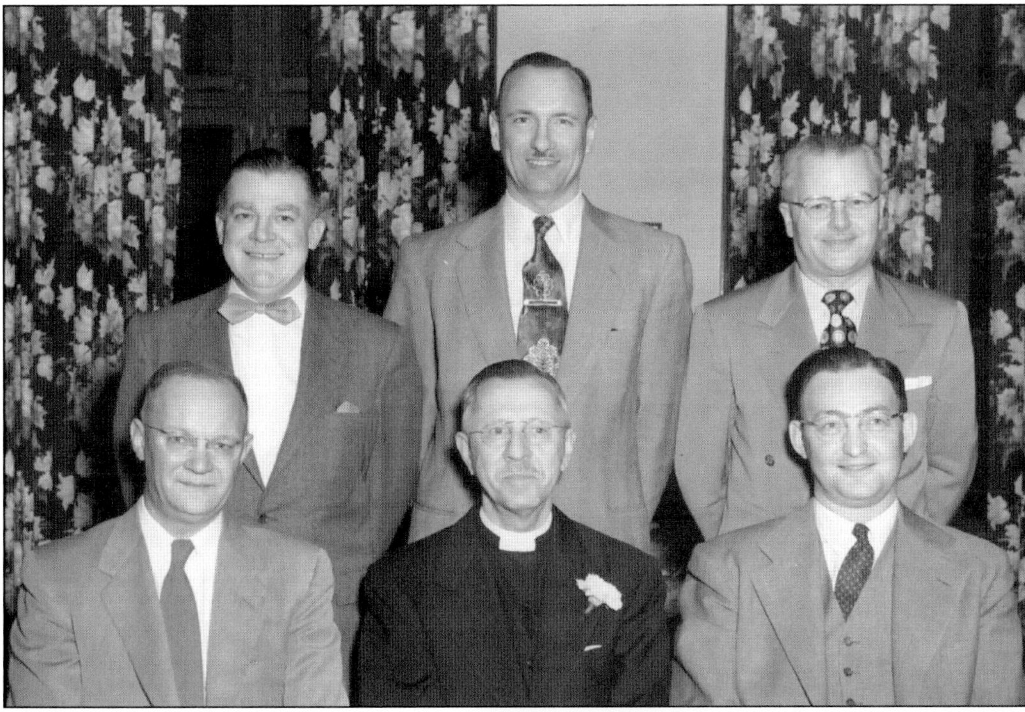

Throughout history, the bonds and friendships formed within a church on Sunday have extended into the parishioners' lives during the next six days. It was also not uncommon for a shared religious background to give one a leg up in matters of business. Pictured here are Parkside parishioners and Pastor Fleck. They are, from left to right, (first row) Ward Flach, Dr. John Fleck, and William Henderson; (second row) George Sautere, William Boehmke, and Howard Landsheet.

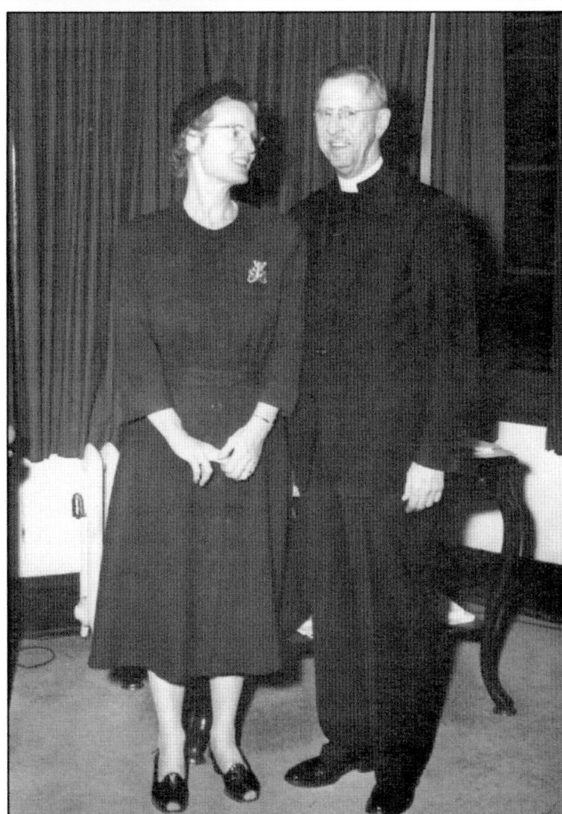

On January 7, 1940, the congregation of Parkside Lutheran Church honored Reverend and Mary Fleck with a reception and tea for their 10th anniversary serving the church. Charter members of the church, as well as more than 350 people from the Lutheran community, attended the festivities, which included musical numbers by church soloists, a violinist, and a cellist.

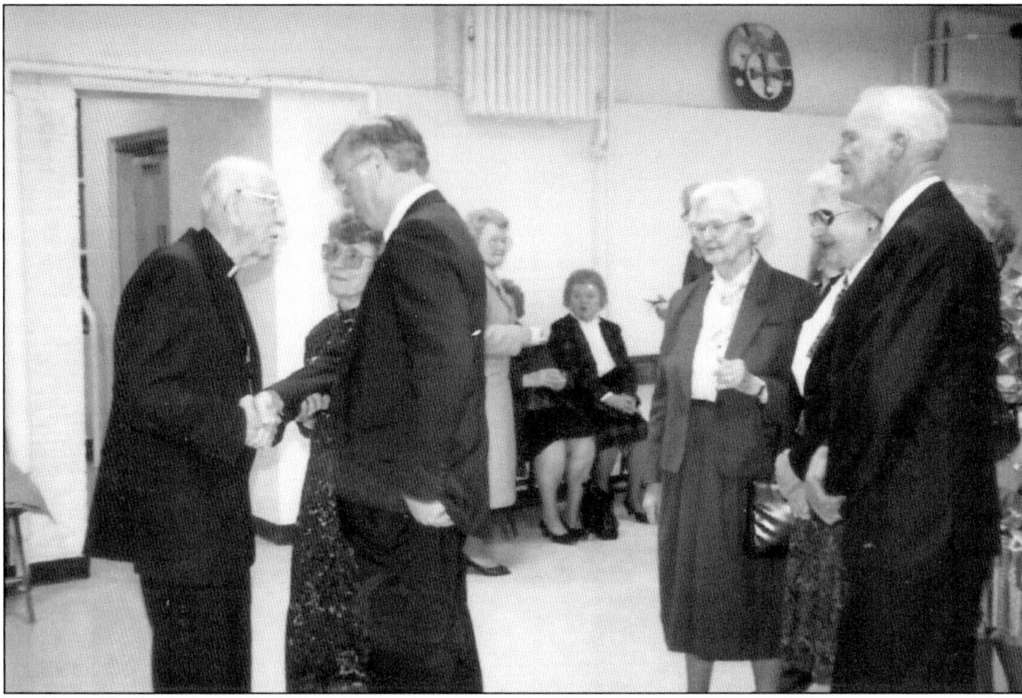

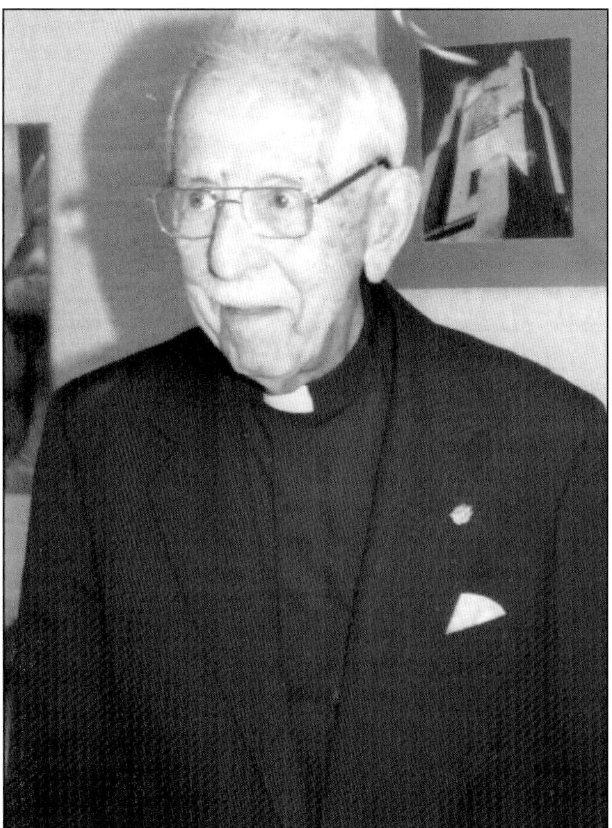

On November 11, 1990, Parkside celebrated "John Fleck Sunday" with a church service and reception. The following year, Pastor Fleck (far left) won four gold medals in the US National Senior Sports Classic at age 99. By finishing the 1,500-meter race walk in 19:39, he became the oldest person to ever qualify for the national games. He was also the only person in his age bracket.

Iconic Parkside Lutheran Church pastor Dr. John Fleck (1891–1992) turned 100 on October 3, 1991. In addition to his years of service as a Lutheran pastor and his participation in competitive swimming events (50 meters, 100 meters, and 400-meter freestyle), Dr. Fleck also served his country as an Army chaplain during World War II.

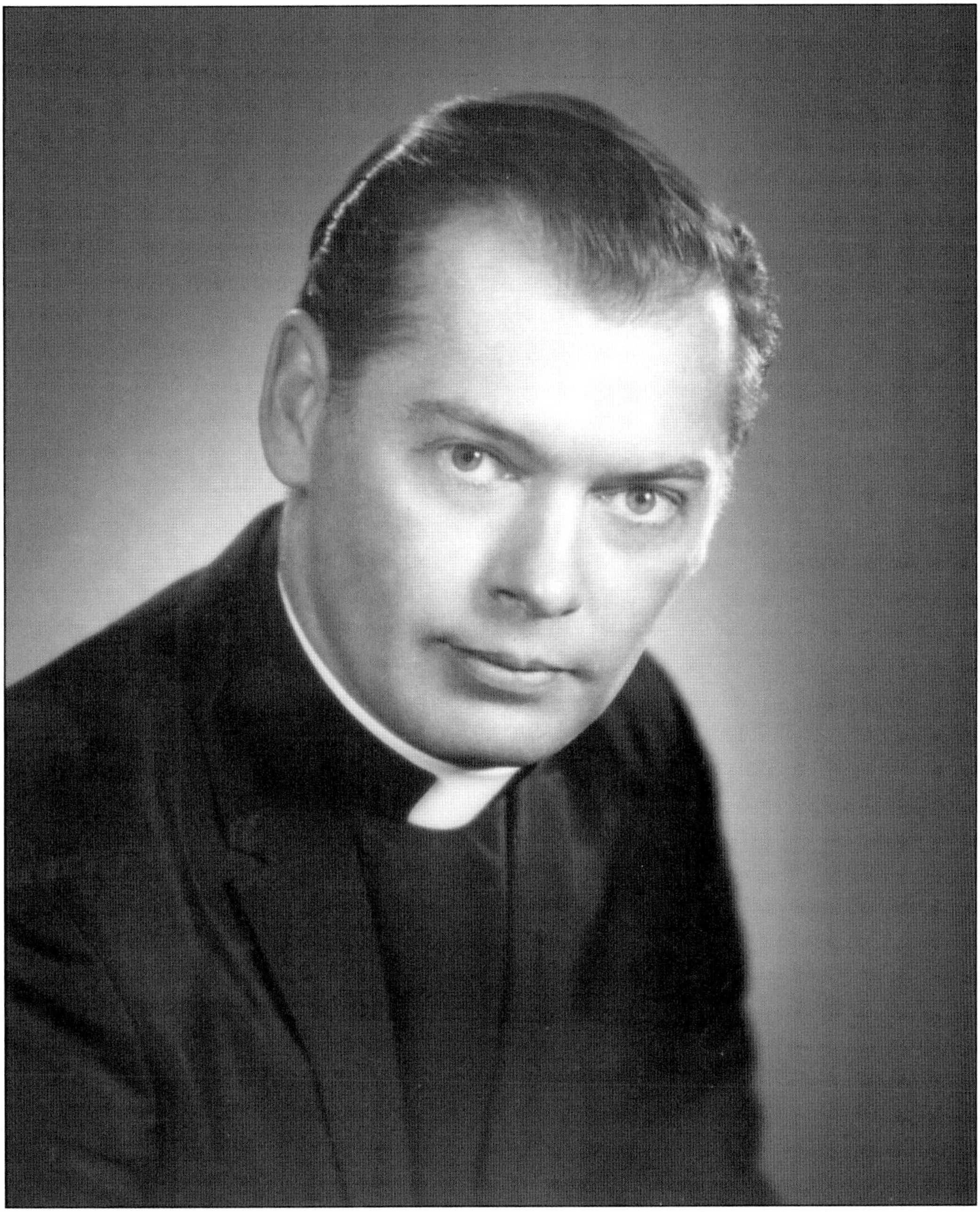

The Reverend Edward Kersten Perry was officially called to Parkside Lutheran Church as an assistant pastor on January 19, 1949. According to church documents, his annual salary was $2,700. Although he left Parkside in 1951, he returned a decade later when he was called as pastor in 1962. In 1965, the Niagara Frontier District of the Lutheran Church in America elected Reverend Perry as its new dean. As the district's top officer, he coordinated the work of nearly 40 churches. On February 6, 1988, Dr. Edward Perry was installed as bishop of the Upper New York Synod. He served in this capacity from 1988 to 1992. Although his career took him all over the state, in a letter to the congregation in the 1990s, Reverend Perry said the following of Parkside: "wonderful memories, wonderful building which has always been my emotional home; ever wonderful people."

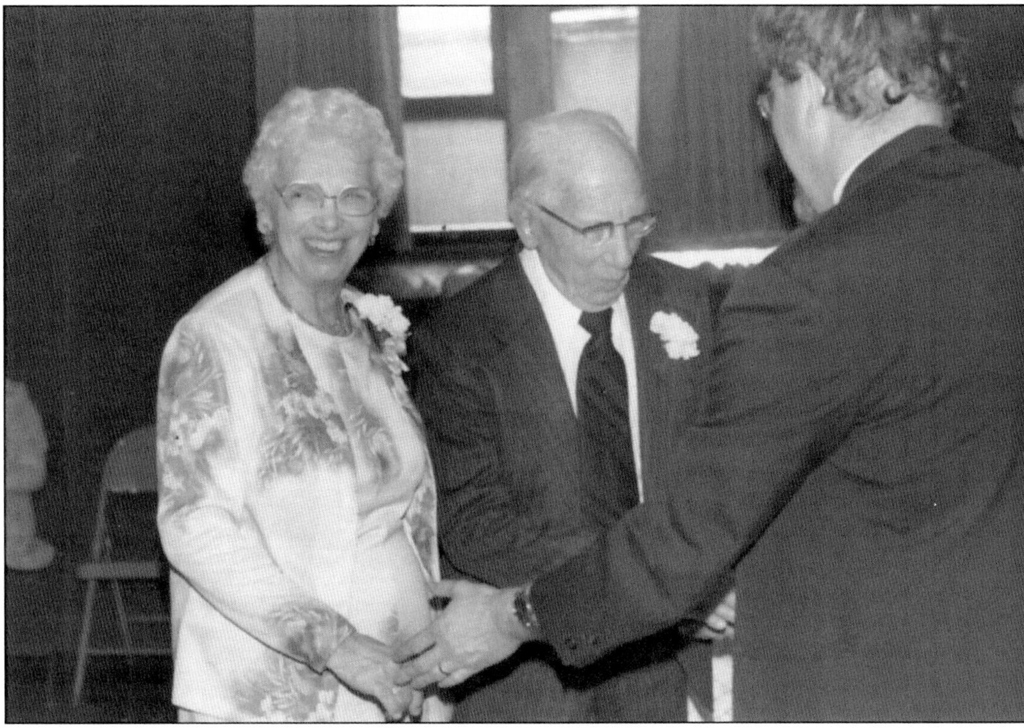

The Reverend Eugene Stowell was called to Parkside in 1963 and served until 1967. He was the first pastor of Ascension Lutheran Church in Snyder, served for 30 years at Resurrection Church in Rochester, and a was a member of the Hartwick College Board. Reverend Stowell is pictured here with his wife, Viola.

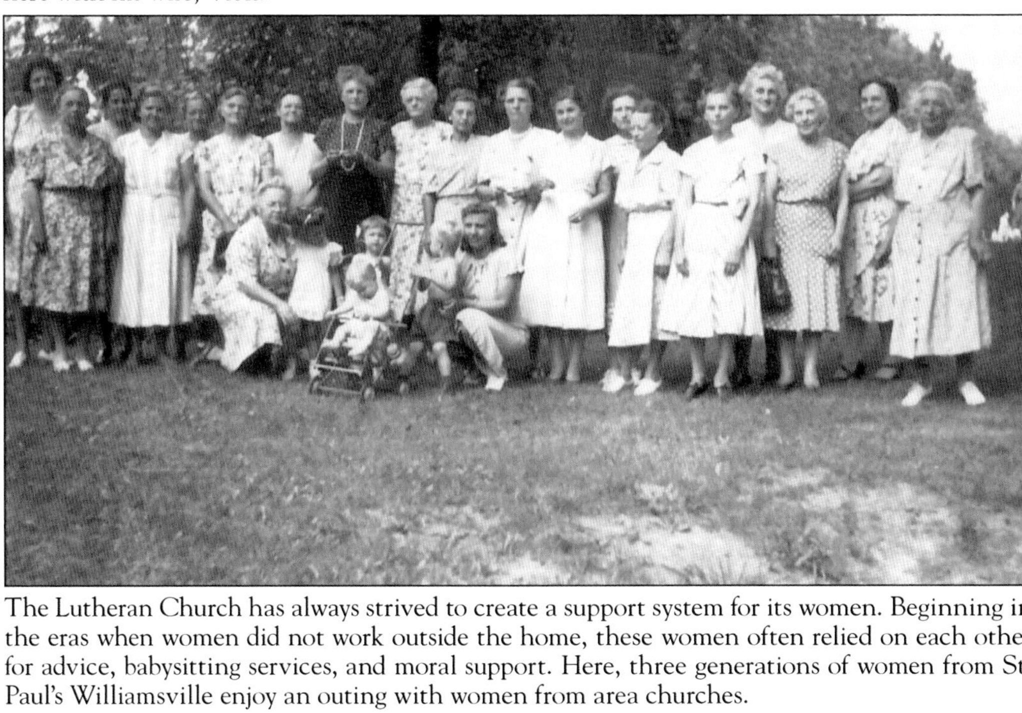

The Lutheran Church has always strived to create a support system for its women. Beginning in the eras when women did not work outside the home, these women often relied on each other for advice, babysitting services, and moral support. Here, three generations of women from St. Paul's Williamsville enjoy an outing with women from area churches.

By the first few decades of the 20th century, many churches were fortunate enough to have families with deep congregational roots. At St. Paul's in Williamsville (established in 1869), families such as the Landels already boasted three generations by 1916. Fred and Julianna Landel began attending in the late 1800s with their five children. Their son Charles was confirmed in 1901 and later married Irene Schoelles. The couple had three daughters. Although daughter Vera was lost to illness as a baby, Dorothy and Lois remained lifetime members. The photograph at right depicts Charles and Irene Landel with daughter Dorothy and newborn Lois at Lois's baptism in 1931. Below, Charles Landel (left) and Reverend Hartman (right) enjoy a gathering at the Landel home following the ceremony. Today, the family has reached its sixth generation at St. Paul's. (Both, courtesy of Julianna Woite.)

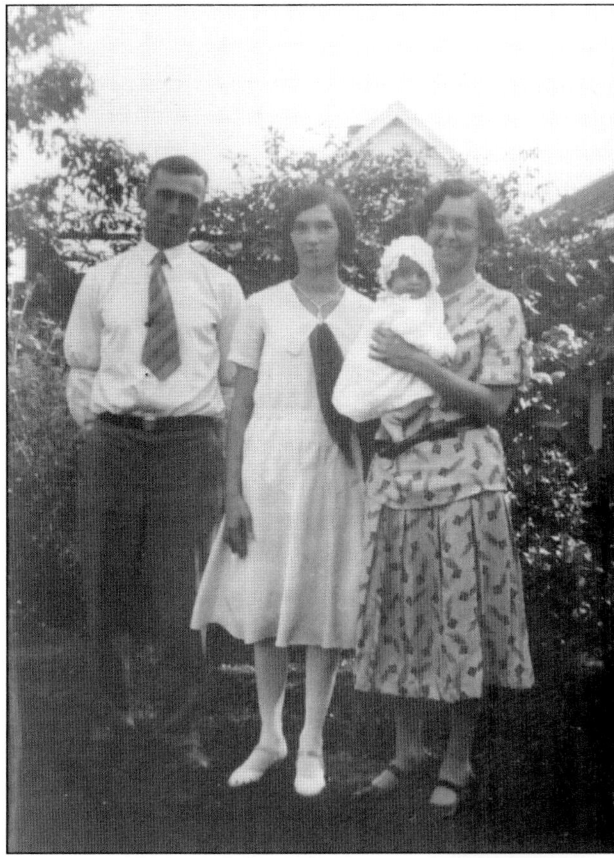

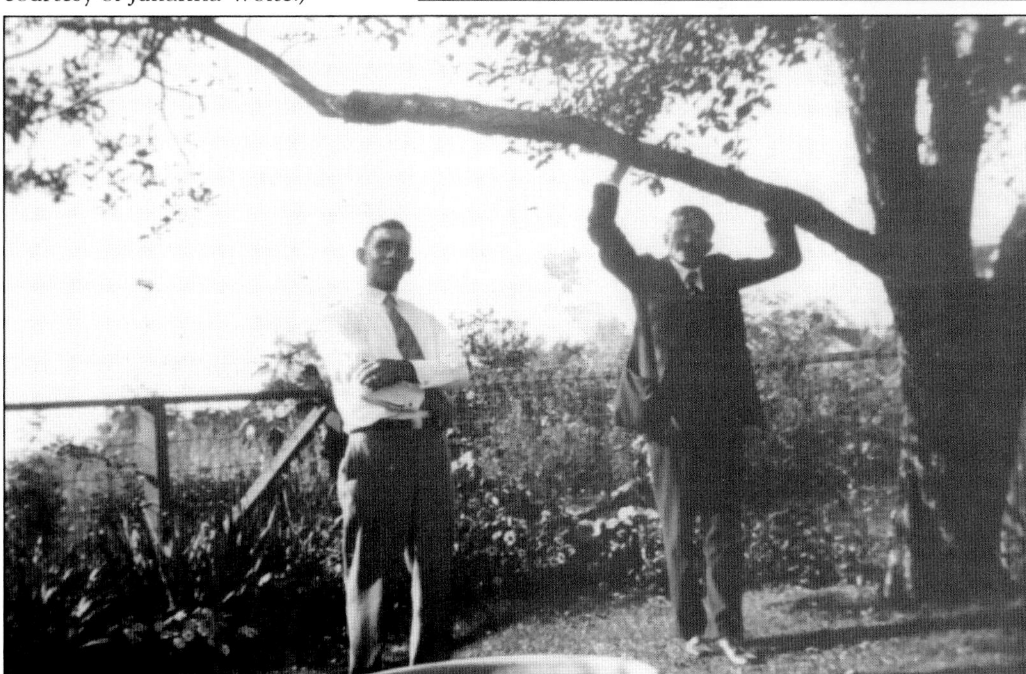

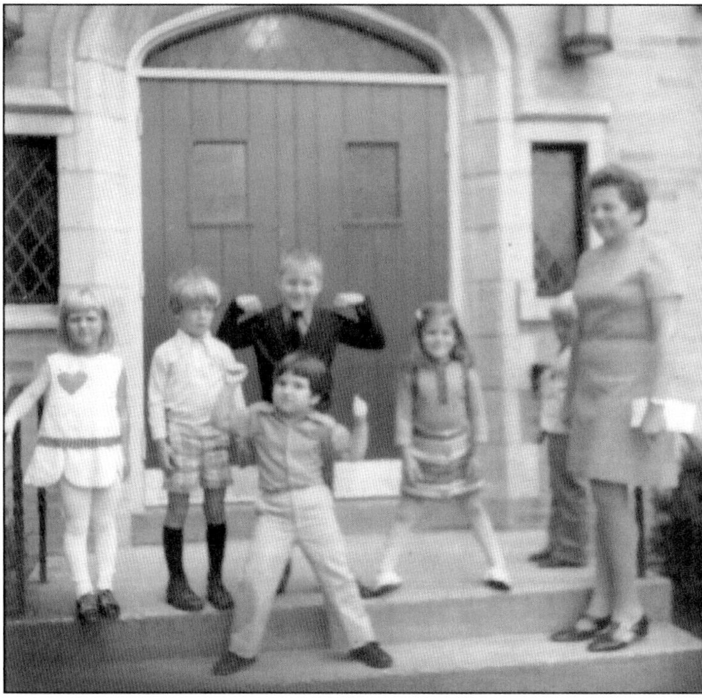

Following the call of Pastor Carl G. Olin Jr. in 1967, St. Paul's in Eggertsville experienced a steady growth in membership, especially among youth and young adults. Aiming to increase their involvement in the congregation, youth representatives were appointed to the council for the first time in 1970. This September 1972 photograph highlights the exuberance of the St. Paul's youth.

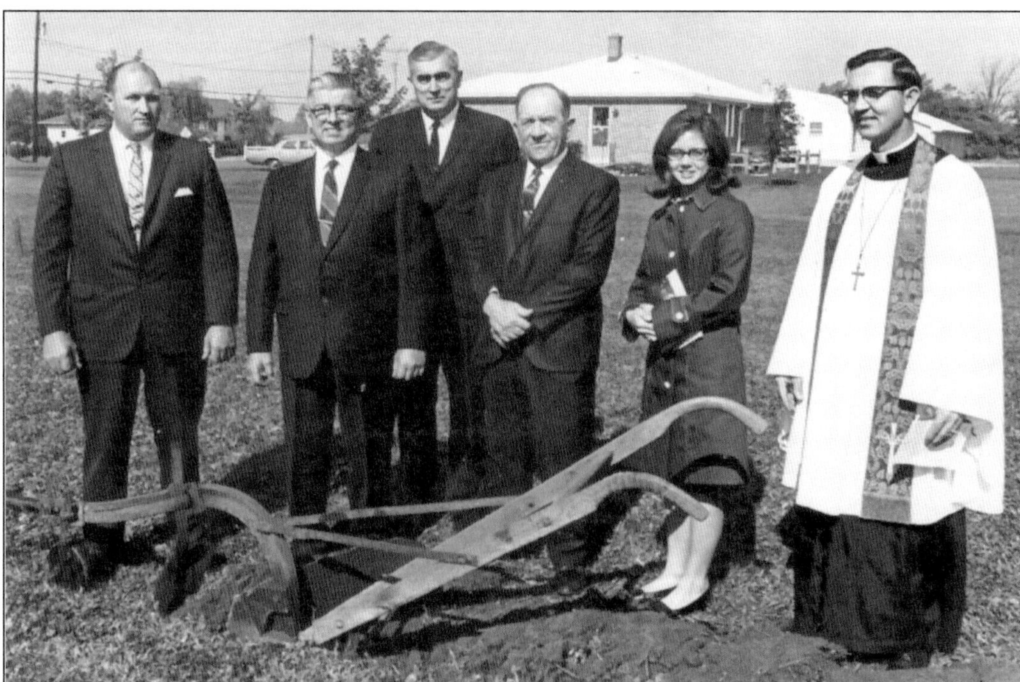

Area churches experienced tremendous growth in the 1950s and 1960s. Churches that began as small "country" congregations enjoyed the growth of the suburbs but found their facilities lacking in space. St. Paul's in Williamsville was forced to knock down the adjacent parsonage to construct an addition to the Sunday school. Seen here, the congregation of Trinity in South Newstead broke ground in 1969 to construct a new church building across the street.

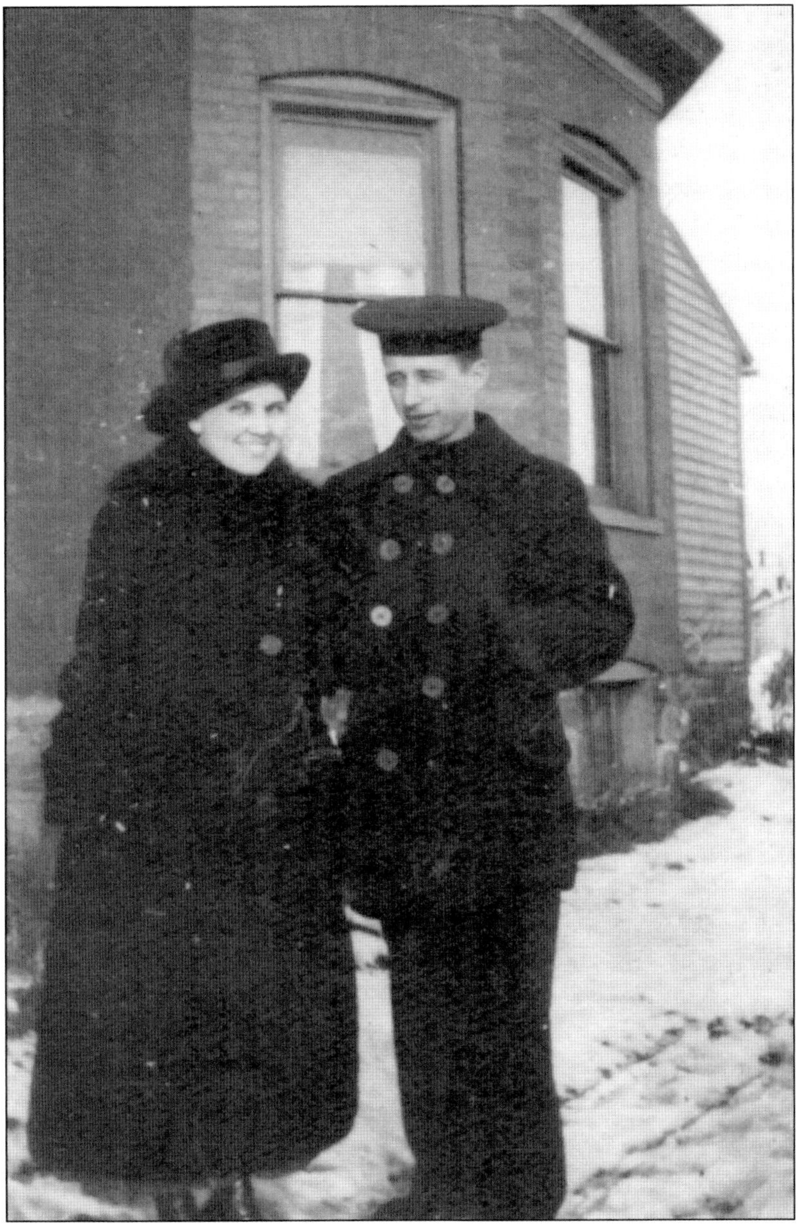

The church faced difficult times in the early 1900s. Most notably, in 1918, the United States entered the war in Europe, and many parishioners found themselves called to service. A state law had mandated the sole use of English in schools, and the country was seeking to distance itself from anything that resembled German sympathy. This included German-speaking churches. In 1933, Edgar W. Krauch offered this remembrance in St. John's 100th anniversary history publication: "How can we express the sorrow and grief that now entered the lives of our people, when the trumpets sounded and the call was issued for all the boys of draft age? For war had been declared against Germany. Brother against brother, nephew against uncle, and even son against father! What sadness filled the air and what hearts were torn asunder." Pictured are St. Paul's Lutheran Church, Williamsville, members Herman and Grace Landel, who were married in 1918 while Herman was on leave from active duty in World War I. (Courtesy of Julianna Woite.)

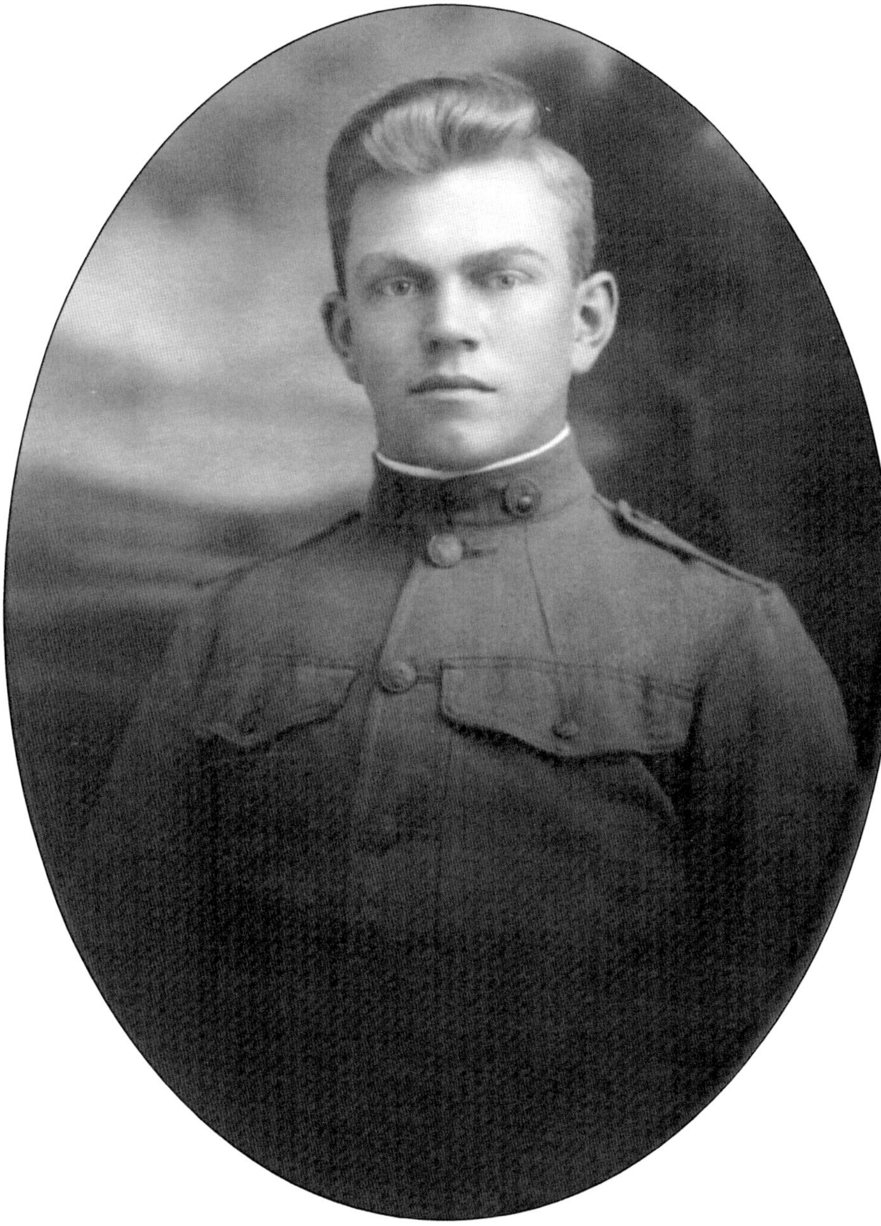

The fellowship of area Lutherans was never more appreciated than during wartime. Arthur Landel (pictured) grew up on a Main Street farm and attended church weekly at St. Paul's Lutheran Church in Williamsville. For soldiers like Landel, their faith and their ties to a home church brought them comfort during some of the war's most trying days. In a letter dated "Christmas 1918," he writes: "I always think of how I used to stand on the church benches and watch the children on Christmas Eve. I think last night was the first Christmas Eve that I didn't attend church since I can remember. Instead I walked post on guard last night and all day so it made for a very long Christmas." He continued to report, however, that "I met the Lutheran Camp Pastor while at Base Hospital and he invited me to services and out to dinner today." In the end, their Lutheran ties brought countless soldiers fellowship and common ground in a foreign land. (Courtesy of Julianna Woite.)

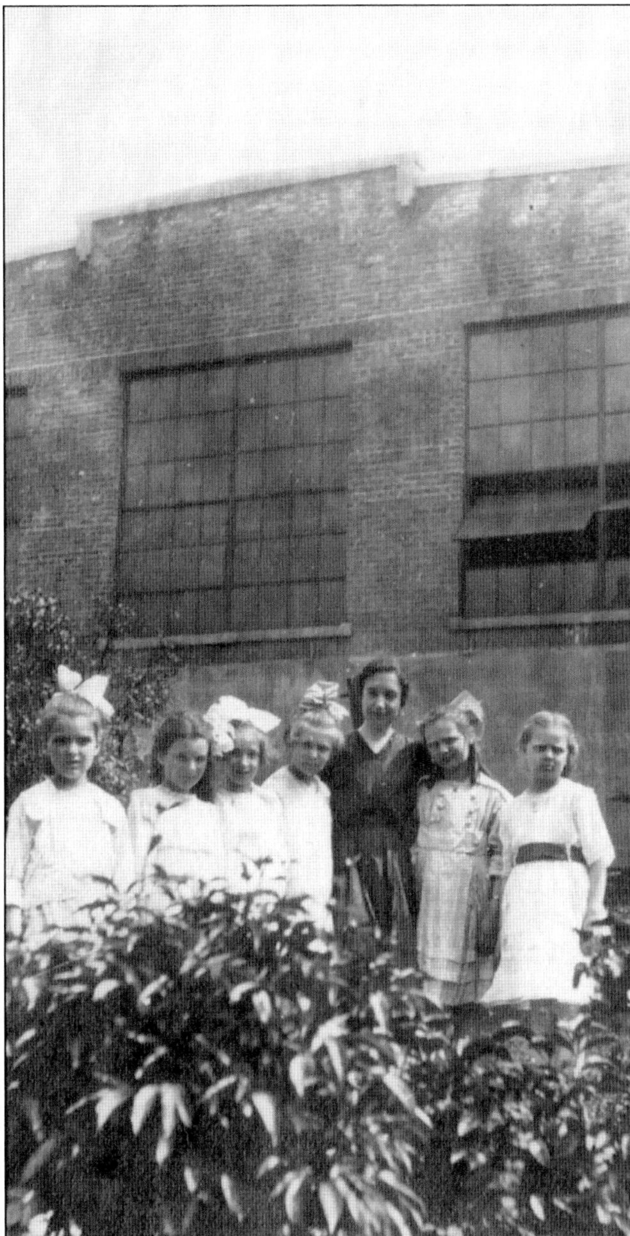

The years 1918 and 1919 saw the influenza pandemic cripple the United States, and Western New York would not be spared. From the fall of 1918 through the summer of 1919, influenza killed more than 30 million people worldwide, including an estimated 650,000 Americans. Locally, infected houses were quarantined, and congregations prayed weekly for an end to the nightmare. By October 1918, however, the disease had reached epidemic proportions in Buffalo. In an attempt to control the spread, gatherings in excess of 10 people were banned by the mayor, and churches, as well as theaters, schools, saloons, and dance halls, were forced to close. For those afflicted, all burials were required to occur within 24 hours and were to be done privately, with only the pastor and immediate family present. Public funerals were strictly prohibited. Here, a 1918 Sunday school class from Holy Trinity enjoys the sunshine, despite the threat of influenza.

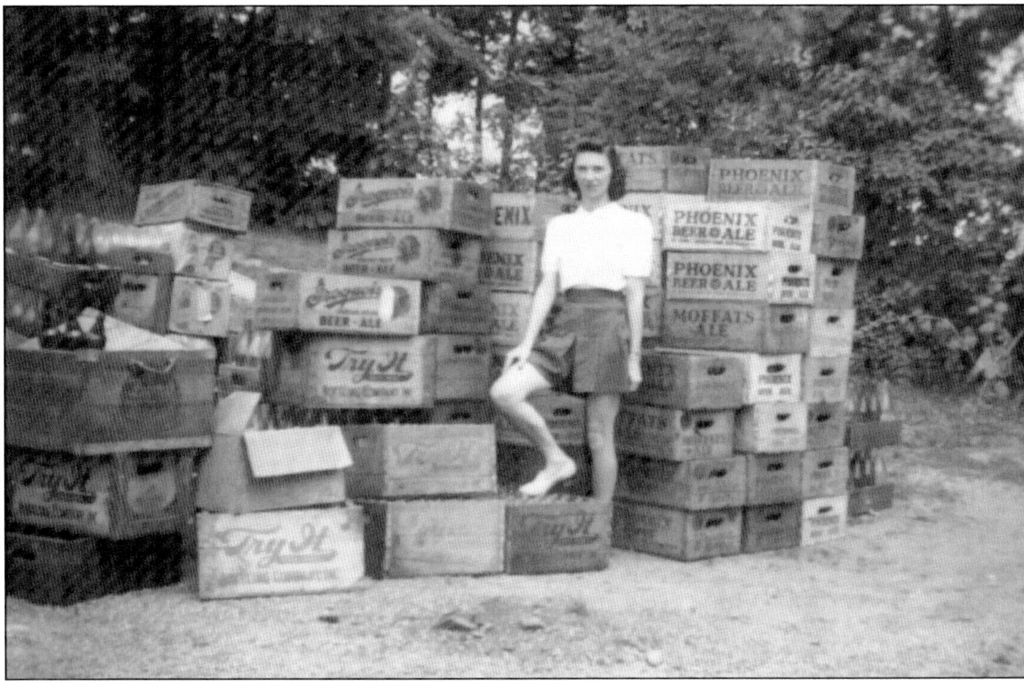

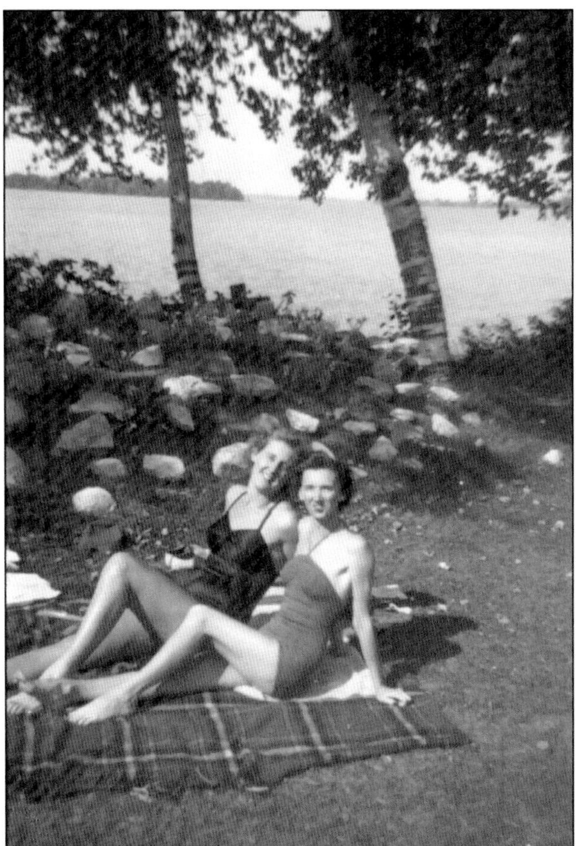

The war years of the 1940s were particularly difficult times for the nation's women. With millions of men involved in the war effort, women on the home front were left to assume new responsibilities and take on new roles. In addition to being single parents and the heads of households, many women entered the workforce in nontraditional roles. Luckily, the church was there to act as a support system. In addition to providing a much-needed sisterhood, women's groups organized activities to help the women relax and restore their mental health. These fun-filled getaways served to rejuvenate the nation's women and allow them to resume their duties refreshed and refueled. St. Paul's Williamsville member Dorothy Landel Shaver is seen above and on the right in the photograph at left. Another St. Paul's member, Arlene Muir, is shown on the left.

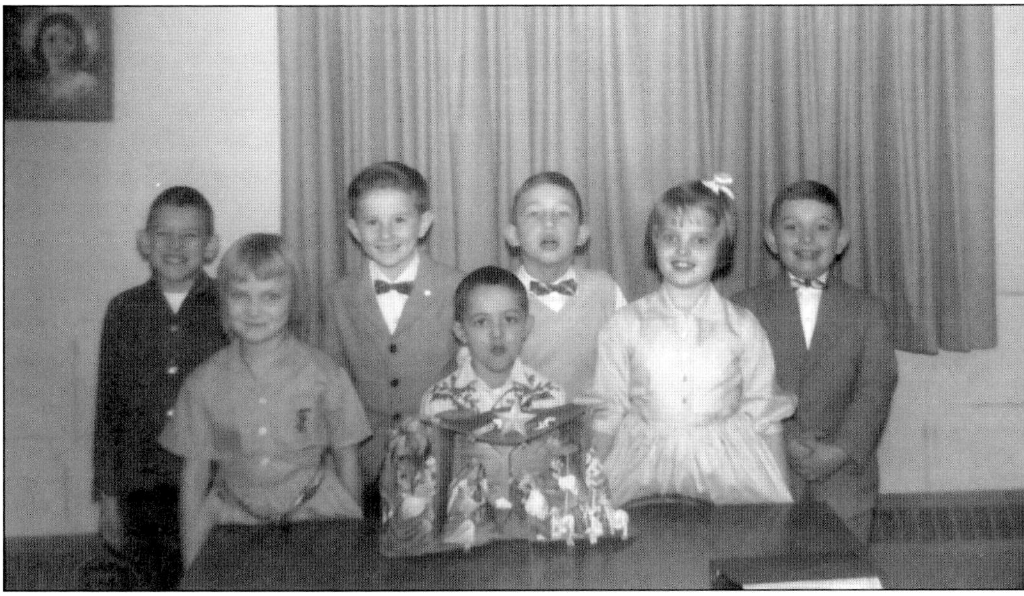

There is no shortage of ways to tell a story, particularly when the tale is as important and popular as the Christmas story. A nativity scene, or crèche, is one of the most traditional ways, with figures representing Jesus, Joseph, Mary, the Angel, the shepherds, the wise men, and the animals. Often, the figures are added throughout Advent in the order in which they appear in the Nativity story, beginning with Mary and Joseph and ending after Christmas with the wise men. In many ways, a Christmas pageant is simply a live-action Nativity scene, with the story told all at one time. Pictured here are children from St. John's Akron in 1958 (above) and 1977 (below).

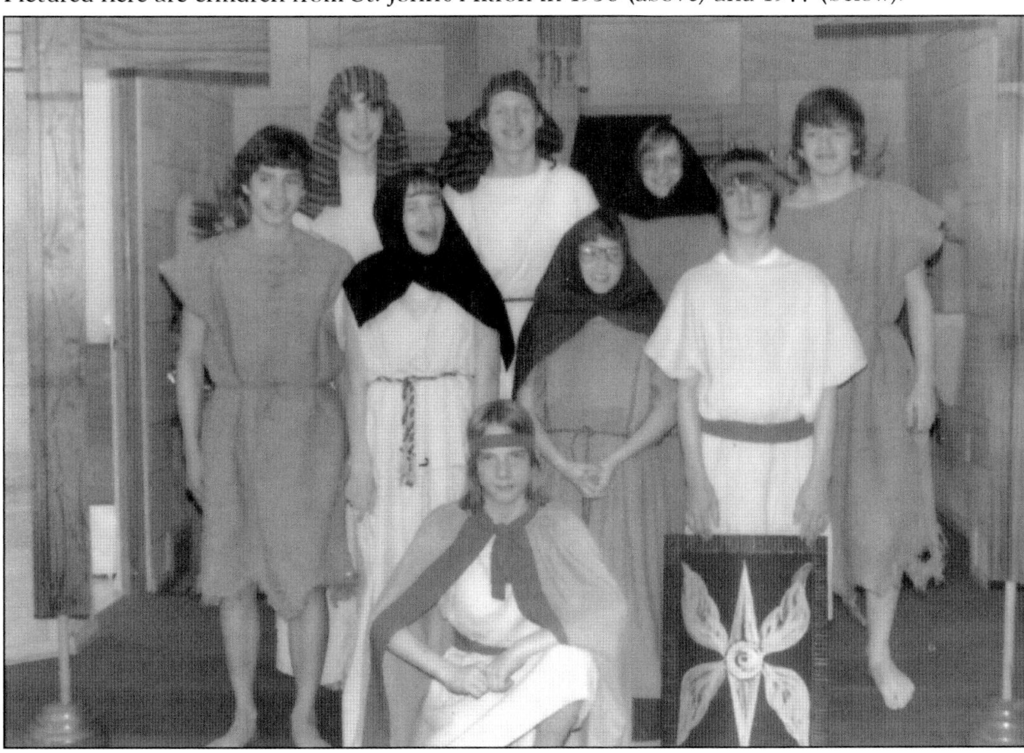

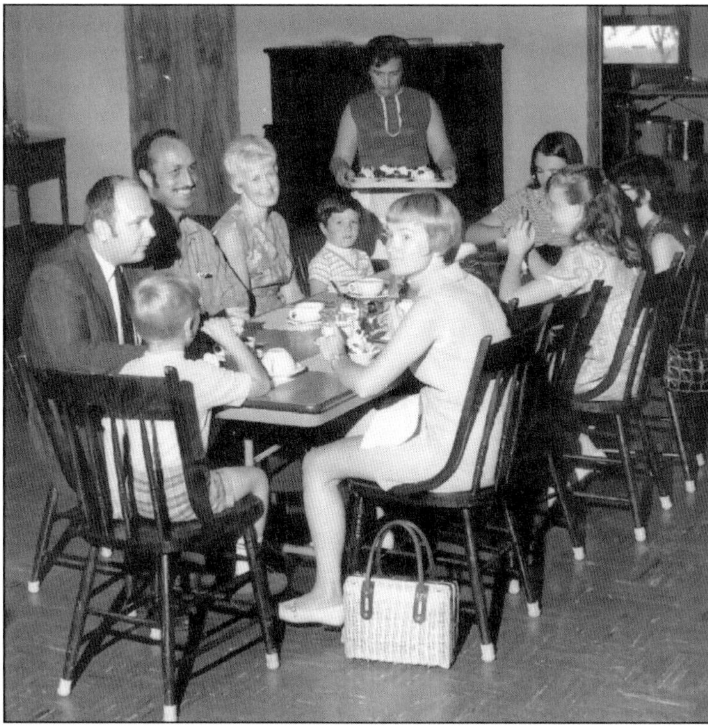

In rural churches, the harvest was a time of great celebration. One of the most beloved traditions at St. John's Lutheran Church in Akron was the annual Strawberry Festival. Pictured here enjoying the festivities are Lynn Brock, Ben Henry, Ann Henry, "Bennie" Henry, Jean Stunnman (serving), Nancy Stunnman, Diane Brock, Daniel Brock, and two unidentified.

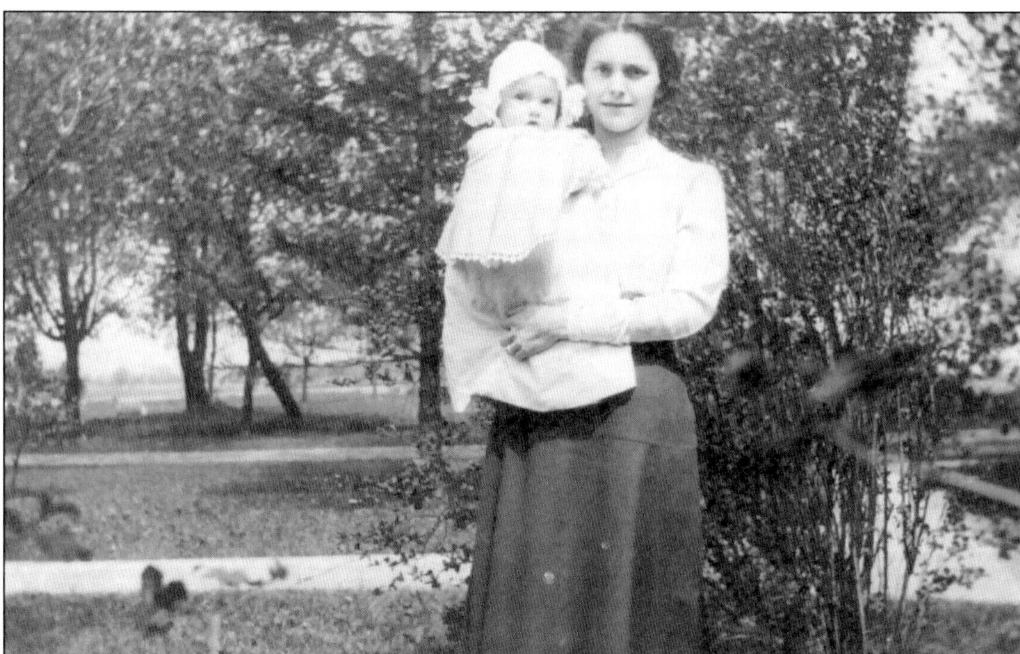

In 1916, Woodrow Wilson was president, George M. Cohan owned Broadway, and the light switch was invented. Although war was brewing in Europe, Western New York churches were experiencing growth. Baptisms were frequent, and in many churches, these children became the first generation to be raised without the German language. Here, Irene Schoelles Landel holds her daughter Dorothy, baptized in the fall of 1916. (Courtesy of Julianna Woite.)

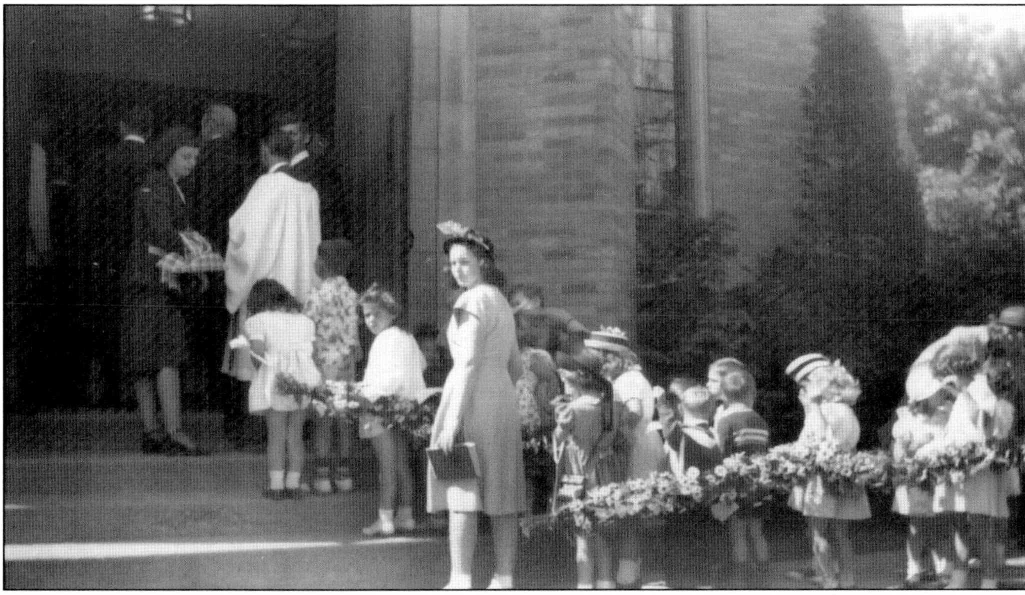

In Matthew 19:4, Jesus says, "Let the little children come to me, and do not hinder them, for the kingdom of heaven belongs to such as these." Lutherans have always embraced this notion, encouraging and welcoming children into church services. Youth-targeted activities such as youth choirs, children's sermons, and even youth-led services have all been incorporated throughout the decades. Another popular tradition has been Children's Day. Above, children at St. Paul's in Eggertsville wait patiently to join in the processional on Children's Day in 1949. At Holy Trinity (below), the youth are seated and ready to begin their Children's Day festivities in 1980.

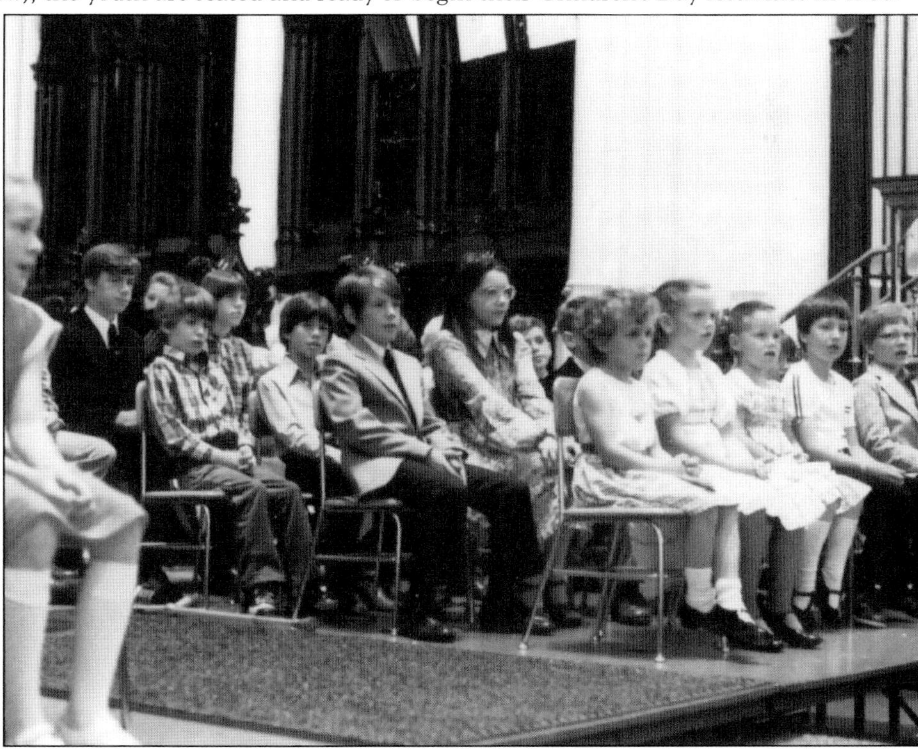

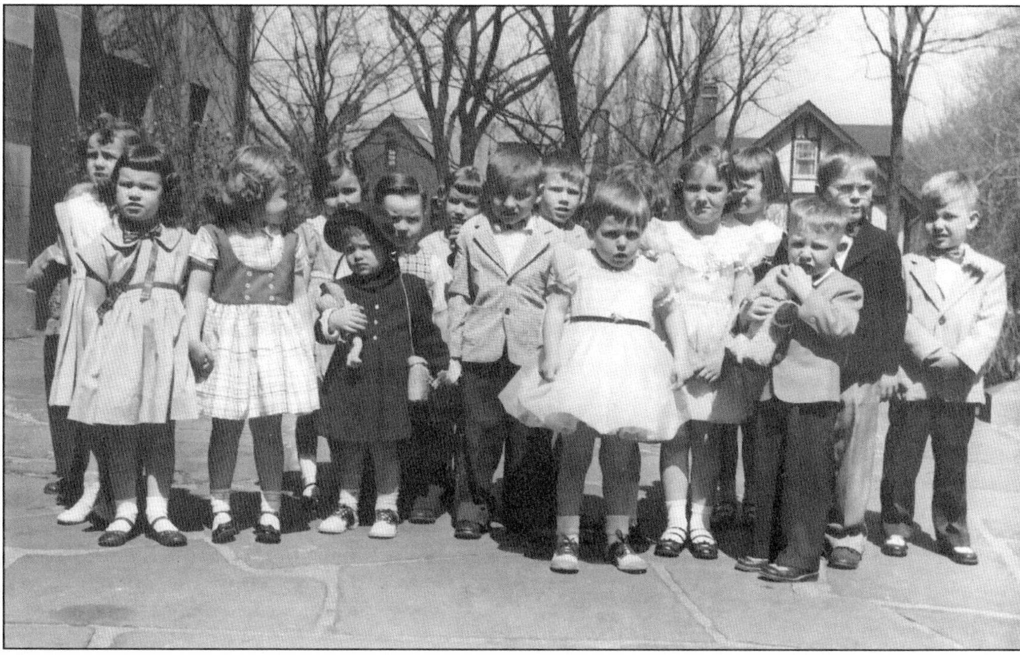

Lutheran children learned at a young age that one was expected to dress up for church. Traditionally, children referred to these outfits as their "Sunday best" or "church clothes." Being appropriately dressed was a way to show respect for the Lord and one's church. Pictured here is the 1955 toddler class of Parkside Lutheran Church.

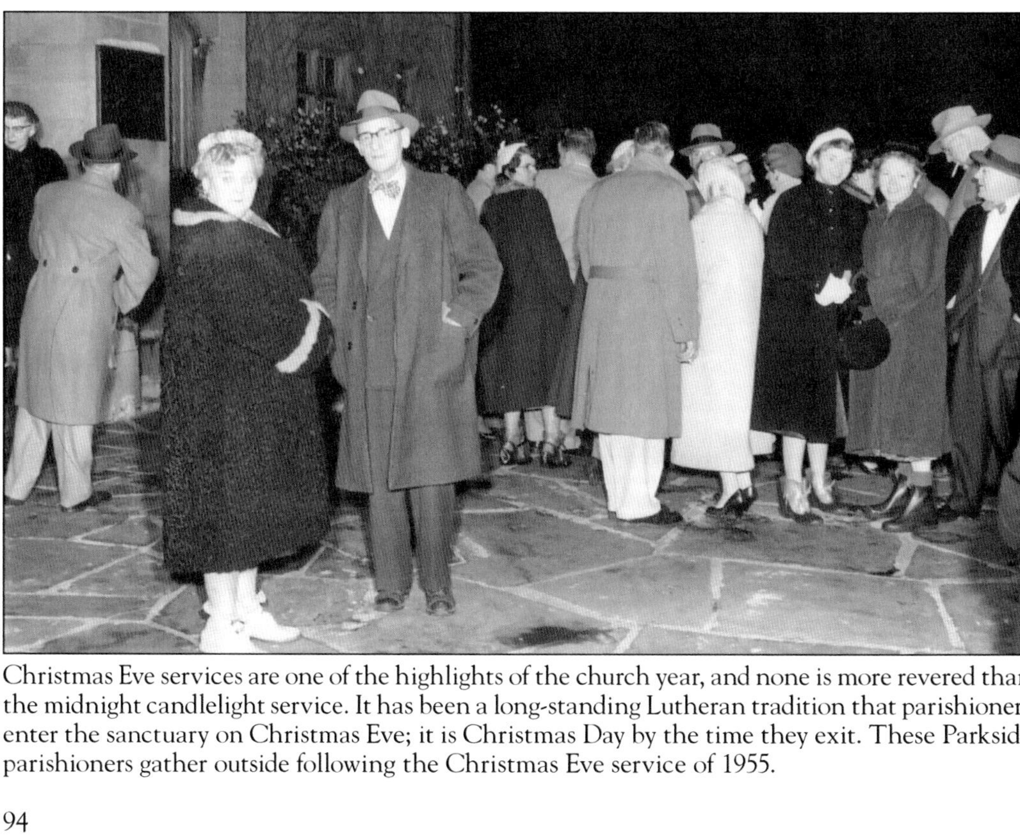

Christmas Eve services are one of the highlights of the church year, and none is more revered than the midnight candlelight service. It has been a long-standing Lutheran tradition that parishioners enter the sanctuary on Christmas Eve; it is Christmas Day by the time they exit. These Parkside parishioners gather outside following the Christmas Eve service of 1955.

According to Martin Luther, "When schools flourish, all flourishes." Therefore, Sunday school teachers have played a vital and revered role in the Lutheran Church. Here, teacher Sally Ammerman (second from left) poses with her students at St. Paul's in Eggertsville. They are Caren Schlack, Linda Heim, Clayt Ackerman, Lee Truby, and Kathleen Hagelberger.

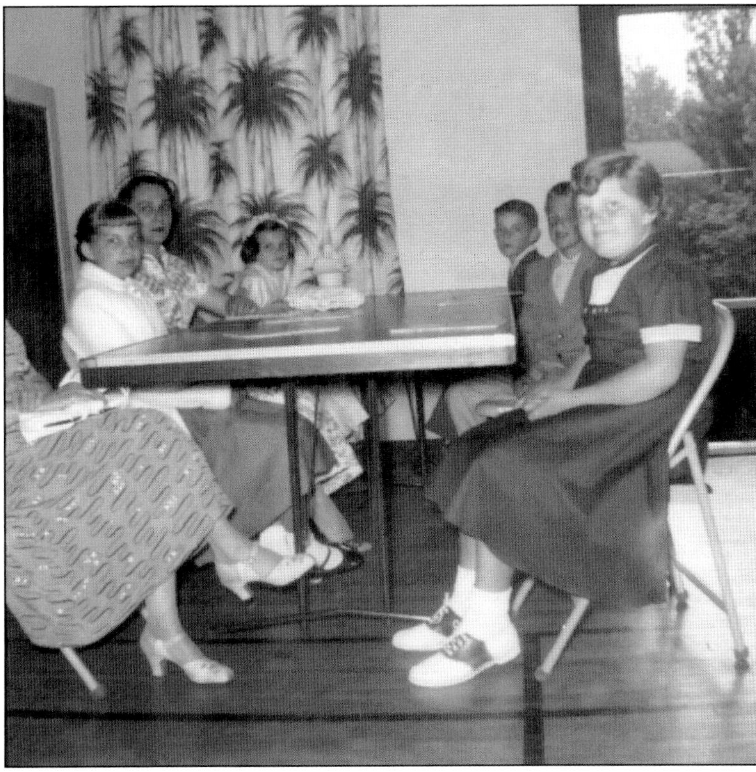

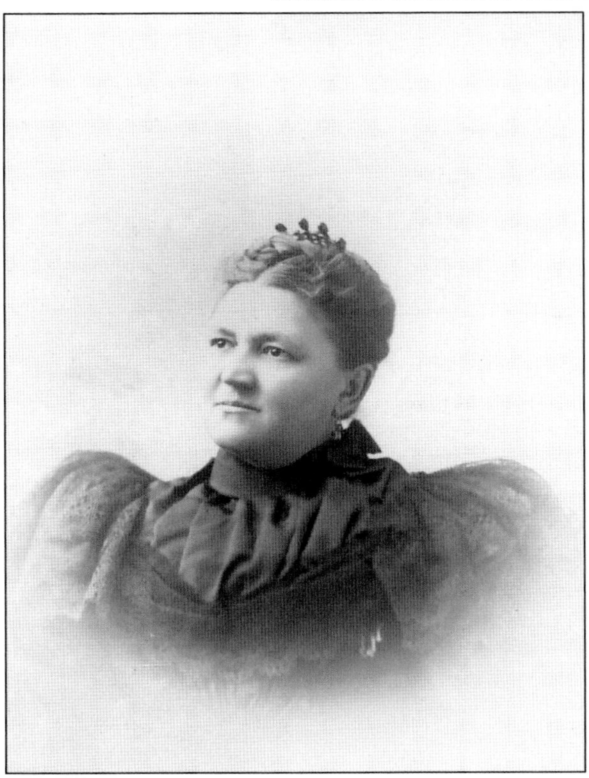

When Martin Luther married Katie Von Bora, a former nun, it directed the course of women in the Lutheran Church forward. Katie was very influential and led the Luther household. Because of this, women in the Lutheran Church have been able to serve in a multitude of ways, at the pastor's discretion, since the beginning of the 19th century. Shown here is a parishioner from St. John's.

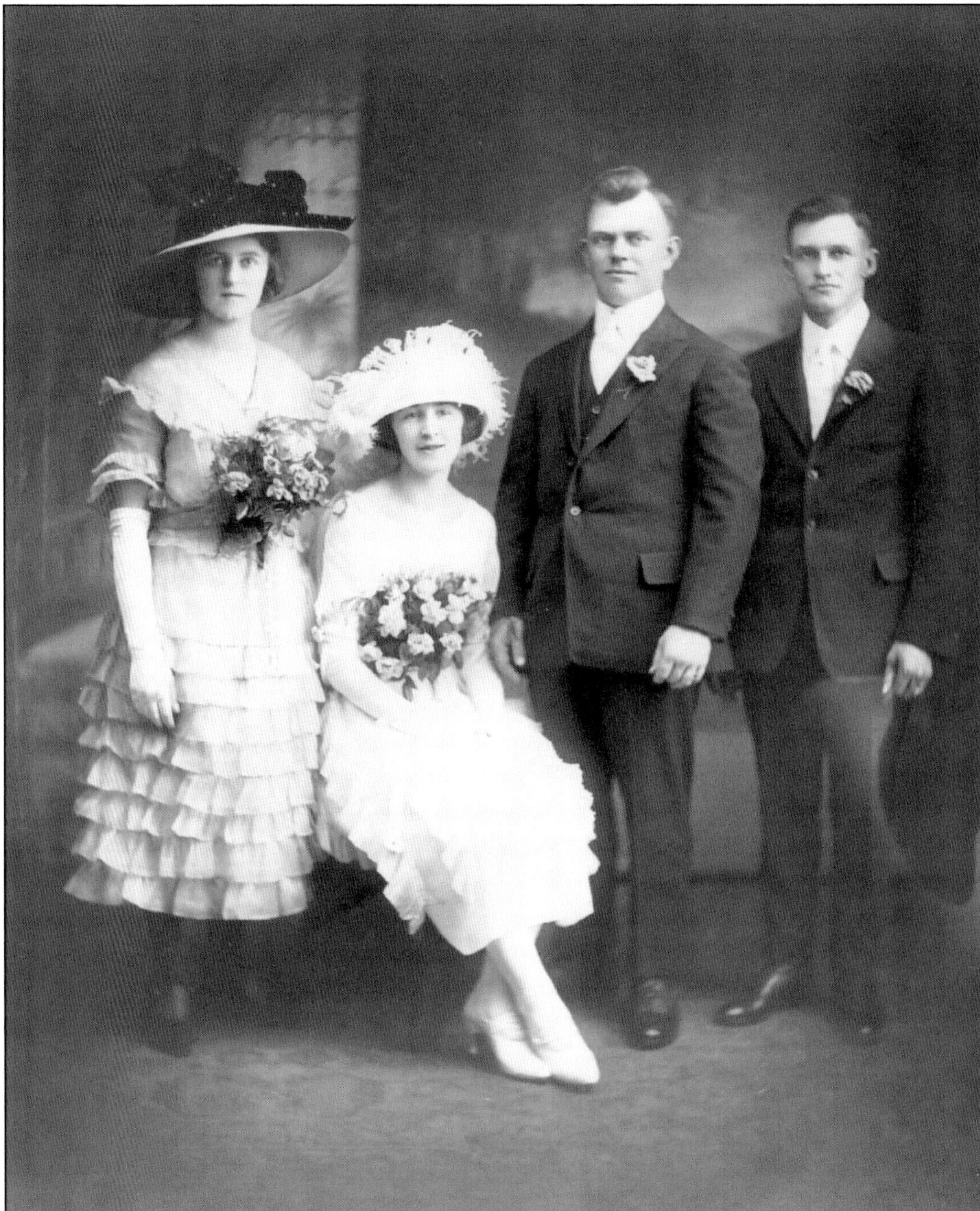

For the first 1,000 years of Christianity, the church did not play a role in marriages. A wedding was seen as a secular arrangement, separate from the purview of the church. This changed when the church began to take on more governmental authority in the Middle Ages. Churches then took on the authority of overseeing and conducting the services as well as the legal aspect of certifying the union. This tradition has continued to this day, and weddings are the only time when pastors and church leaders play a government authorized, legal role. In many ways, weddings are where the separation of church and state is the most tenuous. This is the wedding portrait of Arthur and Margaret Landel. (Courtesy of Julianna Woite.)

Emily Mansperger (right) was married to Dr. William H. Mansperger. They were well-known lay readers at Holy Trinity. In 1948, the dedicated couple gave the church a set of incredible stained-glass chancel windows. Because of their great love for the church, they made many modernizations possible in and around the building. After Emily's death, Dr. Mansperger suggested that a chapel be built in his wife's memory. Sadly, the doctor died only eight weeks after making this donation. With his death, the chapel project was put on hold. However, because of a generous bequest from the physician's will, Holy Trinity was able to purchase the property next to the church and eventually break ground (below) on the Mansperger Chapel.

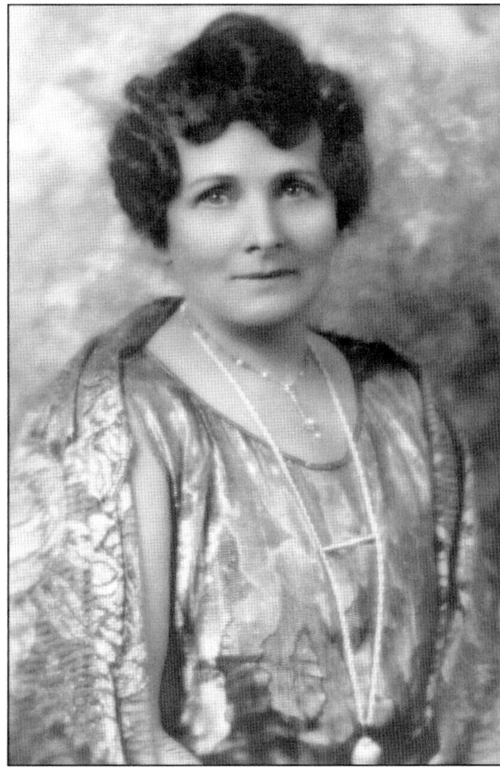

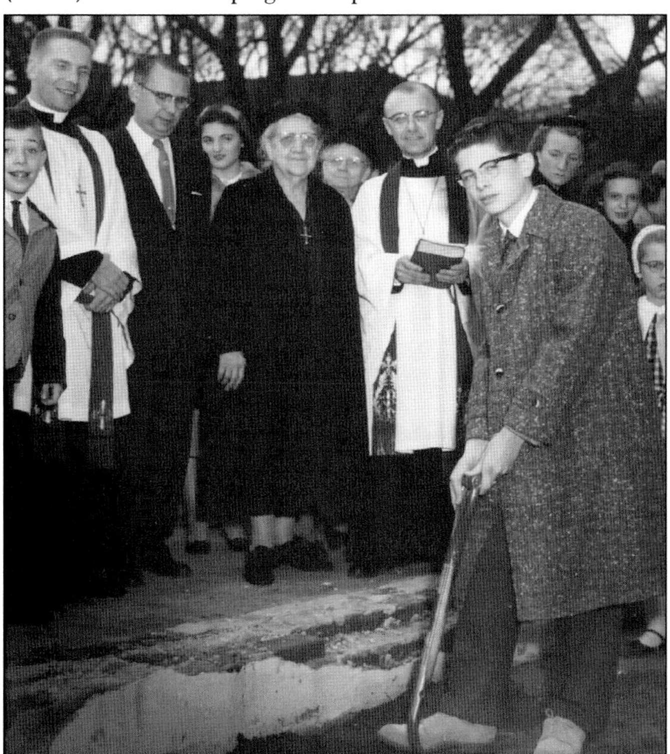

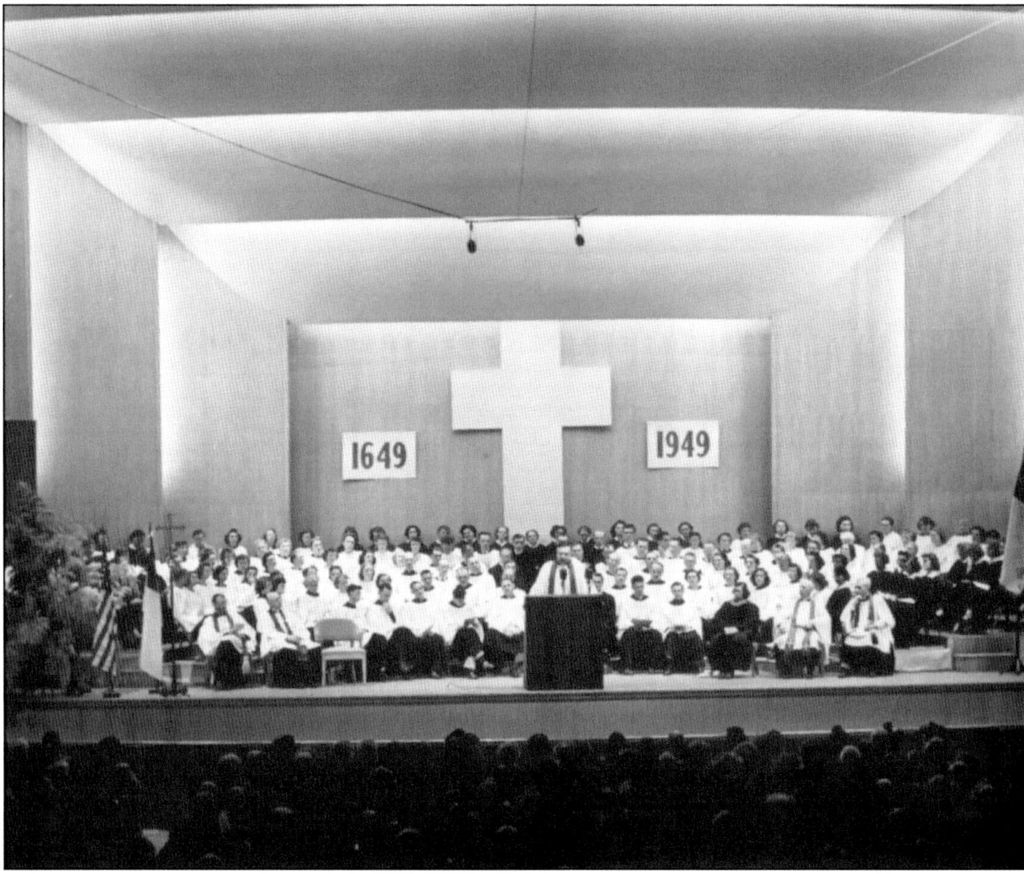

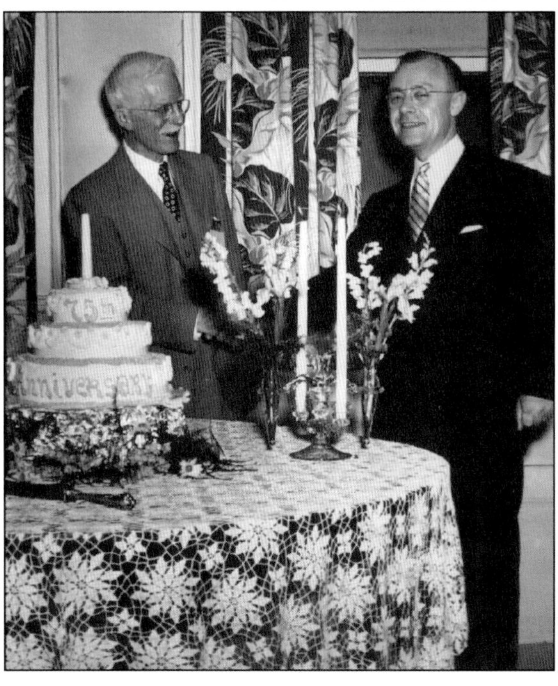

In 1949, area Lutherans celebrated "300 years of Lutheranism in America" at Kleinhans Music Hall. Lutheranism in America had begun in 1649, when Dutch settlers founded the first Lutheran church in the colonies. Lutheranism would change over time, from Dutch to German, and, by 1949, Lutheranism in Western New York had become a melting pot.

Holy Trinity celebrated its 75th anniversary in 1954. During this anniversary year, many new faces came to the church. A few of these faces would leave permanent, positive marks. Otto and Lily Rosin became caretakers of the church, John Becker became the new director of music, and the Reverend Matthew Littleton Winters was welcomed as the new assistant pastor. Dr. Ralph Loew (right) poses at the celebration with an unidentified man.

Susan Roesch is pictured at right getting ready with the help of her father, Charles. J. Roesch, in the Holy Trinity bride's room, new with the chapel complex in 1959. This room provided a quiet place for the bride to reflect and make any last-minute preparations before walking down the aisle. This particular wedding almost did not happen due to national events. On November, 22, 1963, Pres. John F. Kennedy was assassinated. As the nation mourned, Susan waited and wondered if her wedding to Samuel Arthur Mattison, only five days away, would need to be postponed. After meeting with Dr. Loew, it was decided that the wedding would indeed take place as planned (below). (Both, courtesy of Arthur and Susan Mattison.)

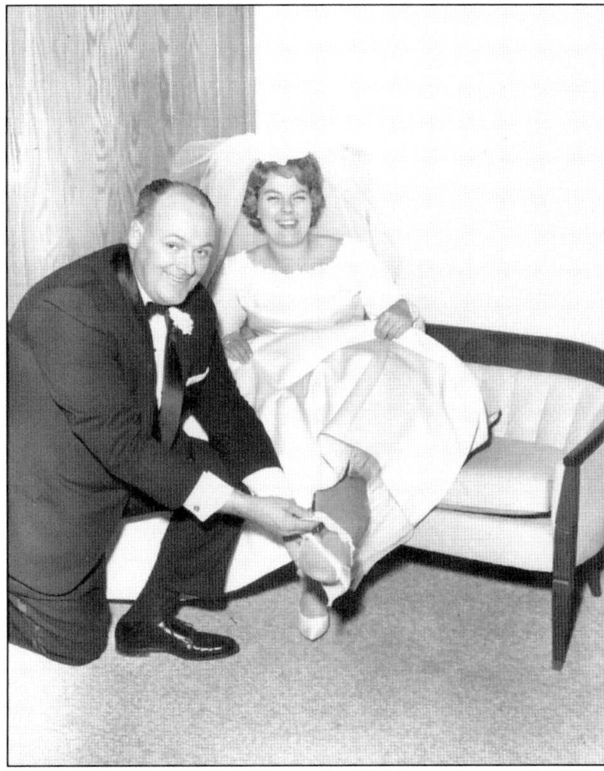

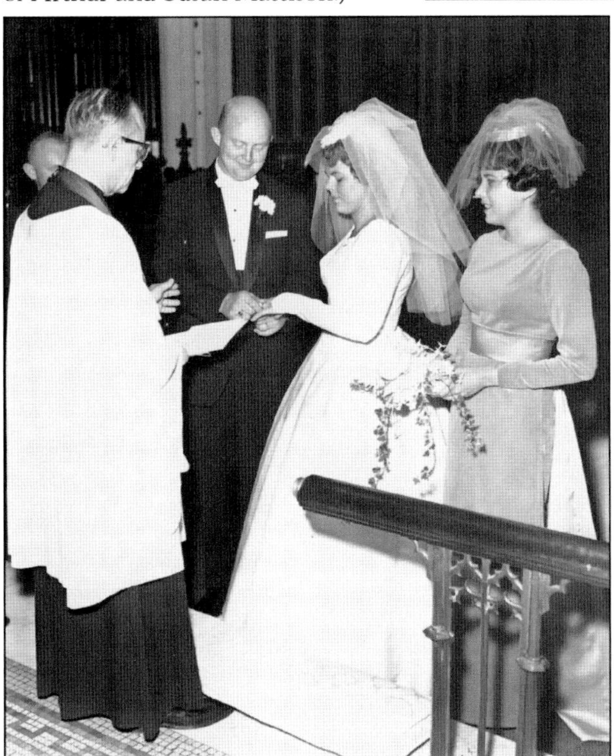

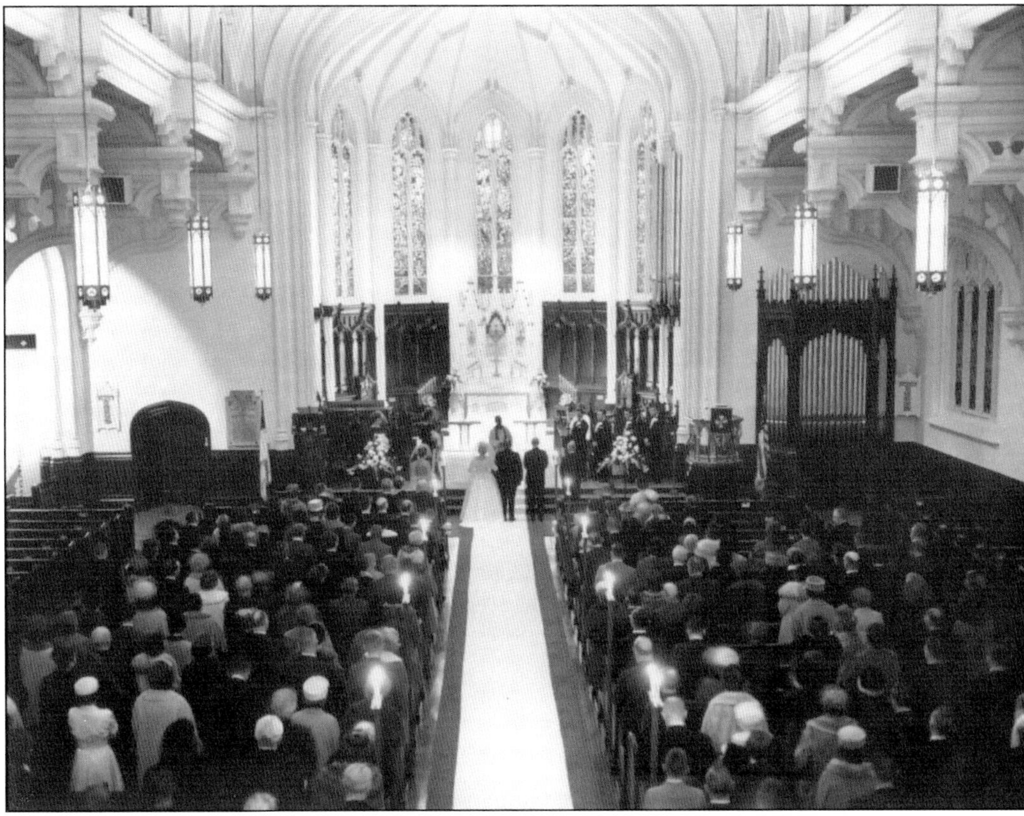

On Wednesday, November 27, 1963, Dr. Loew officiated the wedding of Susan Charlotte Roesch and Samuel Arthur Mattison. Susan was the daughter of Charles J. Roesch, who, with his brother William, owned Charles E. Roesch Meat Stand at the Broadway Market. At that time, the Broadway Market was closed on Wednesdays and Sundays. For the prosperity of the business, the only day Susan could get married was Wednesday. (Courtesy of Arthur and Susan Mattison.)

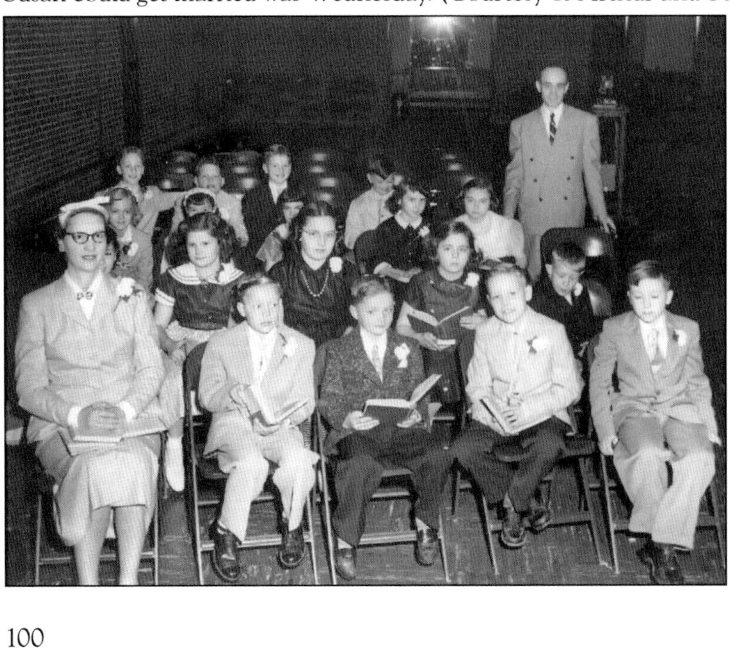

It has always been a priority of Lutheran churches to keep children actively involved. In addition to Sunday school classes, children have been encouraged to attend church services with their parents or class. These Parkside Sunday school students are seated with their teacher, Louise Kinkle. An unidentified superintendent stands in back. This photograph was taken on Easter Sunday, April 10, 1955.

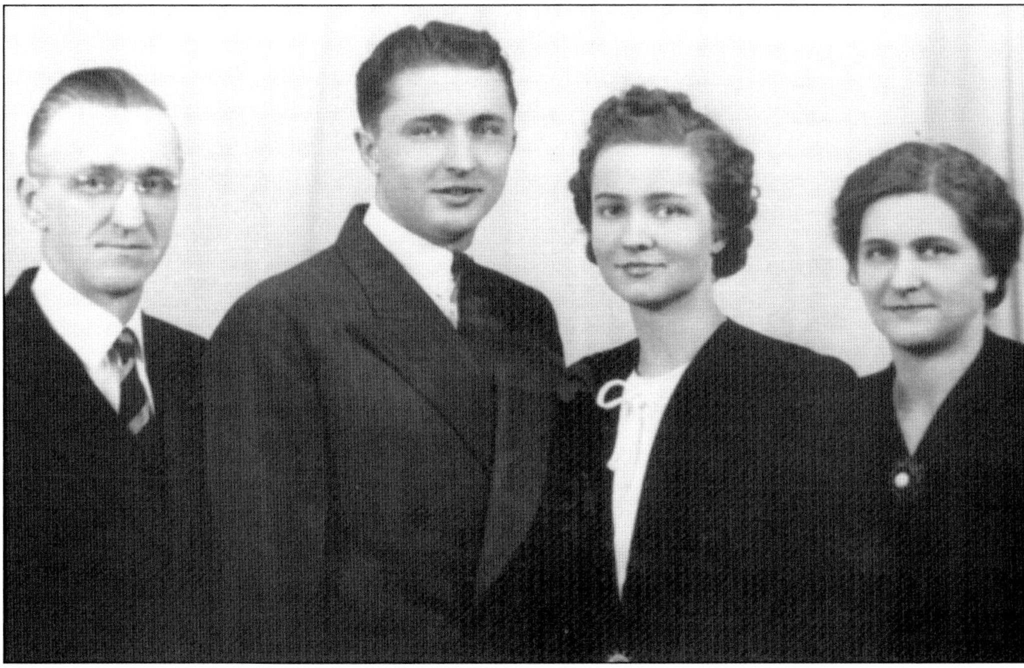

When a pastor is called to a church, so, essentially, is his or her immediate family. Being a member of the pastor's family involves unique challenges. Although the pastor is the one called to serve, there is still a lot of attention paid to the family as well. Because of this, many spouses and children of pastors have found themselves with various leadership roles within the church. Pictured above is Pastor Heuer (left), who served St. John's Akron, and his family, Bernard (second from left), Gertrude (second from right), and Minnie. Shown below is the Reverend Franklin Jensen, pictured with his family at Holy Trinity.

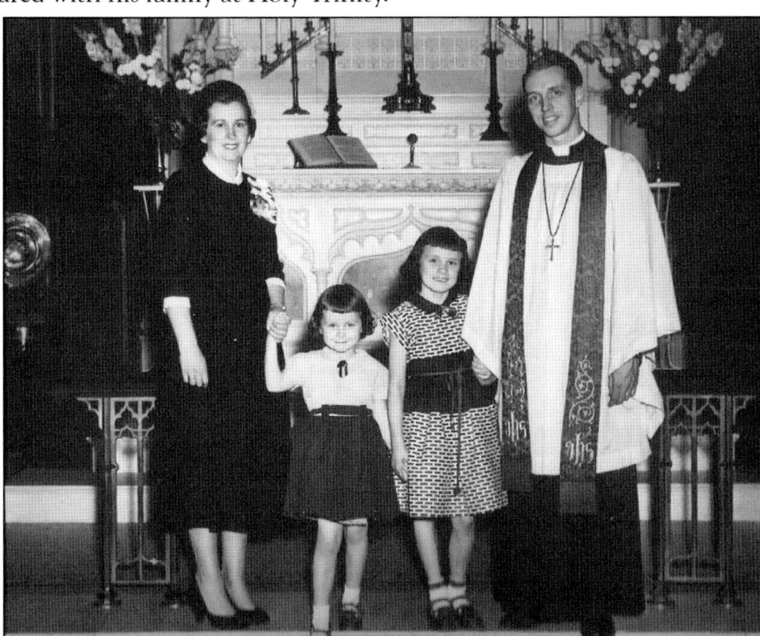

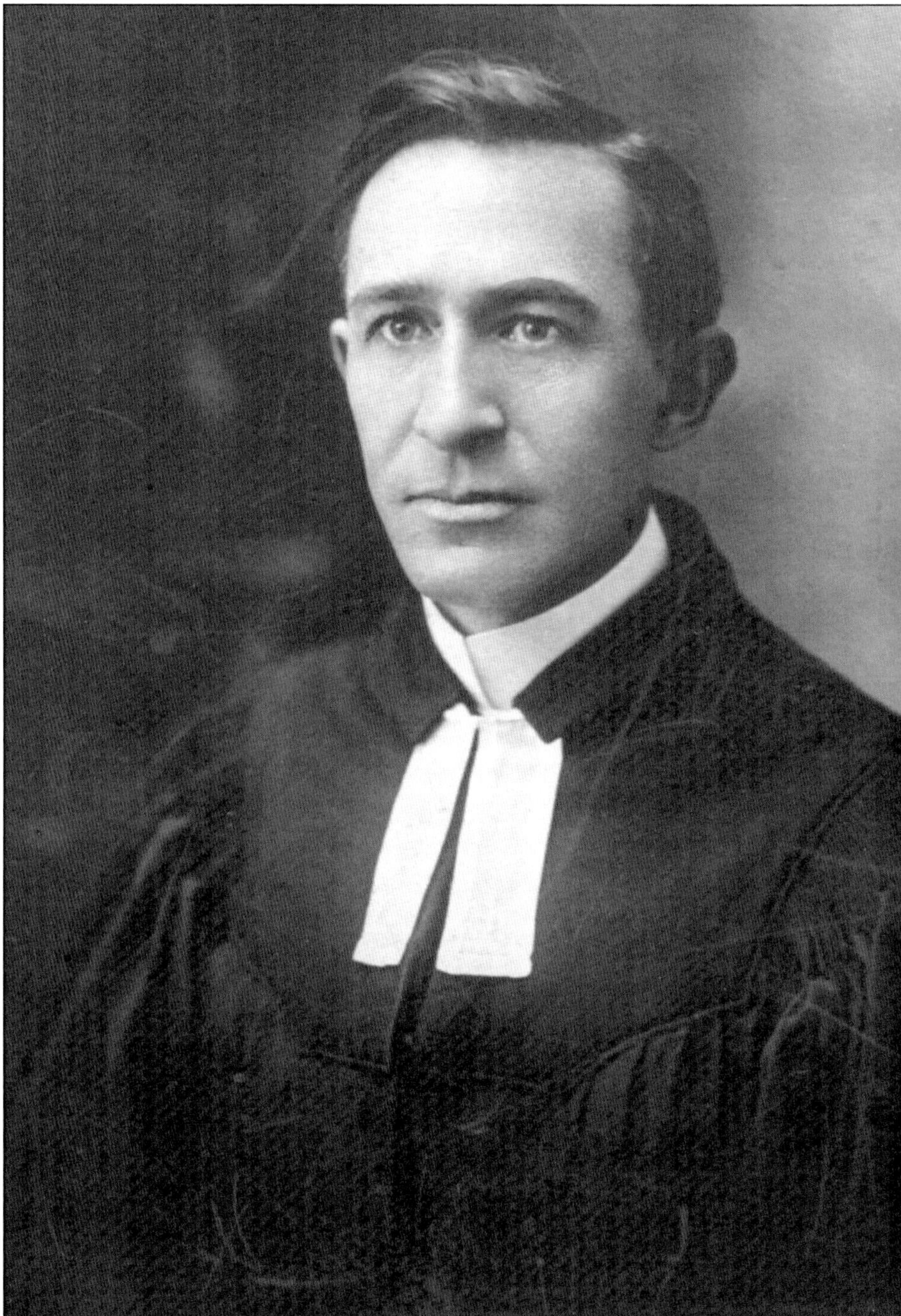

When America declared war on Germany and entered World War I, a concerted effort was made to "Americanize" things that were traditionally seen as German. Everything from sauerkraut to dachshunds received new "American" names. Most Lutheran churches stopped using German in their services as part of this movement. On top of having to change years of tradition, churches needed to acquire new hymnals, Bibles, record books, prayer books, and any other written materials that may have been in German. Pictured here is Pastor Bartell, who served Trinity South Newstead from 1905 to 1918. He led the congregation into this monumental time of change.

The last quarter of the 20th century was a time when the church began to seek its post-Christendom identity. Individual churches were challenged with redefining what exactly their new identity would be. St. John's Akron began to focus more intentionally on its youth. Pastor Willman began serving St. John's Akron in 1976 and remained with it for almost 25 years as it forged this new identity.

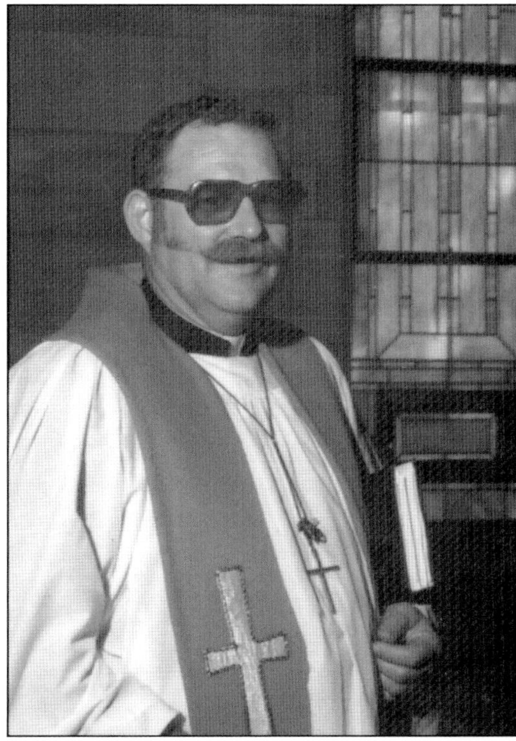

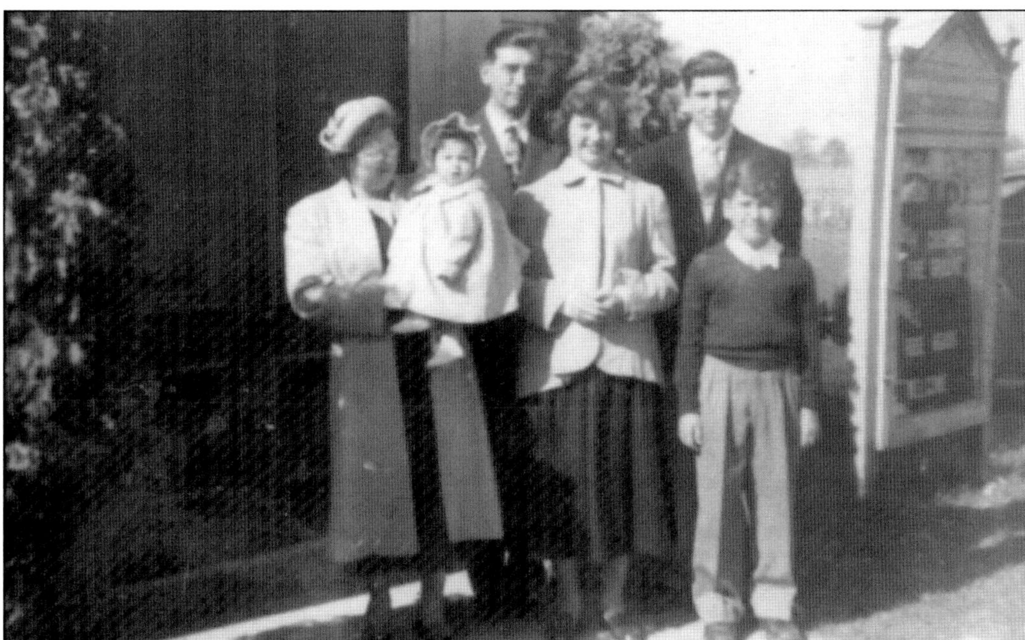

A challenging moment in the life of a congregation is when a pastor leaves. The congregation not only has to say farewell to their leader, but also has to begin the "call process" to identify and hire the next pastor. Pictured here are Pastor John Winters (second row, left) with, from left to right, Helen holding a baby, Pat, Paul, and David, on the day he delivered his farewell sermon at St. John's Akron in 1951.

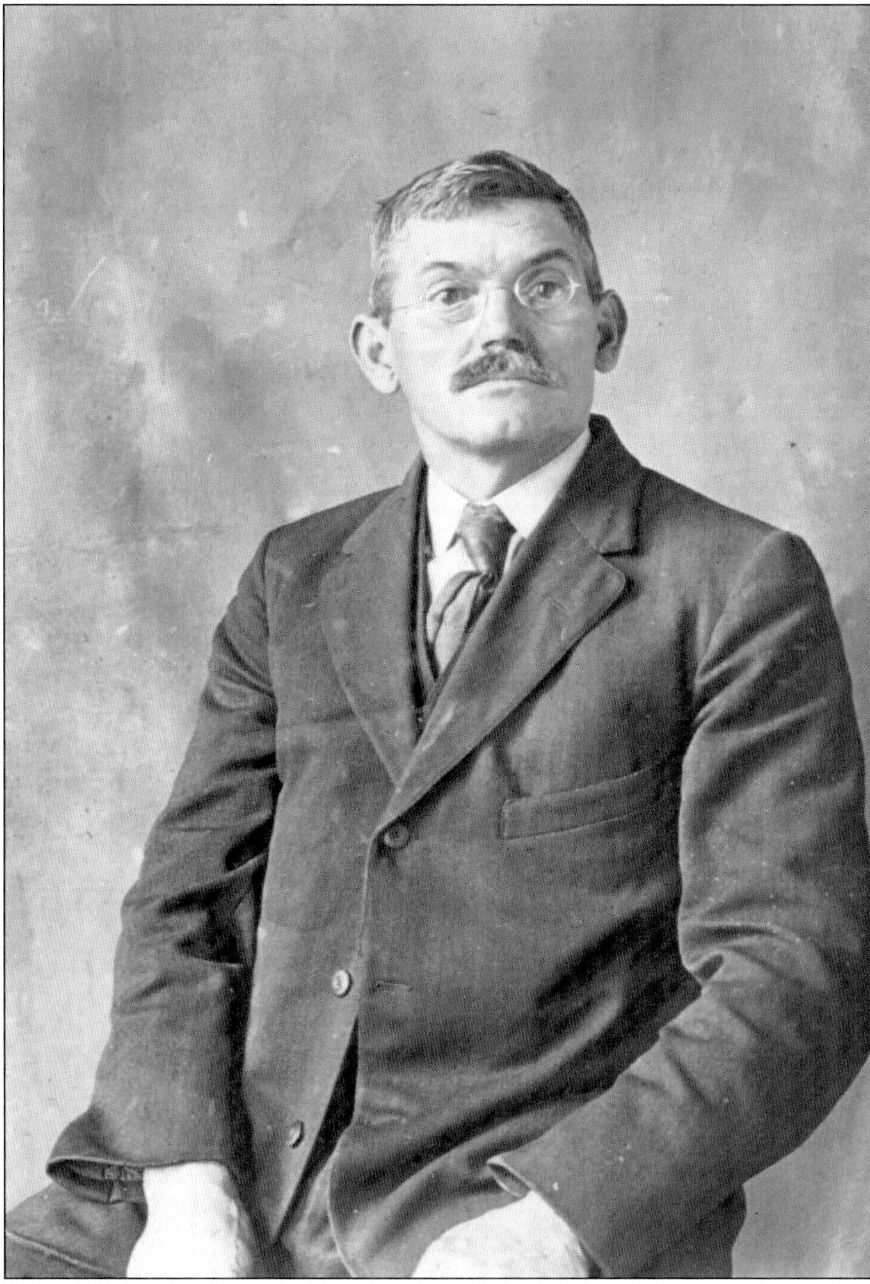

In the early days of Western New York, individual families cared for their own dead, and visitation and funerals took place inside the home. The dead were traditionally laid out in the parlor; more extravagant homes even had a "death door" leading directly from the parlor to the yard. Death doors were used because it was considered bad luck for the dead to exit the house through the same door the living used to enter. Once the deceased was removed from the house, some families would visit the church. But in most cases, the body would be taken directly to the family cemetery. Pictured in 1912 is John B. Schoelles, a member of St. Paul's in Williamsville. Following his death in 1939, he was laid out in the family home at 101 Highland Drive before being buried in Williamsville Cemetery. (Courtesy of Julianna Woite.)

The job of organist has traditionally been a very revered position in the Lutheran Church. In addition to accompanying the weekly services, an organist typically served as director of the congregation's music group as well. This could include organizations such as the chancel choir, children's choir, and handbell choir. Shown here is the organist of Holy Trinity, William Benbow, in 1916.

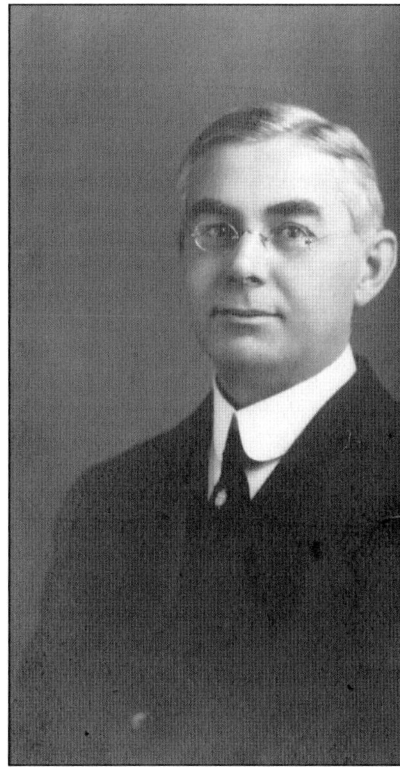

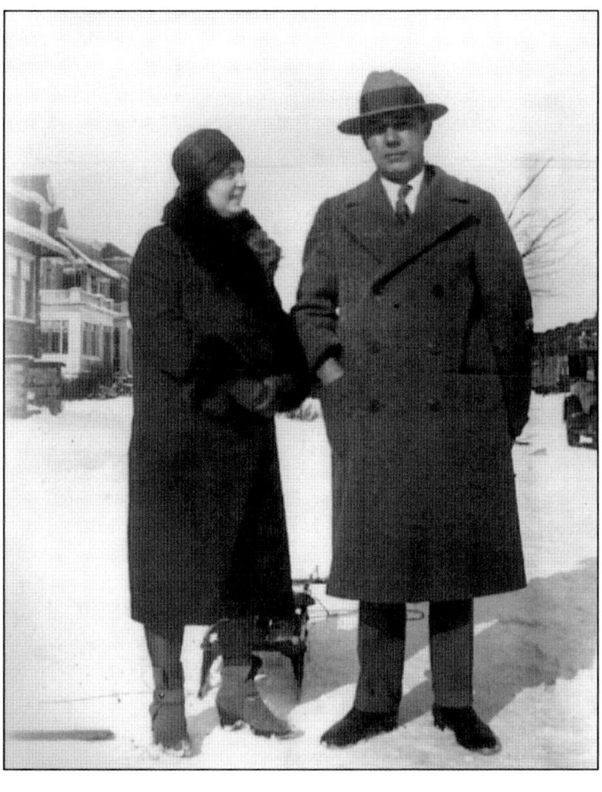

Pictured are members of the "City Church," St. John's Akron, Vi and Harry Neumeister. Even by the early 20th century, Trinity South Newsted and St. John's Akron stood in close proximity. The reason for this was that the two congregations were seen as having distinct personalities. Trinity was the country church, and St. John's was the city church.

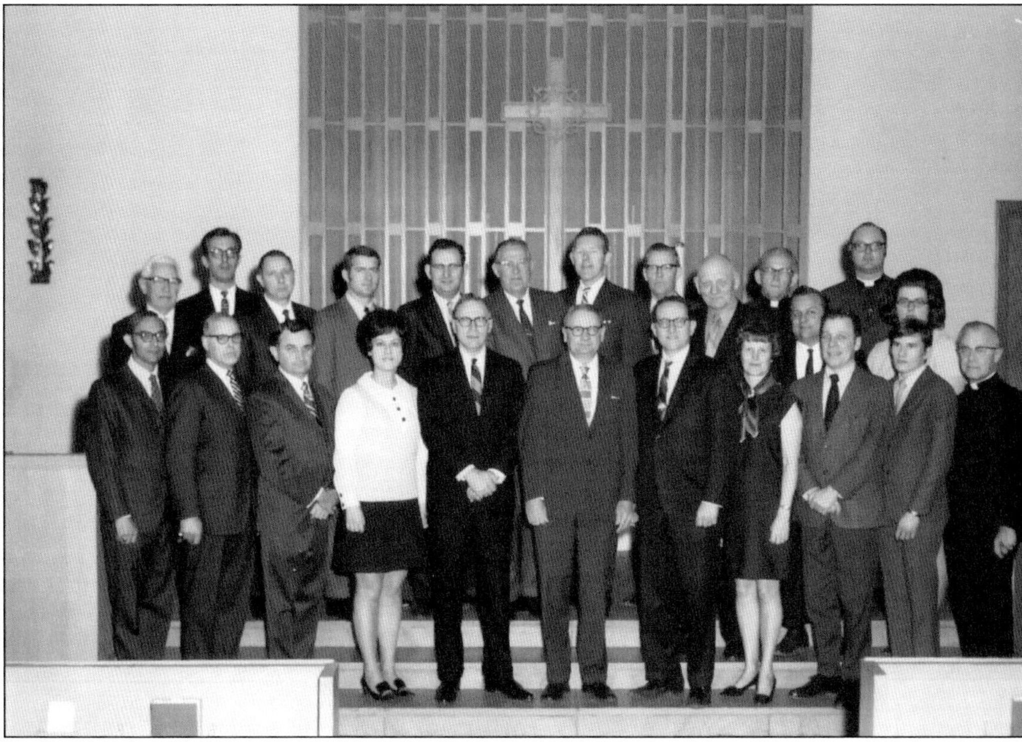

As with most institutions in the country, the original Lutheran churches operated under male leadership. The church council was male, committee heads were male, and, certainly, the pastor was male. Women were not even allowed a vote in church business. During these times, women would have to be content to serve in women's groups or perhaps be an organist or secretary. As times evolved, however, women found themselves elected to councils, becoming ordained, and even serving as bishops. Pictured are the Holy Trinity Church Councils of 1969 (above) and 1970 (below). Of note is not only the presence of several women, but also of one very young woman. Oh, how times have changed!

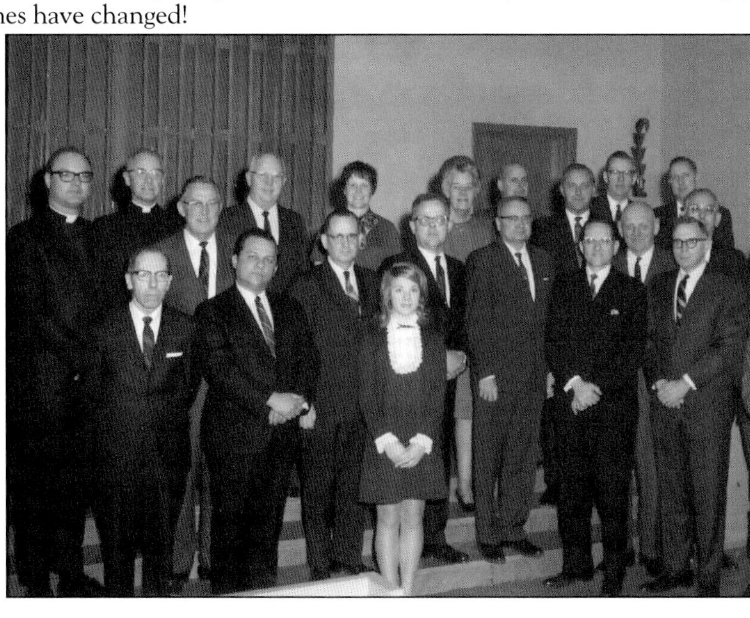

Four

Community Outreach

The Lutheran Church in Western New York has always focused on community outreach. In the early part of the 19th century, this outreach was often focused on meeting the needs of the congregation itself. The reason for this was that Western New York and America in general were in a period known as Christendom. The beginning of the baby boom was the high-water mark of Christendom. But, just as those boomers, upon reaching adulthood, would bring change to the country, so, too, did they bring change to the church. The 1960s was a time of questioning institutions and norms, a time of changing the status quo. Being a part of a church was seen as less of an expectation and more of a personal choice. This led to a change in how the church carried out its mission and served the community. This meant that the church had to begin to reach out and serve the particular needs of the community. This resulted in congregations looking to the neighborhoods around them and asking, "How can we help you?" When a congregation was able to properly identify and meet those needs, powerful and life-changing service occurred. Congregations served young and old, members and strangers, and focused heavily on those who had never darkened a church door. It was through this community outreach that the church began to rediscover itself amid a shifting culture.

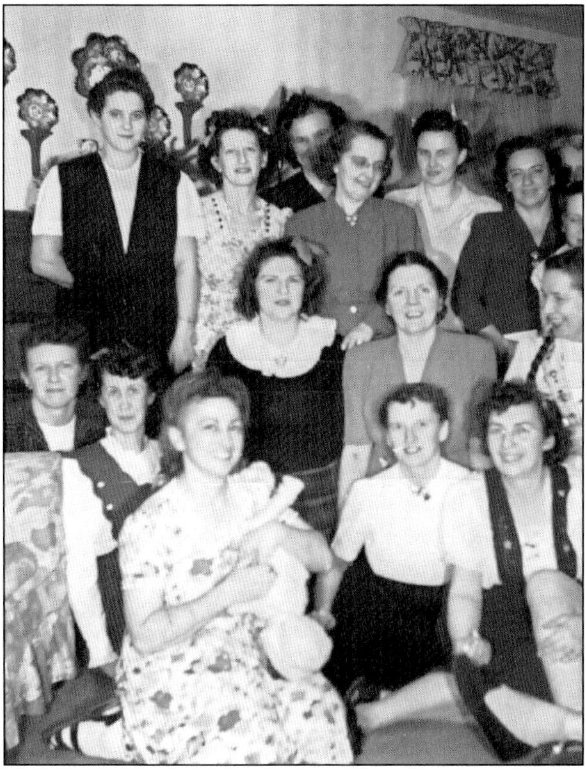

Social groups have always played a vital role in the fellowship of the Lutheran Church. Since their inception, social groups have provided parishioners with a built-in cluster of like-minded individuals with which to socialize. At St. Paul's Lutheran Church in Williamsville, the Gold Band Society was very popular among the members. As the name indicates, the group was for married couples and was geared toward recreational activities. This group proved to be a tremendous support system for couples, especially those with young children. Pictured at left is the Gold Band Christmas Party of 1955. Seen below is another of the group's infamous "theme parties." Here, members dressed as children, met with Santa Claus, and even took turns on Santa's lap.

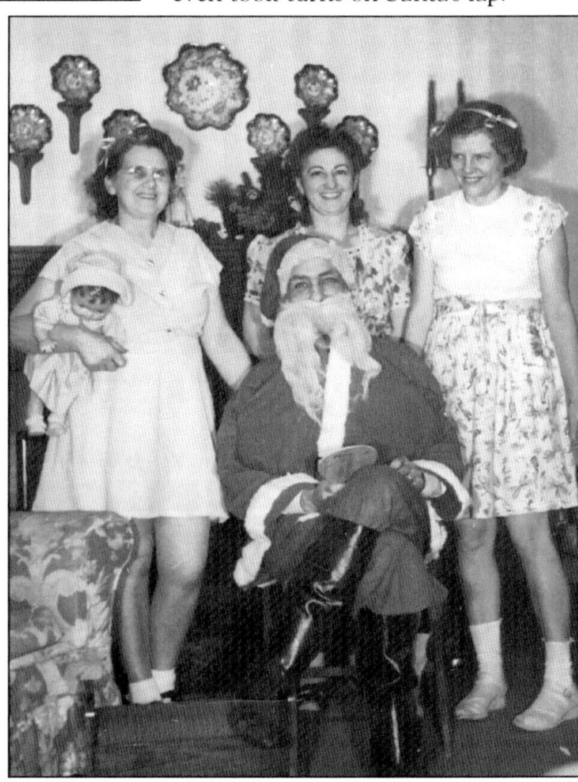

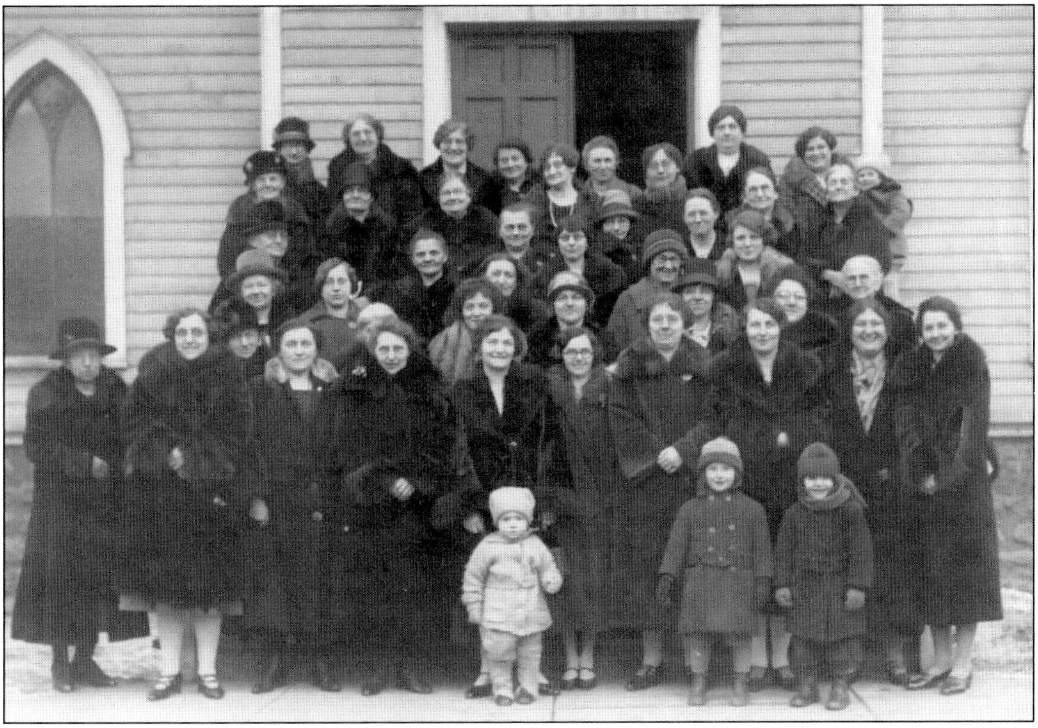

Since the late 1800s, one of the more popular community service opportunities has been the Ladies Aid. According to a written history from St. Paul's in Eggertsville: "These ladies met as a social group, an entertainment group, a charitable group, and a support group They also pitched in eagerly and enthusiastically to help wherever they were needed in the congregation and community. They held regular fundraisers, and it was not unusual for the congregation to look to them when special items needed to be purchased. They sewed, quilted, cooked, baked and cleaned." In congregations across Western New York, members of the Ladies Aid met faithfully, served their community, and enjoyed the fellowship of their friends. Pictured here are the St. Paul's Williamsville Ladies Aid of 1923 (above) and the St. John's Buffalo Ladies Aid of 1943 (below).

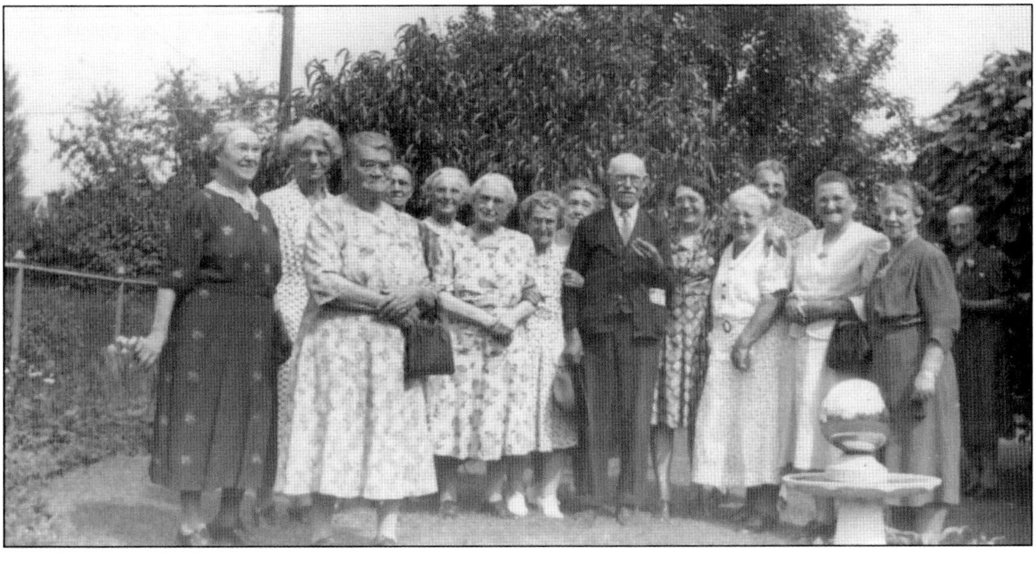

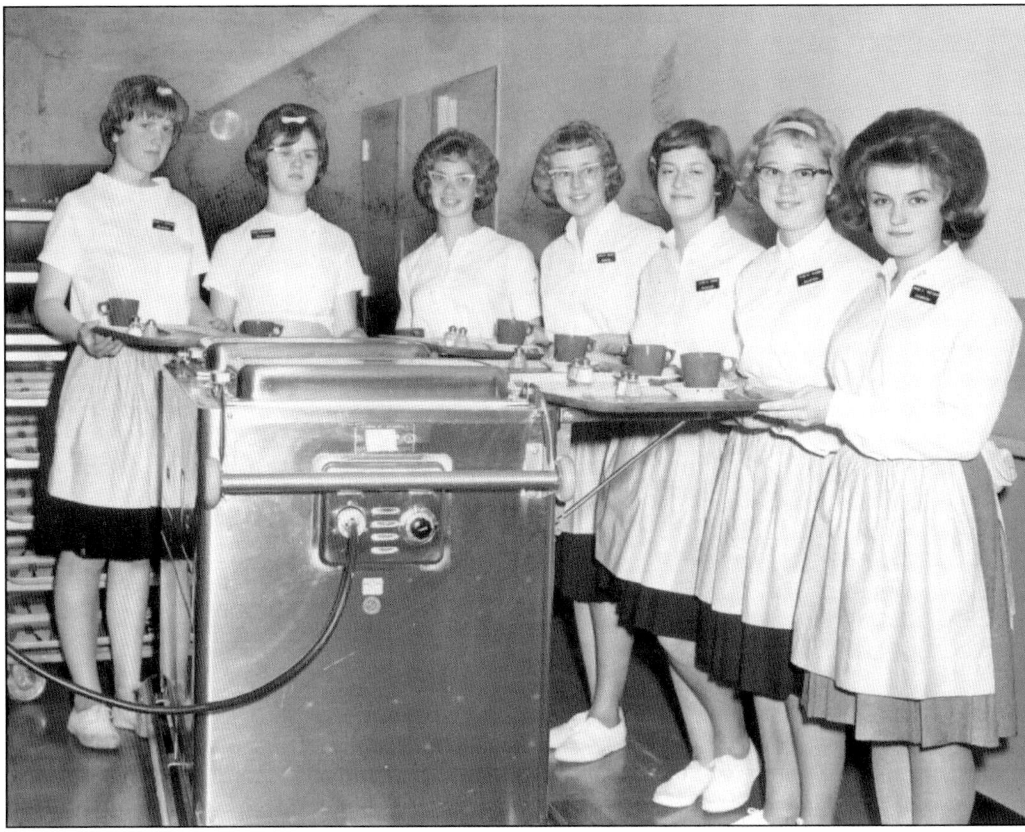

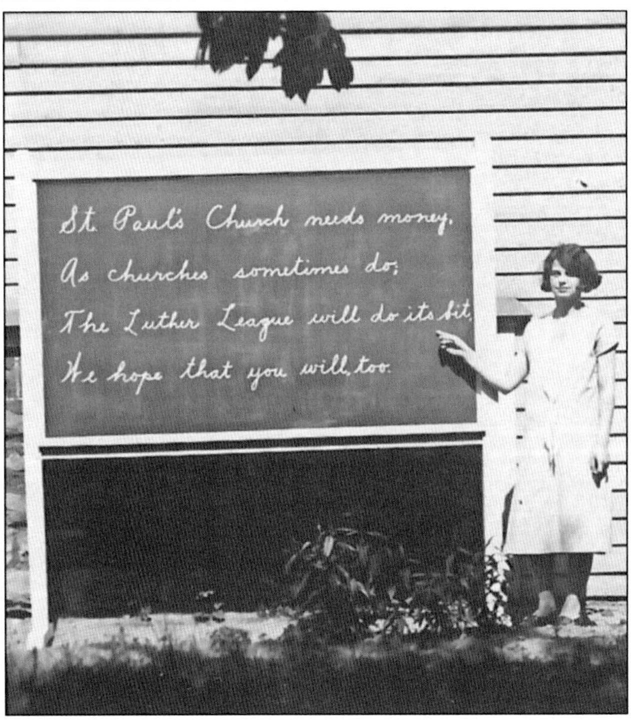

Lutheran youth were also involved in community service, starting at an early age. Operating under names such as the Luther League and Lutheran Youth Organization, young people would volunteer for a broad spectrum of projects, ranging from manual labor to singing for local shut-ins. Each church would have its own chapter, and members would engage in activities both with their chapter as well as with the entire Luther League community. Pictured above are members of the Jewett, Menge, Hansen, and Gelinas families, serving meals to the underprivileged. At left, a member of St. Paul's works on fundraising, with a sign that reads: "St. Paul's Church needs money / As churches sometimes do; / The Luther League will do its bit / We hope that you will too."

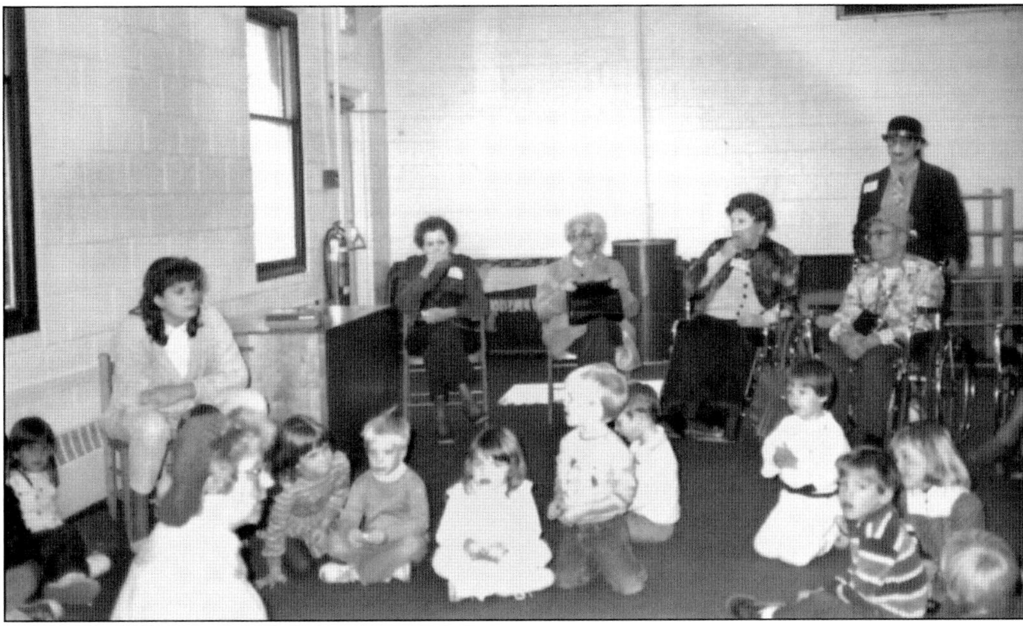

Pastor Hunneshagen was given the task of starting a new church in the early 1970s. He began by asking the community what they needed. The answer he heard most was affordable child care and jobs. Lord of Life was built as a church and a child development center (CDC). The congregation built "The Big Room," which served as the sanctuary on Sunday and as childcare space the rest of the week.

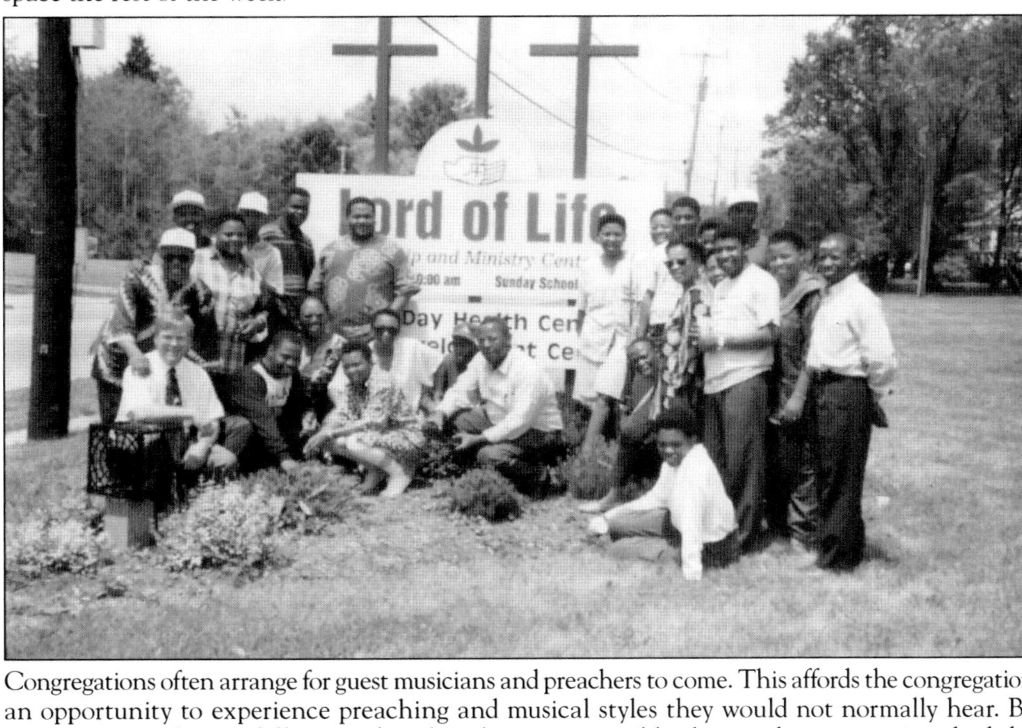

Congregations often arrange for guest musicians and preachers to come. This affords the congregation an opportunity to experience preaching and musical styles they would not normally hear. By inviting guests from a different cultural or denominational background, congregations had the opportunity to broaden their horizons. Here, Lord of Life is visited by a Baptist choir.

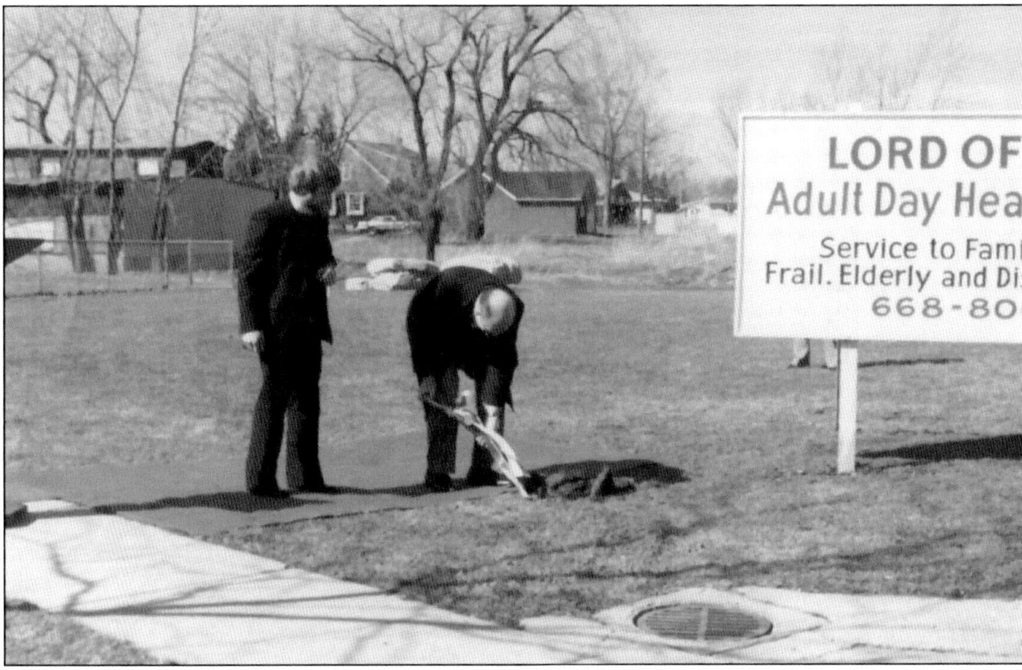

By the early 1980s, Lord of Life's CDC was exceeding the congregation's expectations. It was decided that it was time to once again ask the community what it needed. The response this time was help with elderly family members. The beginning of "the sandwich generation" ushered in a time when families were caring for their own children as well as their aging relatives. Families were looking for safe and productive places for these relatives to go during the workday. To meet this growing need, the adult day health center (ADHC) was designed, and ground was broken, ushering in a new way for the church to serve its community.

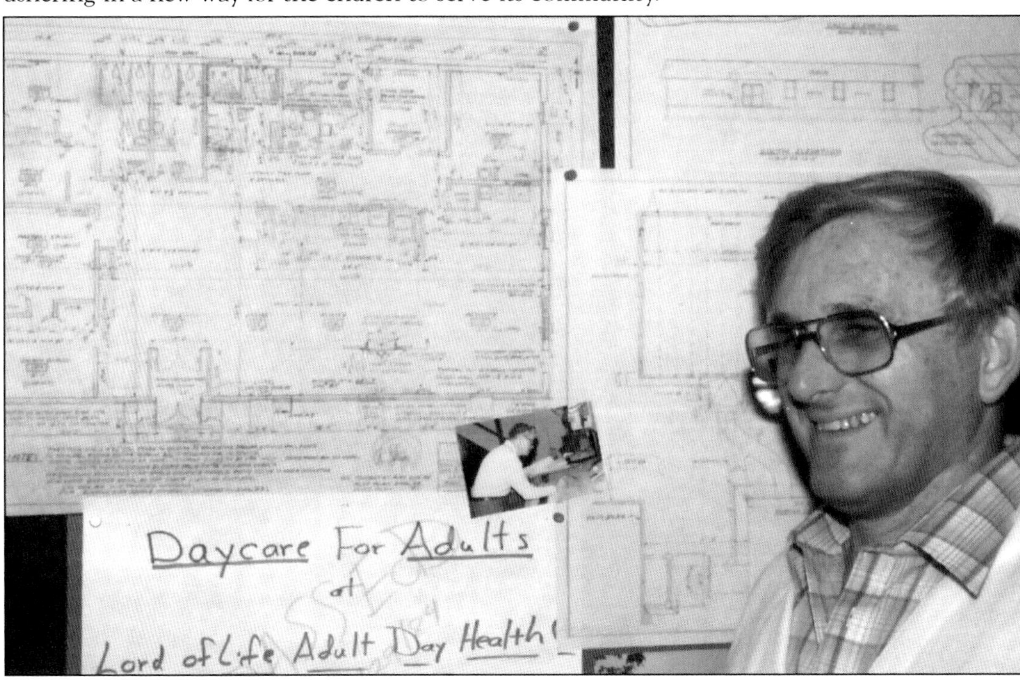

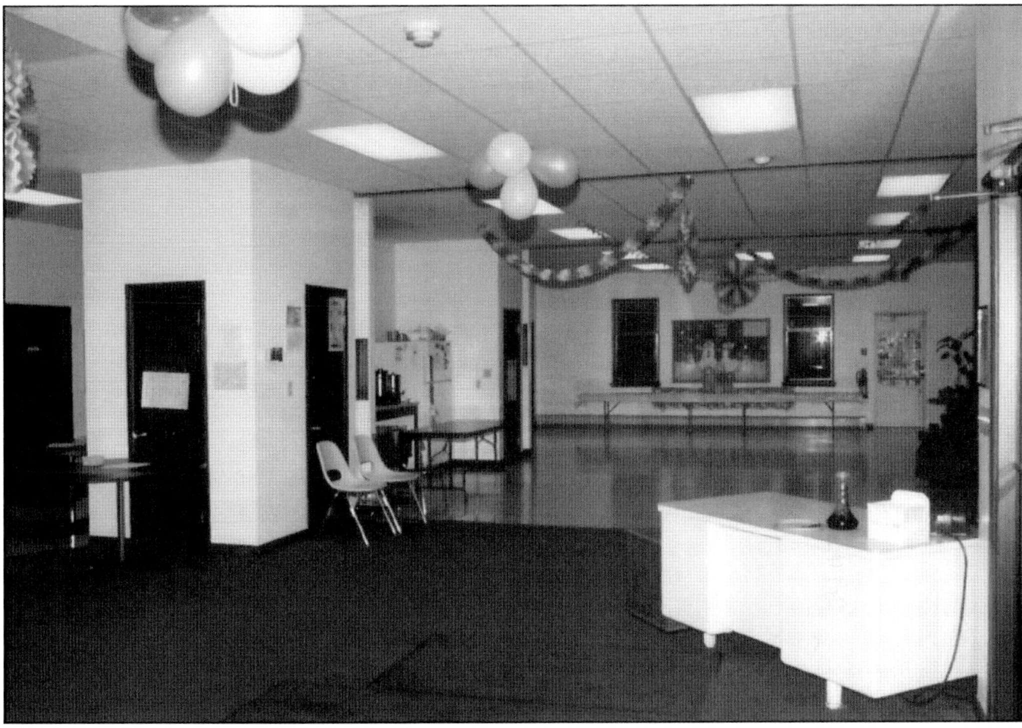

When the ADHC opened its doors and placed its sign in 1982, it was the first facility of its kind in Western New York. No facility had existed to service the needs of the community in this way. The activity room (above) would serve as the main room of the program. There was nursing care available at all times, and skilled caregivers supported the participants as they engaged in various activities, including games, social time, and music. Lord of Life invited outside entertainment as well, bringing everything from music to magic, to the delight of the participants.

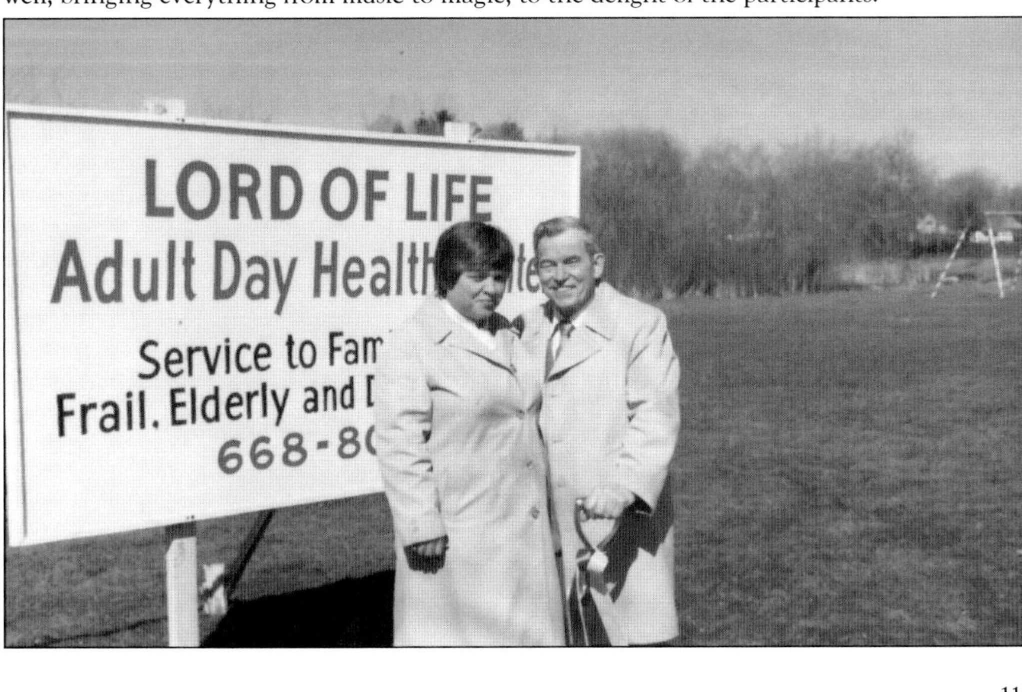

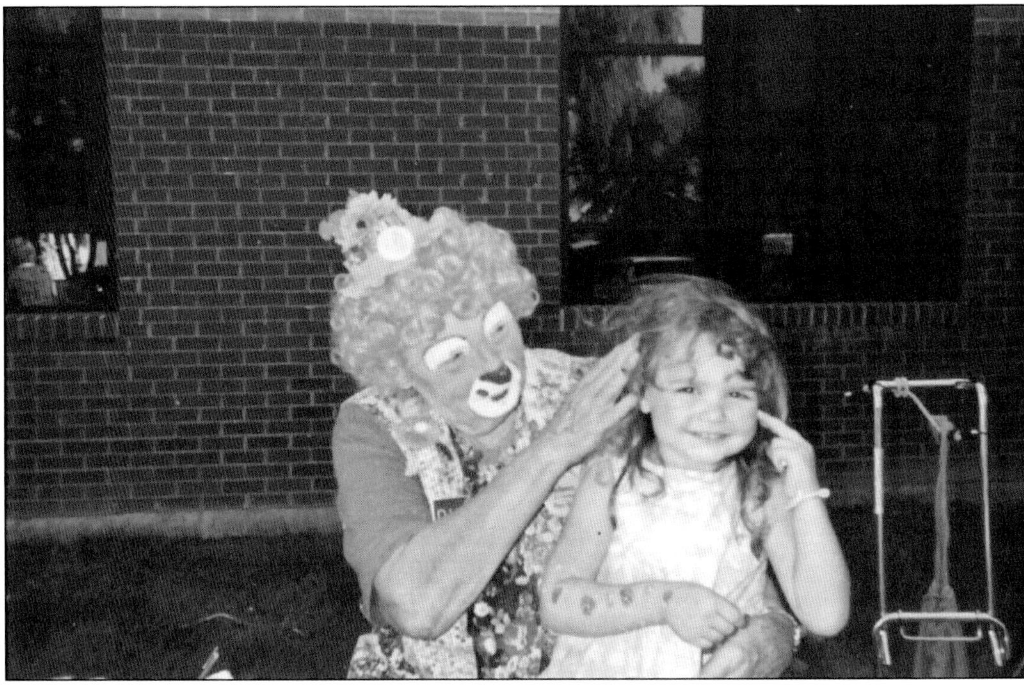

With a child center and an adult center on the same property, Lord of Life had an intriguing opportunity. It was afforded the ability to incorporate programming that allowed its participants, young and old, to interact and brighten each other's lives. Here, a CDC participant and an ADHC participant share a moment of fun.

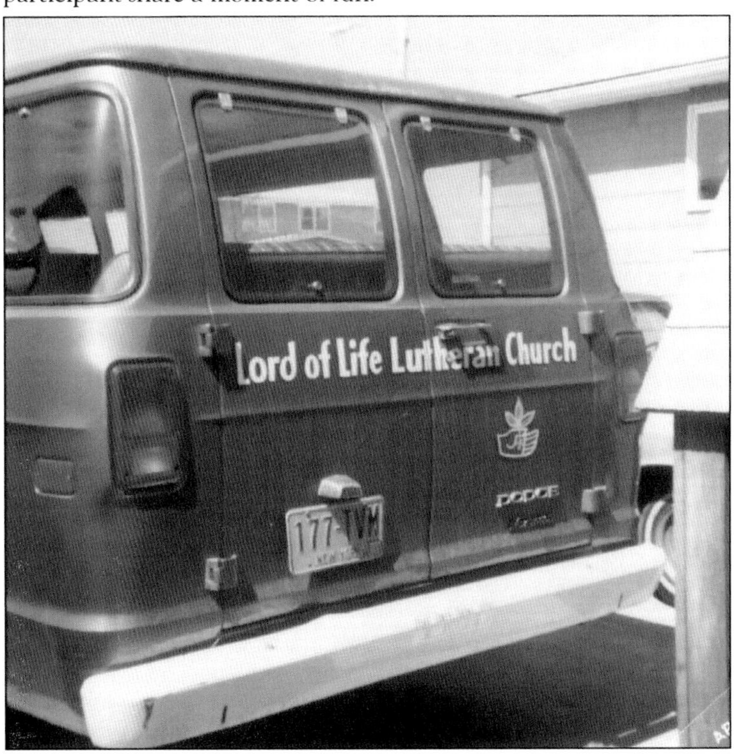

When Lord of Life began the adult day health center, one of the obstacles identified was transportation. The leadership knew that some families would not be able to comfortably transport their loved one to the facility. Lord of Life purchased a van so it could pick up and drop off participants. Pictured here is one of its earliest vans.

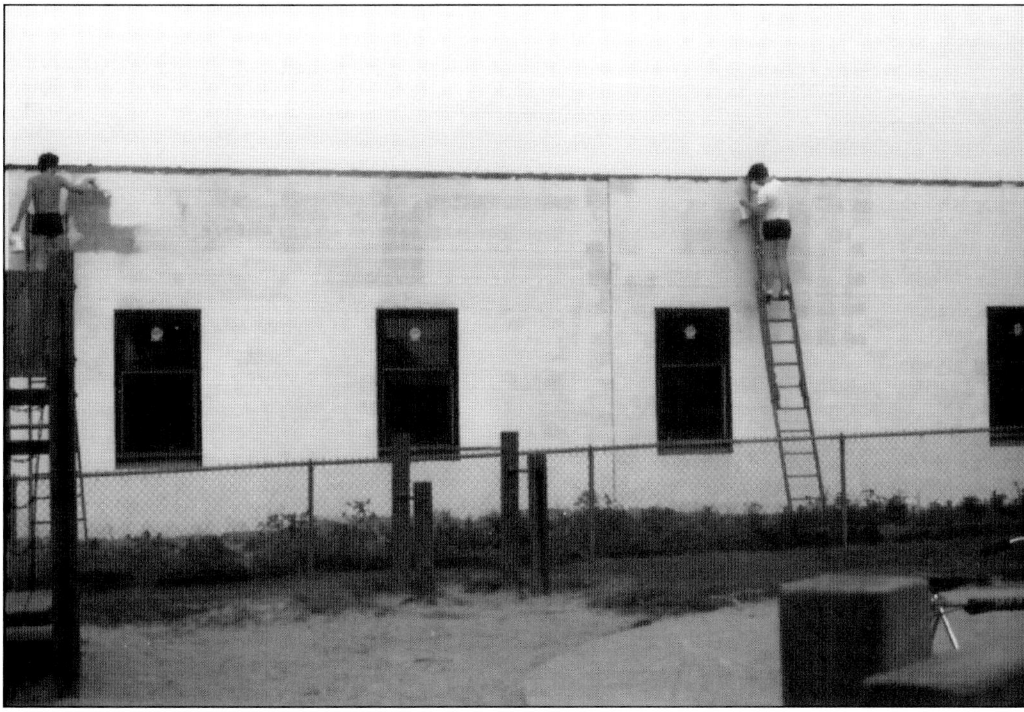

Construction has always been an expensive proposition, and, just as often, church budgets are tight. For this reason, generations of Lutherans have taken matters into their own hands, volunteering their time and pitching in to lower the labor cost of construction. Here, members of Lord of Life help to paint its facility.

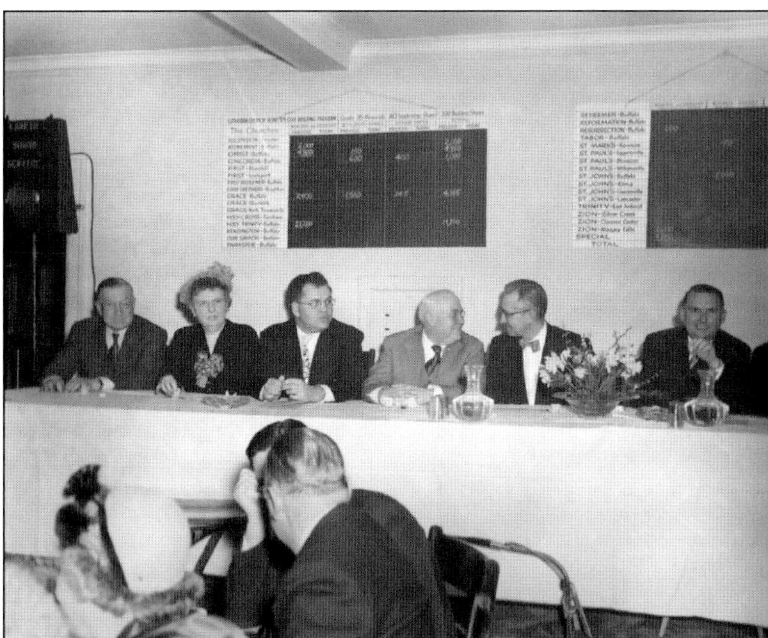

Churches regularly reach out to support their older members. This outreach took on new form when, in 1956, the Niagara Lutheran Home was opened. The original facility was a nursing home capable of housing 60 people. The opening of the facility was supported by area Lutheran churches, including through the funding drive pictured here.

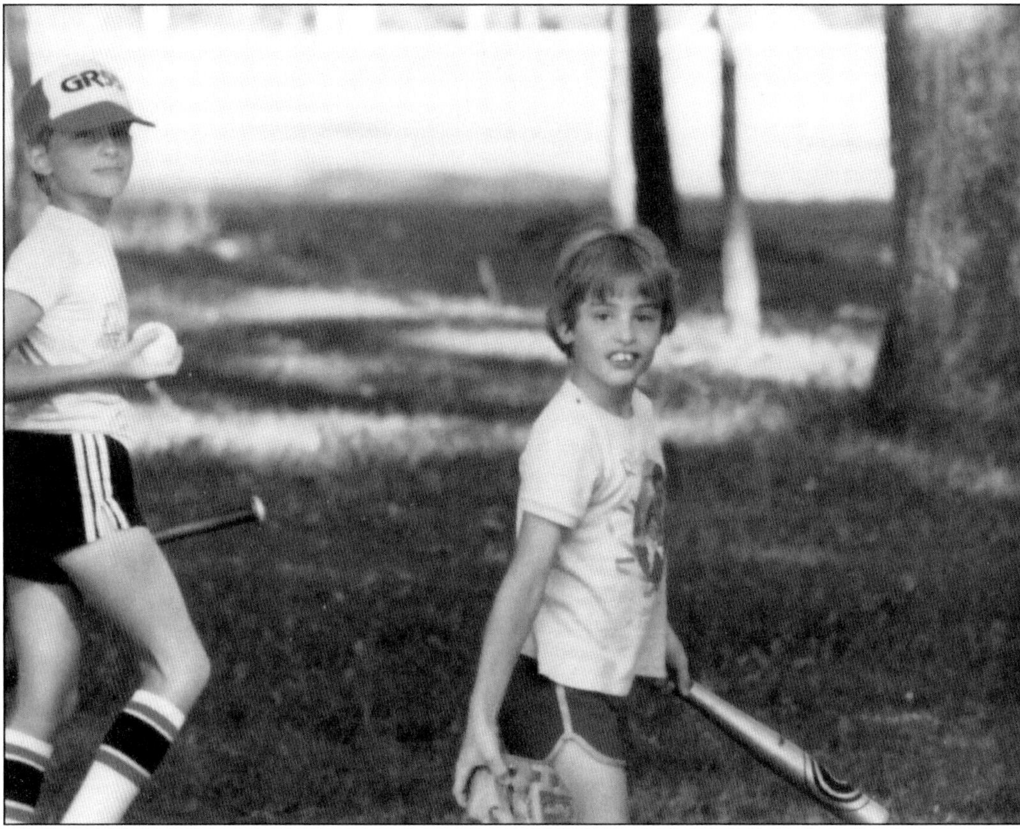

Outdoor ministries play an important role in Lutheranism. Since the 1930s, Lutherans in Western New York have supported Lake Chautauqua Lutheran Center (LCLC) as a place for those ministries. Located on 160 acres directly across the lake from the historic Chautauqua Institute, LCLC has served generations of Lutherans. It offers summer camps, retreat space, year-round programming, as well as ample space for a church picnic. LCLC has been seen as a place to escape the everyday hustle and bustle of life and explore faith in a quieter place. Such ministries have been particularly effective at inspiring leadership, with many clergy having had positive experiences at LCLC.

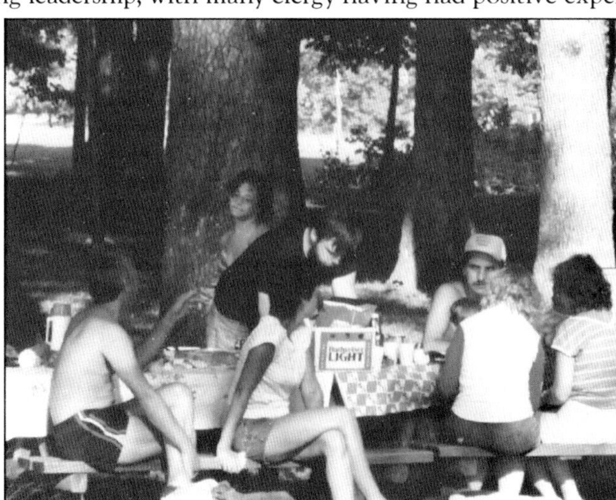

Dr. Ralph Loew provides insight into nature to a group of LYO (Lutheran Youth Organization) members at Lake Chautauqua Lutheran Center in 1969. The young parishioners made many positive memories at LCLC. Seen here in white hats, Cheryl Roesch (left) and Kathy Gibson (right) fondly learn from their respected pastor. Roesch speaks warmly of her times at LCLC, learning, worshiping, and forming new friendships with her peers.

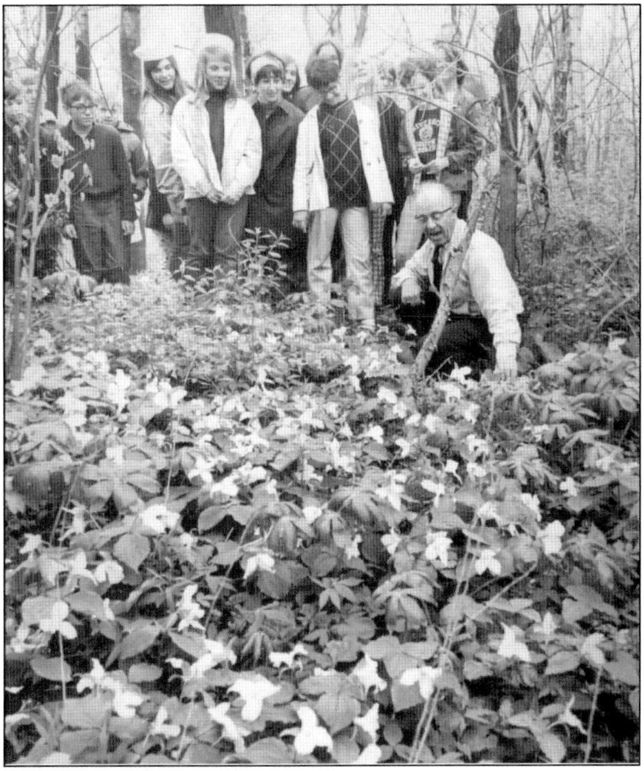

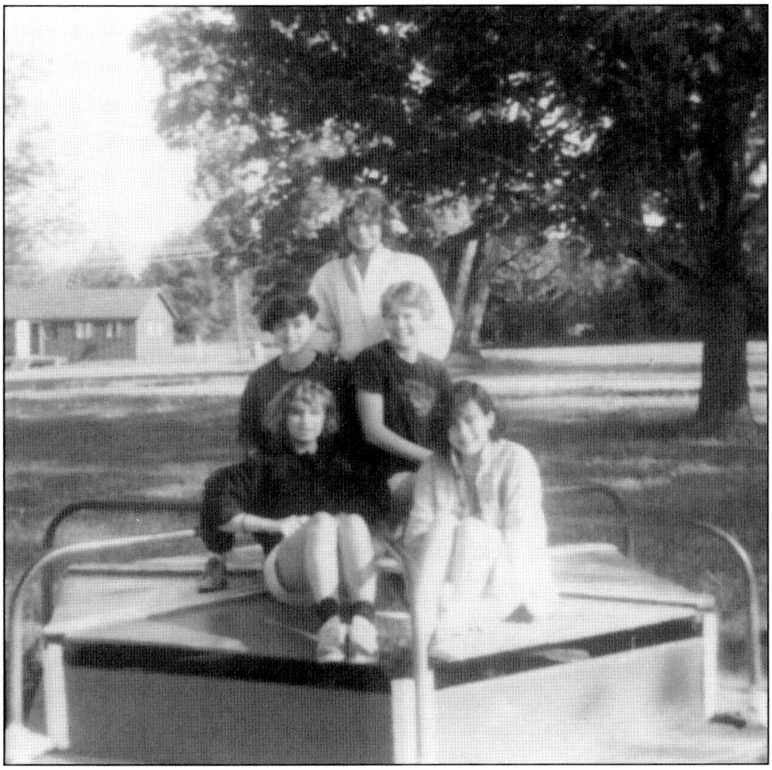

For throngs of youth growing up in the Lutheran Church, nothing foreshadowed the beginning of summer like the Lake Chautauqua Lutheran Center's (LCLC) annual "Work Weekend." It traditionally took place over Memorial Day weekend. Dedicated youth would tackle various maintenance projects and ready the camp for summer. Among those shown here are Kathy Brunett (second row, left), Corinne Johnston (second row, right), and Karen Keiffer (third row) in May 1985.

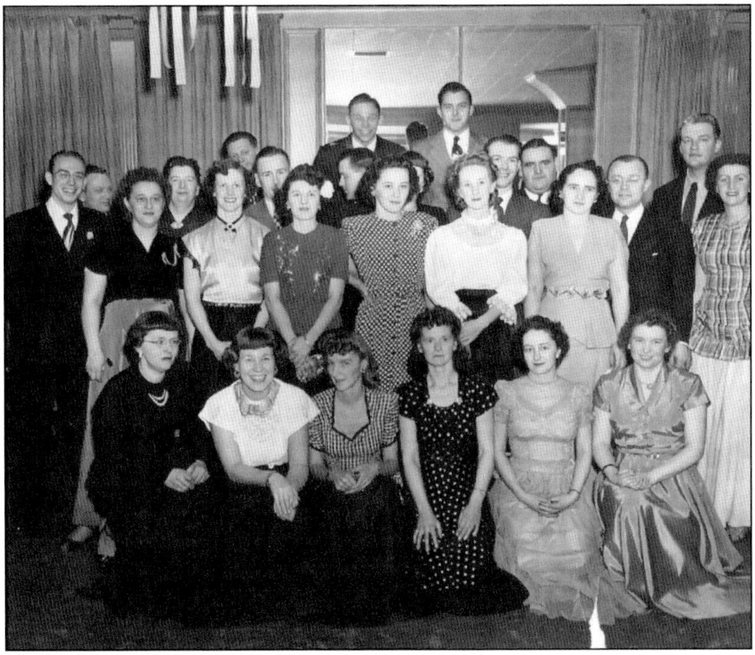

In the early 1950s, Dr. Ralph Loew (second row, second from the right) was very supportive of the formation of a Parent Club at Holy Trinity. This club morphed into Mother's Club. It met monthly, planning fundraisers and social events. Popular gatherings included the luncheon/fashion show and the yearly dinner, when husbands were invited. Mother's Club donated the funds to decorate the 1957 edition of the bride's room.

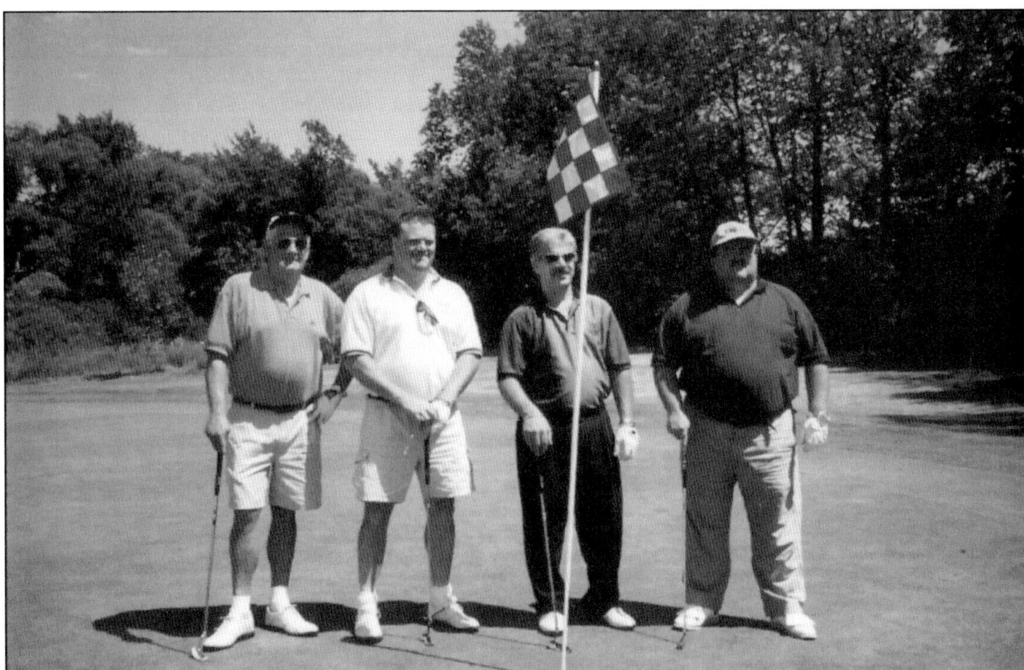

The Lutheran Charities Golf Classic brings together golfers from Lutheran churches across the region. The tournament acts as a fundraiser for the various organizations supported by Lutheran Charities of WNY, which includes LCLC and Lord of Life's ADHC. The tournament gathers Lutherans together in the spirit of charity and fellowship for some wholesome competition. The event is known for being a good time, with an even better purpose.

Five

Moving into the Future

The end of Christendom has left churches searching for a new identity, which has begun to be addressed in part through outreach. However, cultural and societal change continues. Today, the church is growing into what has been called "the postmodern church." The postmodern church continues to focus on God and to preach and teach the Gospel, but in new ways that reach out to people of changing expectations and perceptions. In the early 2000s, many protestant churches forged a "full communion" agreement, which in part means that Lutheran pastors can serve churches of varying denominations, and Lutheran churches can be served by pastors from other denominations. Local churches have found ways to work together, including three congregations merging to become "CrossRoads Lutheran Church." In addition, 30 minutes down the road, Trinity South Newstead and St. John's Akron began a process of consolidation as well. Churches are also finding new ways to worship and new places to worship in. There have been church services in parks, as well as pub churches and churches in various community spaces. Church leaders are also finding new ways to engage the community, such as "Pub with a Purpose," an event in which several local pastors act as servers at the Buffalo Brew Pub to raise money for charity. All of these are ways the church is exploring what exactly it will mean to "be church" as it moves into the future.

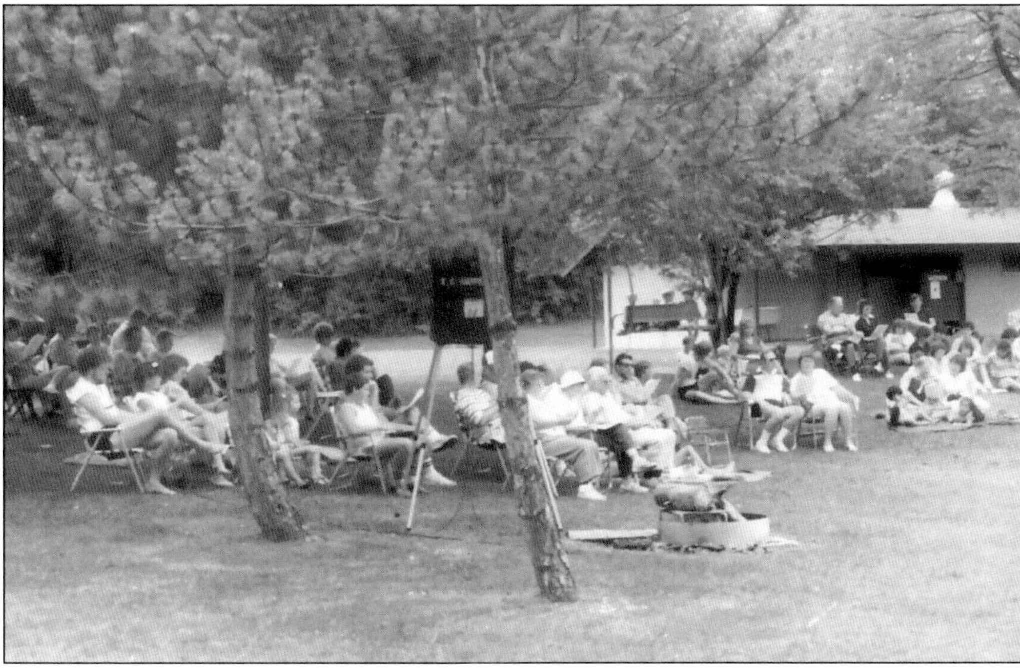

With the end of Christendom in the 1960s, the Lutheran Church had to find new ways to keep people enmeshed in their congregation. While leaders accepted that the church was no longer the social center of the community, they desperately sought ways to keep parishioners active and involved. Ideas included offering nontraditional music and expanding operating hours to alternate days of the week. For some, success would lie in taking the church back to its roots—taking it outside. At St. Paul's Lutheran Church in Williamsville, for example, parishioners enjoyed a yearly "campout." Seen here is a church service (above) and subsequent volleyball game (below) in the summer of 1985.

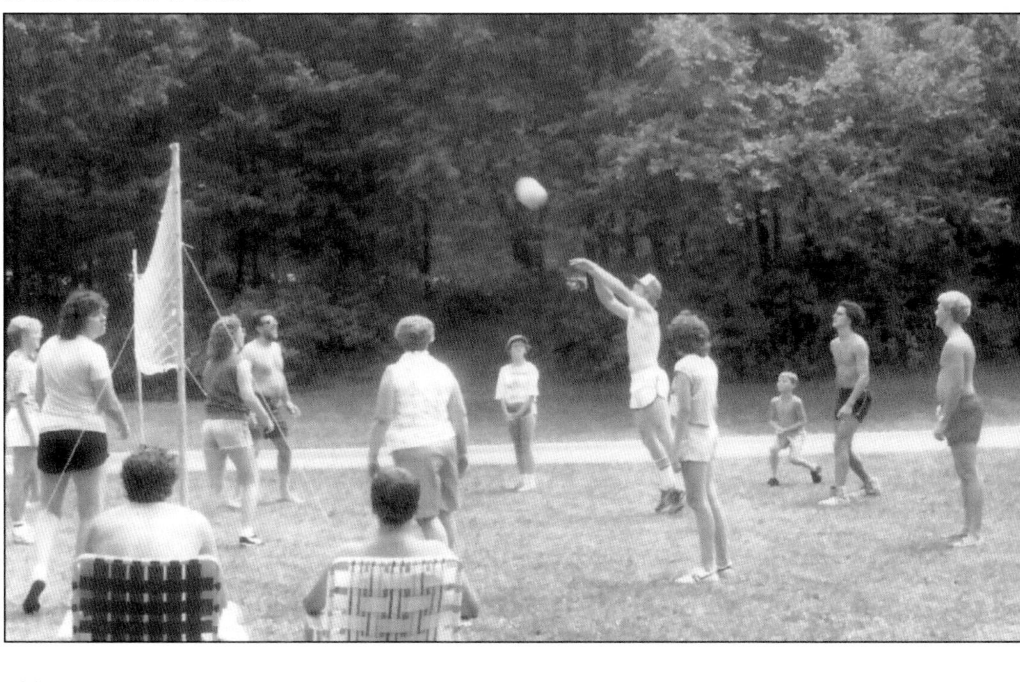

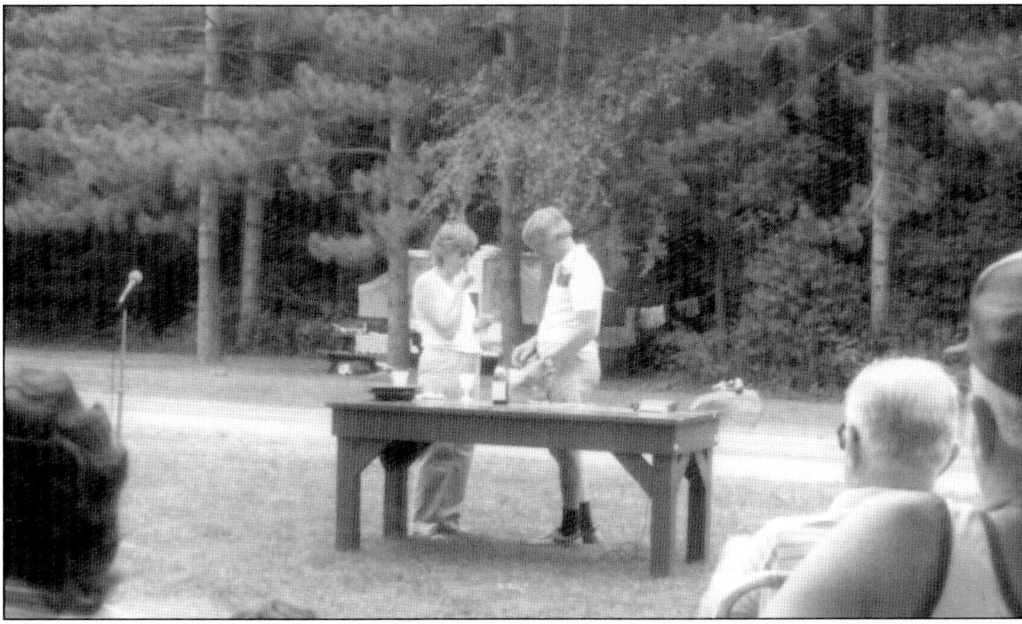

Convening at a campground in Sprague Brook, New York, the people of St. Paul's spent the weekend reconnecting with nature and each other. Games were played, picnics were arranged, and songs were sung around a roaring campfire. Young and old were attracted to these gatherings, and congregational bonds were invariably strengthened. Above, Pastor William F. Seibert and his wife, Phyllis, prepare communion on Sunday morning from a table on the grass. Below, they distribute it to an abundant circle of worshipers. Pastor Seibert, who served St. Paul's from 1971 to 1986, saw his task as "helping believers bridge the gap between the Christianity of Sunday and the real life of the other six days."

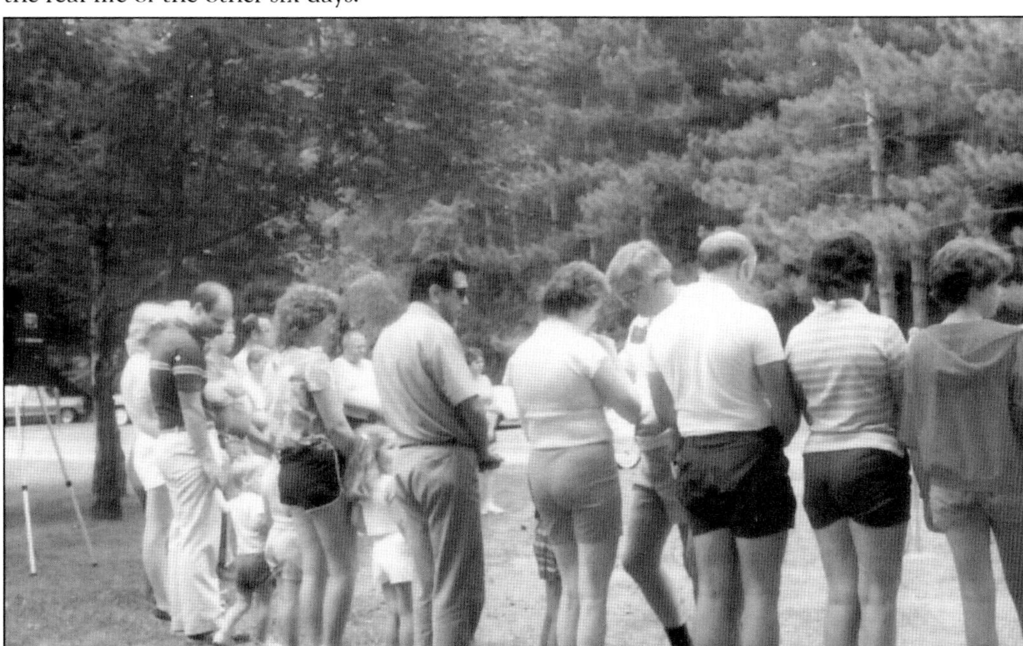

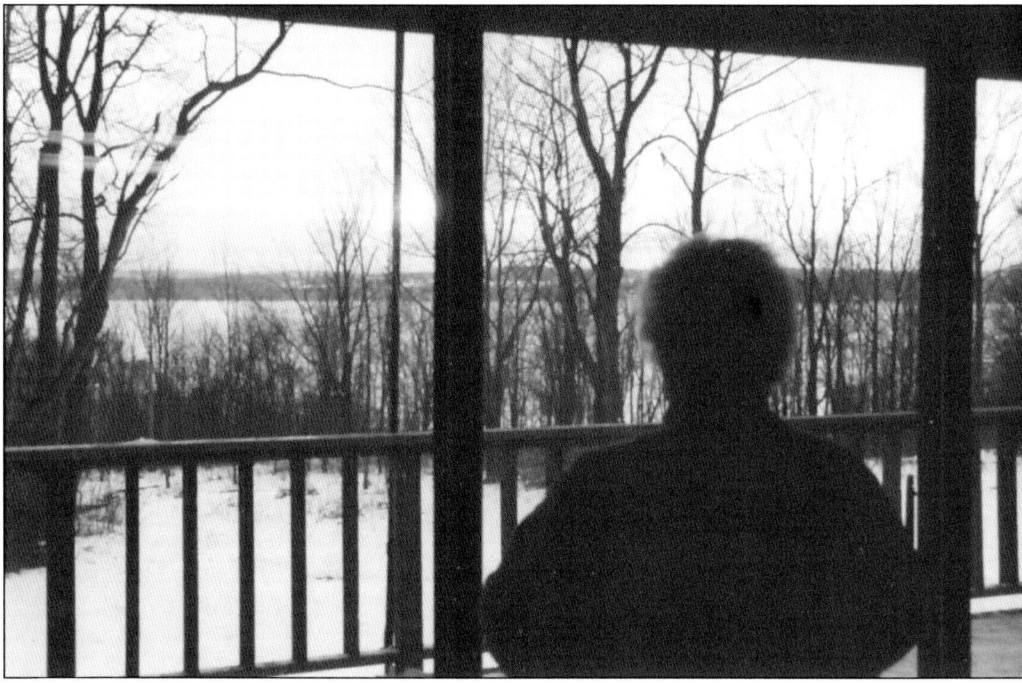

LCLC had long stood for Lake Chautauqua Lutheran Camp. With the construction of the Retreat Center, however, the second "C" was transformed, and LCLC was now Lake Chautauqua Lutheran Center. The Retreat Center was LCLC's first fully winterized, year-round facility. Its construction allowed LCLC to expand its programming and bring in a broader range of groups. It can accommodate large groups and has ample meeting space, dining facilities, and an unparalleled view of the lake (above). It has hosted congregations, family reunions, clubs, church councils, and many more types of groups. Below, participants of Lord of Life's winter congregational retreat spend some quiet time and enjoy their view of the surroundings.

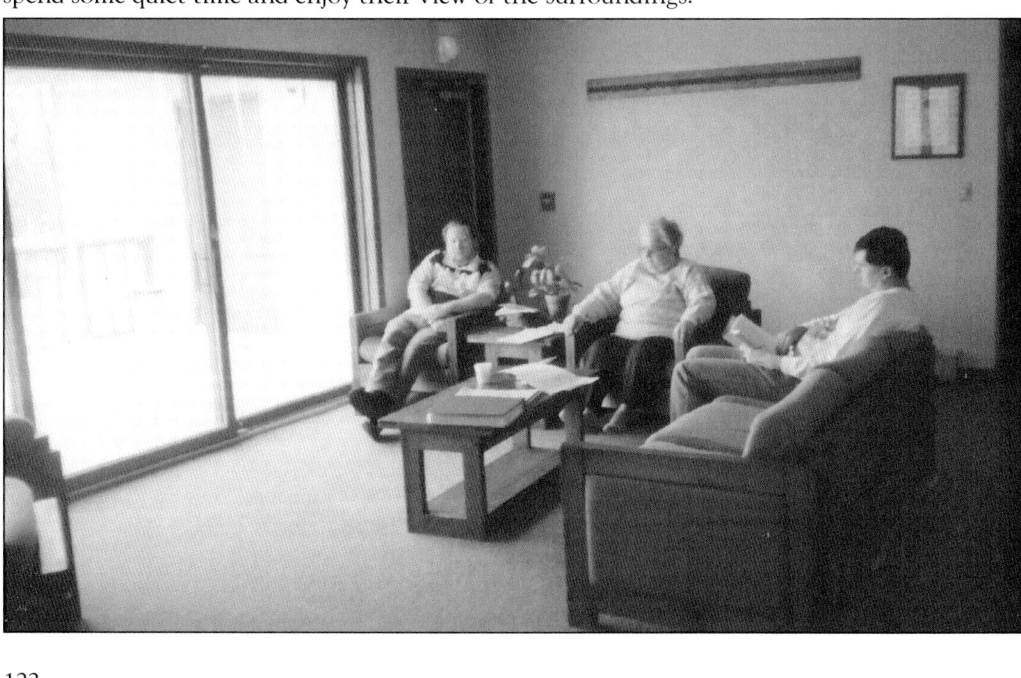

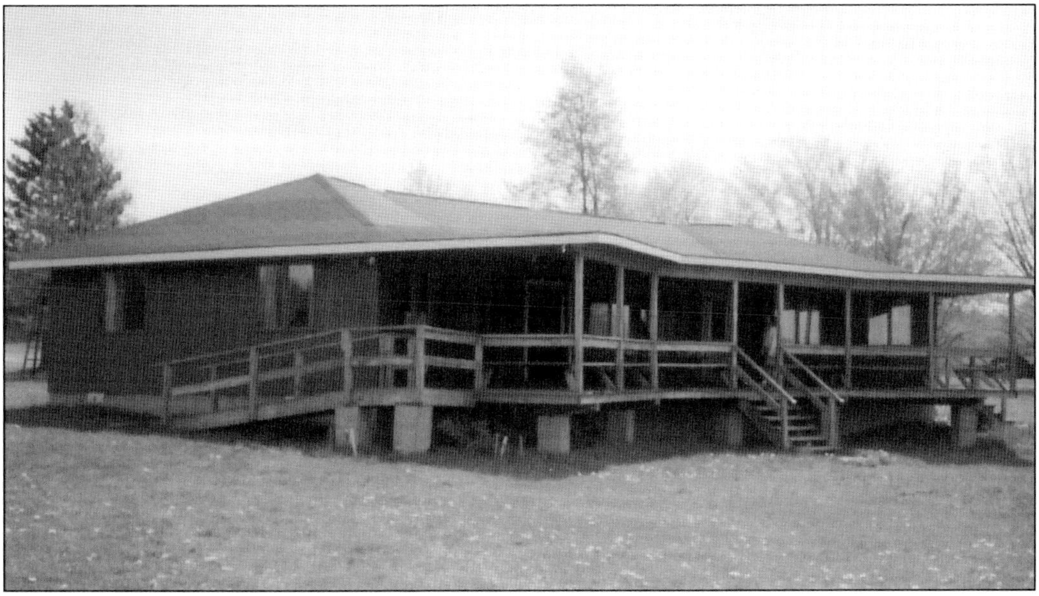

As LCLC continued to expand its programming, Redeemer Lodge was built. The cabin was the only facility onsite with its own bathroom and kitchen. During the summer months, it served to house campers participating in summer-camp programs. In the spring and fall, it allowed for groups looking to use the camp to not have to travel to a separate bathhouse and afforded groups the ability to prepare their own meals.

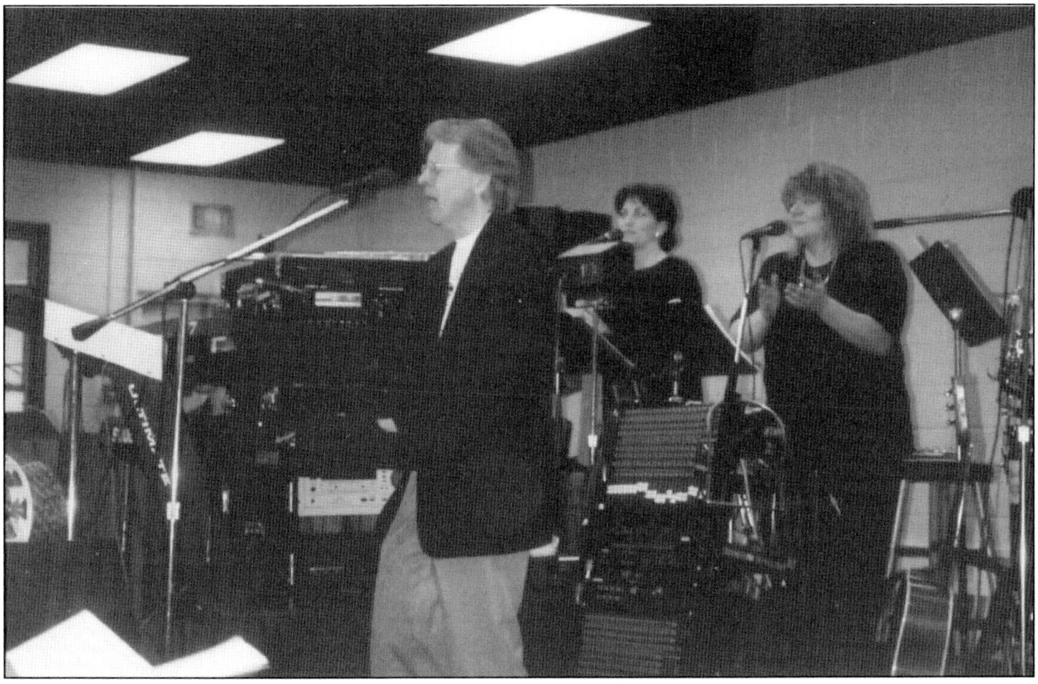

According to Martin Luther, "Next to the Word of God, the noble art of music is the greatest treasure in the world." As the world began to change, however, church music needed to change with it. Many churches began to explore contemporary alternatives to traditional worship music. The Praise Band at Lord of Life, born in the 1980s, is one such example.

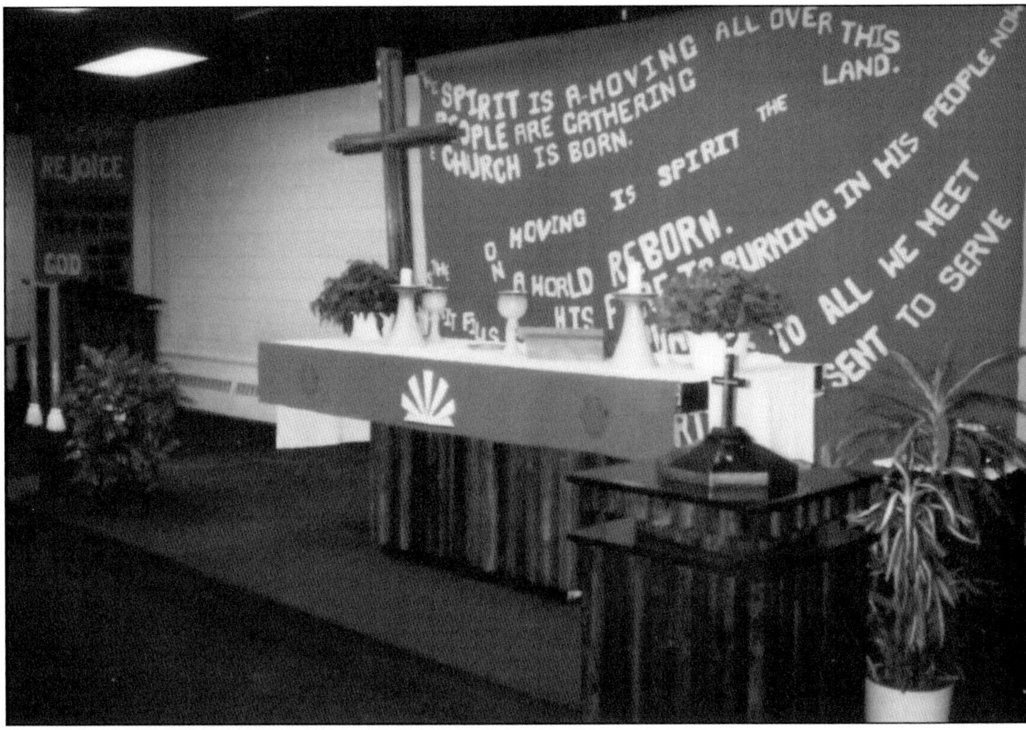

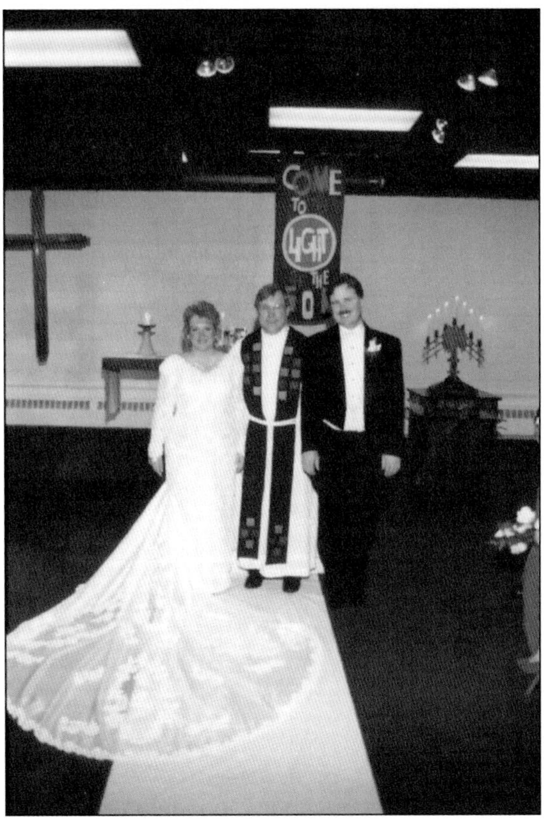

Since Lord of life worshipped in space shared with its child development center (CDC), its sanctuary had a very nontraditional appearance. There was no organ, pews, or stained-glass windows. Each Saturday, a group of volunteers would move toys out of the way, set up chairs, and hang banners to transform "the big room" into a sanctuary. The altar was pushed to the side of the room during the week to allow the CDC the room it needed for its programming. This routine continued for more than 20 years, until a dedicated sanctuary space was constructed.

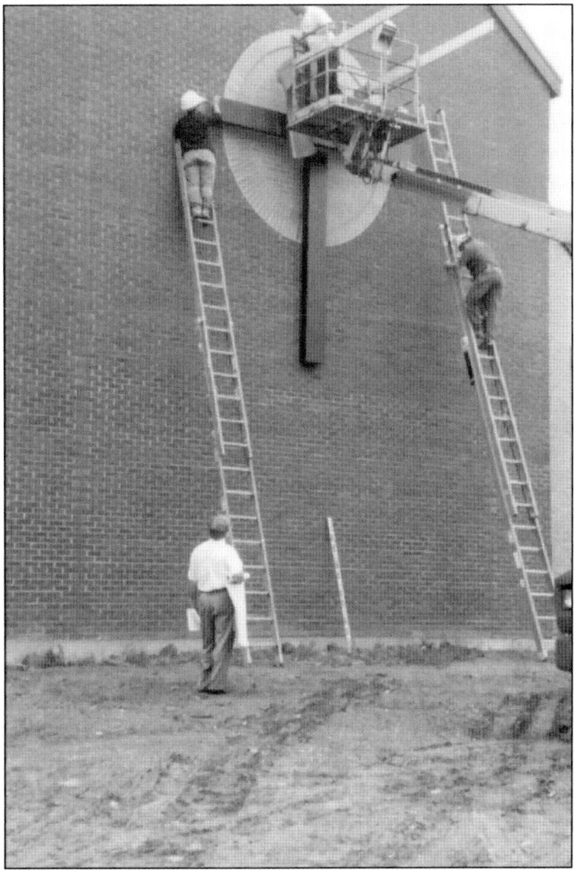

The CDC and the ADHC occupied the same property, but they were not connected; an open space separated the two. It was decided that a proper sanctuary and office space should be built between the facilities, thus uniting them. A modern sanctuary was designed and constructed. One of the final acts involved hanging the cross (at right). It faces Borden Road. The neighboring lot was purchased, and its house was razed (below). The lot was turned into a field, creating an outside space to be used by the church as well as the two centers.

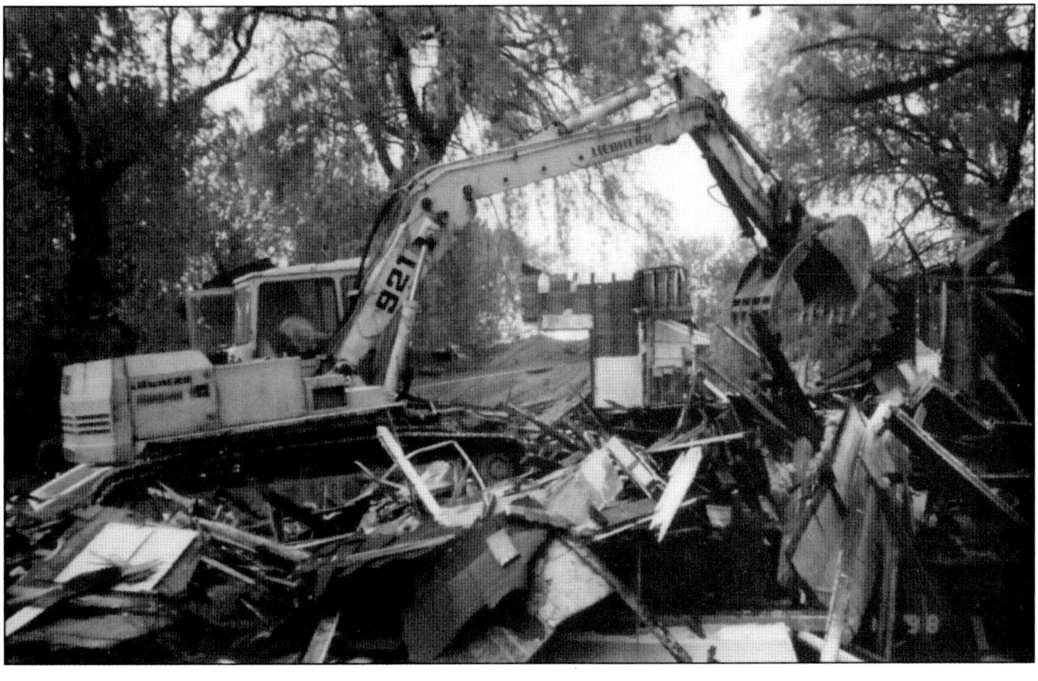

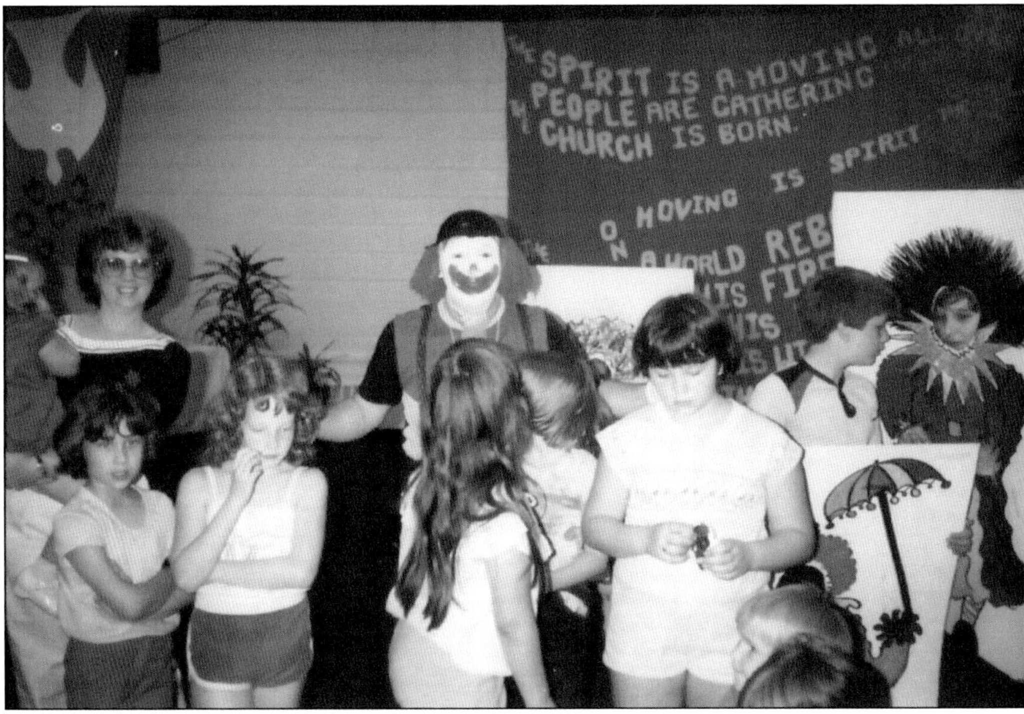

Churches often look for new and innovative elements to add to their worship service. Congregations aim to create new experiences and memories by incorporating these varied ideas. Some ideas are more avant-garde than others. Here, Lord of Life participants engaged in clown worship: a service led by clowns and mostly done with pantomime.

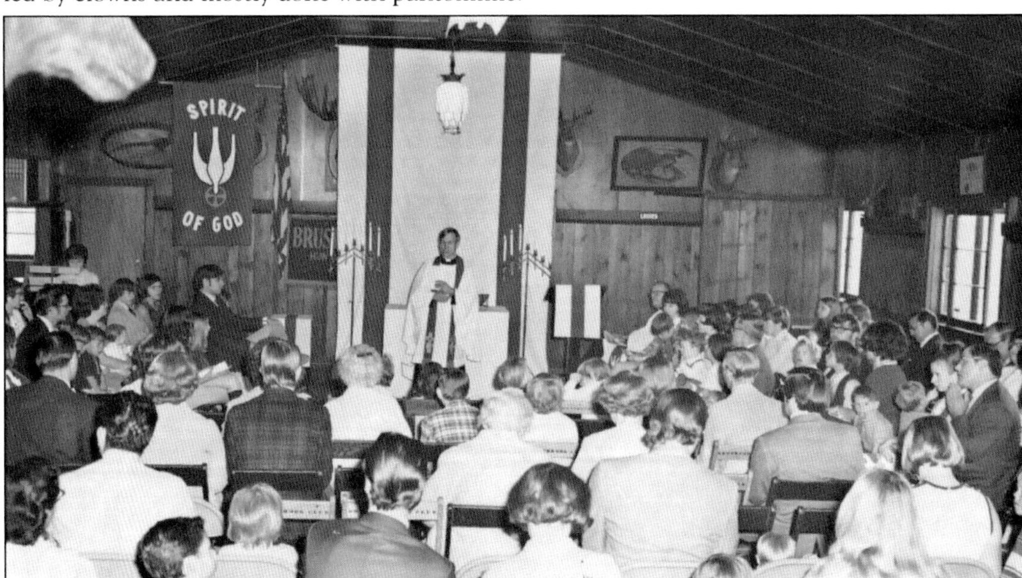

When Lord of Life began holding worship services, it did not yet have its own building. Because of this, its earliest services were held at a hunting lodge (pictured). Note the animal heads mounted as trophies behind a makeshift altar. Member Pauline Newhouse noted that the space often smelled like stale beer and smoke, a nod to the space's use the rest of the week.

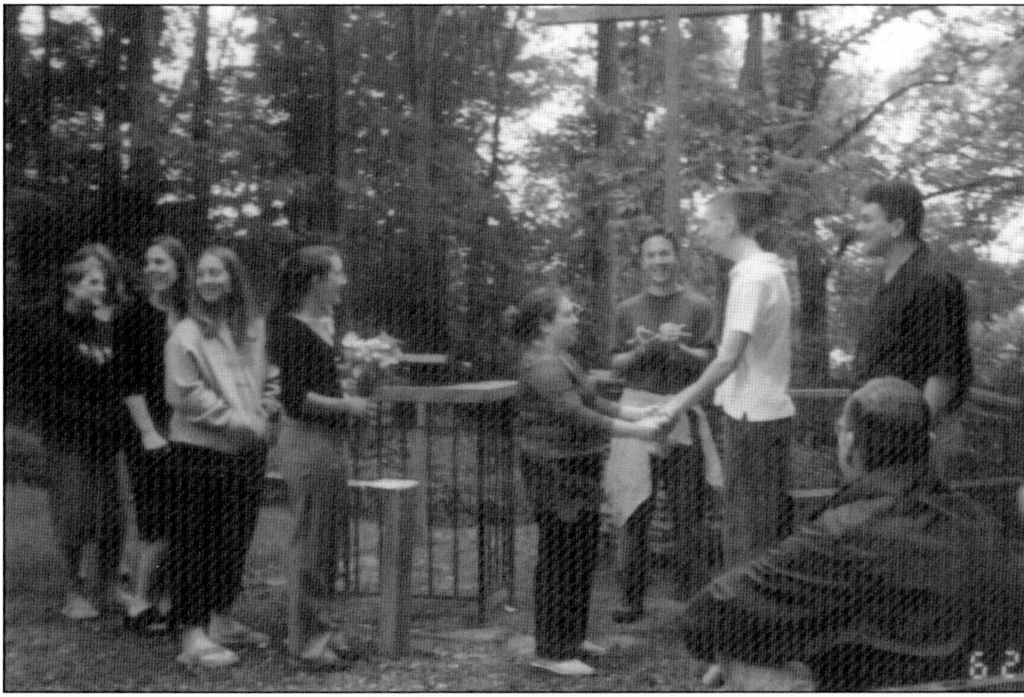

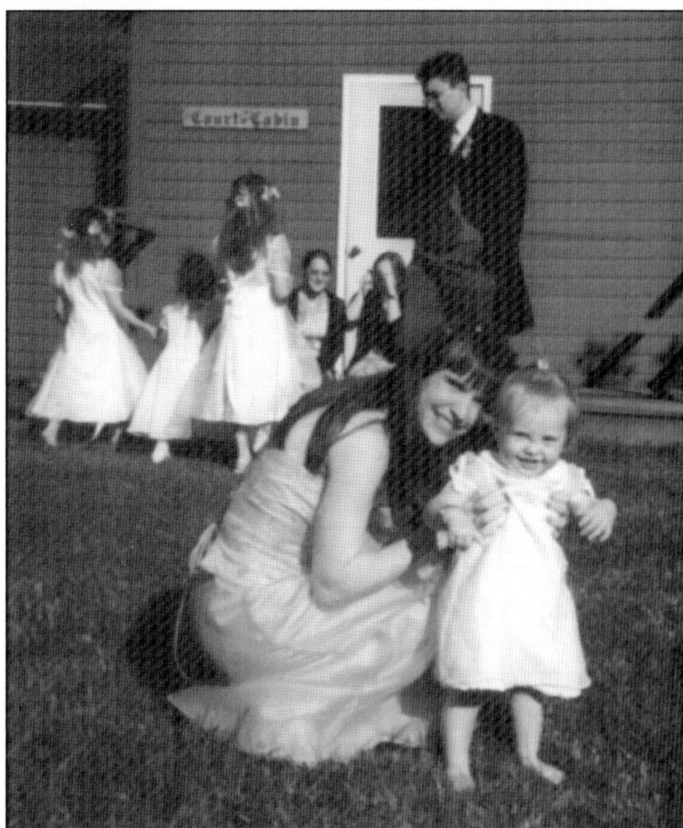

LCLC has been vital in providing a place for campers and the staff of primarily young adults to explore their faith and how that faith will impact the way they live their lives. Consequently, LCLC has played host to many life-changing decisions and events. One unexpected side effect has been that LCLC has hosted many weddings. People who have met and fallen in love there have returned for their wedding services. Pictured above are author Jamie Retallack and Olivia Hess at their 2004 wedding rehearsal in LCLC's outdoor chapel, presided over by Rev. Steve Biegner. At right, author Julianna Fiddler-Woite and daughter Victoria pose for a photograph at the wedding reception the following day, on LCLC's A Field. (Both, courtesy of Julianna Woite.)